THE CRITICAL RESPONSE
TO GEORGE ELIOT

Recent Titles in
Critical Responses in Arts and Letters

THE
CRITICAL RESPONSE
TO GEORGE ELIOT

Edited by
KAREN L. PANGALLO

Critical Responses in Arts and Letters, Number 11
Cameron Northouse, *Series Adviser*

GREENWOOD PRESS
Westport, Connecticut • London

Library of Congress Cataloging-in-Publication Data

The Critical response to George Eliot / edited by Karen L. Pangallo.
    p. cm. – (Critical responses in arts and letters, ISSN
1057-0993 ; v. 11)
  Includes bibliographical references and index.
  ISBN 0-313-28773-2 (alk. paper)
  1. Eliot, George, 1819-1880 – Criticism and interpretation.
I. Series.
PR4688.C72   1994
823'.8 – dc20   93-41224

British Library Cataloguing in Publication Data is available.

Library of Congress Catalog Card Number: 93-41224
ISBN: 0-313-28773-2
ISSN: 1057-0993

First published in 1994

Greenwood Press, 88 Post Road West, Westport, CT 06881
An imprint of Greenwood Publishing Group, Inc.

Printed in the United States of America

Copyright Acknowledgments

The editor and publisher gratefully acknowledge the following authors and publishers for permission to use copyrighted materials:

Claude T. Bissell, "Social Analysis in the Novels of George Eliot," *English Literary History*, 18 (1951), 221-239. Reprinted by permission of the Johns Hopkins University Press.

Sara Moore Putzell, "George Eliot's Location of Value in History," *Renascence*, 32, No.3 (Spring 1980), 167-177. Reprinted by permission of Sara M. Putzell-Shoemaker, School of Literature, Communication, and Culture, Georgia Institute of Technology, and *Renascence*.

Brian D. Beyers, "*Adam Bede*: Society in Flux," *Unisa English Studies*, 11, No.3 (September 1973), 25-29. This article was first published in *Unisa English Studies*, Vol.XI:3 (1973), and is reproduced here with the permission of the Editor and the University of South Africa.

Mason Harris, "Infanticide and Respectability: Hetty Sorrel as Abandoned Child in *Adam Bede*," *English Studies in Canada*, 9 (1983), 177-196. Reprinted by permission of the author and *English Studies in Canada*, the official publication of the Association of Canadian College and University Teachers of English.

David Malcolm, "*The Mill on the Floss* and the Contemporary Social Values: Tom Tulliver and Samuel Smiles," *Cahiers victoriens et edouardiens*, No.26 (October 1987), 37-45. First published in *Cahiers victoriens et edouardiens* (University of Montpellier, France), No.26, October 1987, 37-45. Reprinted with permission of the author, copyright 1987 by David Malcolm.

Preston Fambrough, "Ontogeny and Phylogeny in *The Mill on the Floss*," *The Victorian Newsletter*, No.74 (Fall 1988), 46-51. Reprinted by permission of the author and *The Victorian Newsletter*.

Meri-Jane Rochelson, "The Weaver of Raveloe: Metaphor as Narrative Persuasion in *Silas Marner*," *Studies in the Novel*, 15, No.1 (Spring 1983), 35-43. Copyright 1983 by North Texas State University. Reprinted by permission of the publisher.

For my family

CONTENTS

Contents

Critical Response to *Romola*

Critical Response to *Felix Holt, the Radical*

Critical Response to *Middlemarch*

SERIES FOREWORD

Critical Responses in Arts and Letters is designed to present a documentary history of highlights in the critical reception to the body of work of writers and artists and to individual works that are generally considered to be of major importance. The focus of each volume in this series is basically historical. The introductions to each volume are themselves brief histories of the critical response an author, artist, or individual work has received. This response is then further illustrated by reprinting a strong representation of the major critical reviews and articles that have collectively produced the author's, artist's, or work's critical reputation.

The scope of *Critical Responses in Arts and Letters* knows no chronological or geographical boundaries. Volumes under preparation include studies of individuals from around the world and in both contemporary and historical periods.

Each volume is the work of an individual editor, who surveys the entire body of criticism on a single author, artist, or work. The editor then selects the best material to depict the critical response received by an author or artist over his/her entire career. Documents produced by the author or artist may also be included when the editor finds that they are necessary to a full understanding of the materials at hand. In circumstances where previous, isolated volumes of criticism on a particular individual or work exist, the editor carefully selects material that better reflects the nature and directions of the critical response over time.

In addition to the introduction and the documentary section, the editor of each volume is free to solicit new essays on areas that may not have been adequately dealt with in previous criticism. Also, for volumes on living writers and artists, new interviews may be included, again at the discretion of the volume's editor. The volumes also provide a supplementary bibliography and are fully indexed.

While each volume in *Critical Responses to Arts and Letters* is unique, it is also hoped that in combination they form a useful, documentary history of the critical response to the arts, and one that can be easily and profitably employed by students and scholars.

Cameron Northouse

THE CRITICAL RESPONSE
TO GEORGE ELIOT

INTRODUCTION

The articles which constitute this collection all touch upon the theme of the self within society and its interconnectedness. George Eliot's growth, as reflected in her novels, is followed chronologically as she developed and as she explored relative issues such as positivism, Comtian philosophy, the religion of humanity, and concepts of sympathy. There is an attempt to reflect Eliot's ever-evolving social consciousness and to demonstrate how both reviewers and critics of her time and modern-day critics (1970s-1990s) understand the importance of the element of human charity in her novels. The articles included in this book were selected because, although they come from publications from England, South Africa, Canada, America, and France, they all trace precisely the same theme. Such recurring attention to the universal theme of the human condition speaks to readers of all time.

Certainly George Eliot was not the first novelist to explore religious themes of humanity. Her reading of Aristophanes, Plato, and Goethe is well-documented and her work reflects the influence of these readings. However, Eliot distinguished herself from other Victorian novelists in her use of an engaging narrator and realism. These elements of Eliot's style together with the philosophical influences of George Henry Lewes, Auguste Comte, John Stuart Mill, Herbert Spencer, Ludwig Feuerbach, David Friedrich Strauss, and Charles Darwin are what set her apart from other novelists.

Eliot began to explore the then-alternative philosophies when she was in her twenties. Although she adhered to her Evangelical beginnings, her own secular creed was a constantly evolving force in her life. Upon translating Feuerbach's *Essence of Christianity* (1854), Eliot explored the theories which traced the mutual relationships between people. Her readings on Comtian Positivism enlightened her further as she studied the religion of humanity. These influences, coupled with Darwin's theories on natural selection, gave the Victorian reader a new perspective on one's place and function in society. Eliot's references to "fellow feeling" defined, and still defines in today's larger society, the relation of the individual within the interconnected web of the world.

Of singular profound influence on Eliot's novels was the philosophy, writings, and encouragement of her "husband," George Henry Lewes. Lewes' emphasis on the moral value of literature, particularly realism and the psychological forms of such art, aided in Eliot's own philosophy of writing. Although Eliot did not completely believe in the claims of such nineteenth-century sciences as phrenology, her attention to and sharing of Lewes' interests in the sciences of the mind and of human evolution is well-represented in her novels.

The psychological novel was Eliot's vehicle for promoting her ethos of duty and self-renunciation. Edward Dowden, in *Contemporary Review* (August 1872), cites Eliot's penchant for emphasizing duty and everybody's ties to their pasts. "To understand any individual apart from the whole life of the race is impossible." Dowden sees duty as the connection between the self and its external life. As will the many critics who followed him, Dowden quotes from *Felix Holt*, "There is no private life which has not been determined by a wider public life." In *The Fortnightly Review* (1 November 1876), Sidney Colvin, too, refers to Eliot's theme of universal kinship. "Every problem in conduct, every human action and situation, involves some issue or other between personal cravings and instincts and the laws that make for the common good." Colvin goes on to cite the differences between Eliot and George Sand and finds Eliot to be more firmly rooted in her philosophical themes.

In *English Language History* (1951), Claude T. Bissell outlines in his article "Social Analysis in the Novels of George Eliot," Eliot's role as "recorder and reflective observer of man in society." Bissell considers how Eliot dealt with issues of class, family backgrounds, social structure, and status in *Adam Bede, The Mill on the Floss,* and *Middlemarch.*

The impact of the collective historical self upon the historical world--the individual acts which have combined to create civilization--is explored in Sara Moore Putzell's "George Eliot's Location of Value in History," *Renascence* (Spring 1980). "Eliot taught her readers to aspire to meliorate present human suffering and to contribute to the moral evolution of the species." Putzell cites examples of the consequences of past deeds and choices in *The Mill on the Floss, Adam Bede, Felix Holt,* and *Daniel Deronda.*

Written when she was nearly 40 years of age, *Adam Bede*, Eliot's first novel, was well-received and acclaimed for its realism. W.L. Collins, in an essay in *Blackwood's Edinburgh Magazine* (April 1859), finds the story not a religious one but one whose "religious principle is a large-hearted charity." Collins interprets *Adam Bede* as a realistic presentation of all the people that make up rural Warwickshire--the weak, the strong, the vain, the honest; all creating the human community; all deserving of sympathy. In his article for *The Times* (12 April 1859), E.S. Dallas finds that the story points to the theme of man's unity and oneness with one another somewhat like the works of Thackeray but in stark contrast to other novelists and dramatists who see the "differences between man and man." Eliot, however, differs from Thackeray in that she finds, in her characters, qualities of goodness; qualities which warrant sympathy even though the characters may be guilty of being avaricious, dishonest, or even murderous.

Eliot expressed her evolving awareness of the need for human sympathy in a letter to Francois D'Albert-Durade (6 December 1859). She notes her change by stating that the objective of all men should be the "inward life" and the feelings towards "our struggling fellowmen. . . ."

Brian D. Beyers's article, "*Adam Bede*: Society in Flux" in *Unisa English Studies* (September 1973), studies social backgrounds of the diverse classes in the novel. The various circumstances of the social strata contribute to the viability of the Hayslope community in its adaptability and lack thereof. Beyers considers the co-existence of many levels of society and the shared "common humanity." Mason Harris, in "Infanticide and Respectability: Hetty Sorrel as Abandoned Child in *Adam Bede*" in *English Studies in Canada* (June 1983), attempts to make the reader aware of Hetty's role in relation to her limited community. "Eliot's religion of humanity depends on the replacement of Christian revelation with moral education through experience. . .a conflict between self and community is implicit in Eliot's portrayal of Hetty."

Called a "natural history" by its author, *The Mill on the Floss* is concerned with the effects of family duty and obligation of the self, in particular Maggie Tulliver, and the functional abilities of that self within a community as provincial as St. Ogg's. Eliot fervently believed that human beings improve morally by experiencing happiness and suffering; such experience evokes the fellow-feeling which she often referred to in her novels.

Although *The Mill on the Floss* was subjected to comparison with *Adam Bede* and found to be inferior to it, the unsigned review from *The Guardian* (25 April 1860), sees the story as "one of the development of character. . . ." *The Times* article by E.S. Dallas (19 May 1860), praises the work in which Eliot has admirably presented "the sort of life which thousands upon thousands of our countrymen lead. . . ."

David Malcolm raises issues regarding social values, material success and individualism in his article "*The Mill on the Floss* and the Contemporary Social Values: Tom Tulliver and Samuel Smiles" in *Cahiers victoriens et edouardiens* (1987). Malcolm analyzes Tom Tulliver's egoistic individualism in lieu of Eliot's emphasis on charity and fellow-feeling. In "Ontogeny and Phylogeny in *The Mill on the Floss*," in *Victorian Newsletter* (Fall 1978), Preston Fambrough refers to the individual's experience and applies the theory of organicism. "Since human society is a living unity of interdependent parts, the slightest action of any of these human integers theoretically affects the whole and every part, not merely for the present but for all time."

Often called a fairy tale because of its happy ending, *Silas Marner* was the most symbolic of Eliot's works. Here the symbolism of the weaver acts as a metaphor for the individual who binds the many strands of society together.

In a letter to her publisher, John Blackwood, on 24 February 1861, Eliot refers to her theme in *Silas Marner* of "pure, natural human relations." E.S. Dallas, in *The Times* (29 April 1861), praises Eliot's realistic portrayal of even the poorest lot--those poorest in means and in spirit. *The Westminster Review* of July 1861, in an unsigned review, finds a correlation between "characters and their circumstances. . .in which all human beings are influenced by their environment. . . ."

Eliot's narrative persuasion and the interaction of metaphor with this method of narration is handled in Meri-Jane Rochelson's article "The Weaver of Raveloe: Metaphor as Narrative Persuasion in *Silas Marner*" in *Studies in the Novel* (Spring 1983). "The theme of universal interconnectedness. . .is thus presented through the method of narration, itself based in the idea that things can best be understood when viewed 'in the light of' each other."

Romola departs from Eliot's previous works both in setting and time-frame. Sometimes called her "European novel," *Romola* takes place in fifteenth-century Florence when Savonarola had seized government control from the powerful Medici family. The story is of Romola's support for and eventual disillusionment with Savonarola and her own moral progress. An anonymous review, "New Novels: *Romola*" in *The Athanaeum* (11 July 1863), finds the novel to be of a higher level than Eliot's earlier stories. The reviewer believes that the reader, who is looking for something other than a light fiction, will come away from *Romola* with a greater sense of duty and obligation and a desire to move from things which provide only self-gratification. Richard Holt Hutton, in an unsigned review in *Spectator* (18 July 1863) alludes to Eliot's stress on one's obligation to duty and the controversy of the fifteenth-century between Greek scholarship and Christian faith. Eliot's response to Hutton's review in a letter to him dated 8 August 1863 re-affirms her intentions regarding the presentation of "religious and moral sympathy with the historical life of man" within her novels. The anonymous reviewer of *The Westminster Review* (October 1863) finds *Romola* to be Eliot's greatest work because it brings together the theme of moral duty; "no one has so fully seized the great truth that we can none of us escape the consequences of our conduct. . . ."

The father-daughter relationship of Romola and Bardo, the focus of Henry Alley's piece "*Romola* and the Preservation of Household Gods" in *Cithara* (May 1984), refers again to Eliot's philosophy of the importance of the relationship to the past and its "potential benefits to the community at large." Romola's growing sympathy with the individual lives around her--familial and communal--has root in Sophocles' portrayal of Oedipus and Antigone in *Oedipus at Colonus*.

Set in Loamshire in the 1830s, *Felix Holt, the Radical* contrasts the political and personal principles of the characters Harold Transome, Felix Holt, and Esther Lyon. Eliot's analysis of peoples' motives and her realistic presentation of the characters brings the reader yet another glimpse of Eliot's perception of the religion of humanity. Eliot's letter to Sophia Hennell of 13 July 1864 underscores her moral sense and ideals as they are presented in this novel. Frederic Harrison, in a letter to Eliot dated 19 July 1866, reflects on Comte's Positivism. In discussing their Positivist conceptions of society, Harrison and Eliot, in her response dated 15 August 1866, rebut the problems of egoism and "aroused sympathy" in the novel.

E.S. Dallas in *The Times* (July 1866) finds Eliot's style rich but that her strength lies in her ability to deliver characters who cause the reader to share in their ranges of feelings. In contradiction to Dallas, Henry James, in an unsigned review in *Nation* (16 August 1866), alludes to Eliot's humanity and her morality which "is constant, genial, and discreet." James finds fault in *Felix Holt*, with plot and style primarily; however, he sees the novel as a profound expression of her "extensive human sympathy." In her article "George Eliot's Vision of Society in *Felix Holt, the Radical*" in *Texas Studies in Literature and Language* (Spring 1975), Lenore Wisney Horowitz finds that the novel "presents an urgent plea for the present to break free from the control of the past in the definition and solution of society's problems." Wisney refers to industrialism, the first Reform Bill, and evolving political philosophies as the elements of social transition and reform in Victorian England.

Middlemarch culminates Eliot's attention to psychological and social influences on people's conduct and influence on the wider community. Truly a "study of provincial life," the novel weaves together a number of smaller plots which are directed by the characters' impulses and decisions. All of these sub-plots and individuals combine to create a history of the community of Middlemarch, with all of its components interdependent upon each other. In her letter to American author Harriet Beecher Stowe on 8 May 1869, Eliot clarifies her religious point of view as "a more deeply-awing sense of responsiblity to man, springing from sympathy with that which of all things is most certainly known to us, the difficulty of the human lot." John Blackwood's letter to Eliot on 20 July 1871 responds to the *Middlemarch* manuscript and encourages Eliot in her "study of human life and nature."

An anonymous review in *The Saturday Review* (7 December 1872), takes issue with Eliot's moral stance and her emphasis on duty. "If *Middlemarch* is melancholy, it is due perhaps to its religion being all duty. . . ." The Reverend W. Lucas Collins, in *Blackwood's Magazine* (December 1872), finds that *Middlemarch* fails in its religious presentiments. Sidney Colvin's review, in *Fortnightly Review* (19 January 1873), considers future as well as contemporary readers in his review and deliberates on Eliot's philosophies and "spiritual processes."

In "The Moral Imagination of George Eliot" in *Papers on Language and Literature* (Fall 1972), Bert Hornback examines Eliot's portrayal of the weblike universe of *Middlemarch* and her adherence, within the novel, to the ideals of duty and sympathy. George Eliot's moral imagination gives character to these ideals, and the novel demonstrates how these ideals bind men together and "enlarge men's sympathies." Robert Coles, in "Irony in the Mind's Life" in *Virginia Quarterly Review* (Autumn 1973), focuses on the issue of "indefiniteness" and how Eliot shifts from mockery and satire to sympathy, particularly in the character of Bulstrode.

All of Eliot's novels stirred her readers' reactive passions; however, none divided her fans and followers quite so much as her final book, *Daniel Deronda*. Although critics, particularly her contemporaries, disparage the Jewish half of the book, it is as true to her philosophical creed as is the Gwendolen half of the novel. Most criticism of *Daniel Deronda* centers around its Jewish/Christian core.

In "The Strong Side of *Daniel Deronda*" in *The Spectator* (29 July 1876), R.H. Hutton sees the strength of the novel's plot and finds that *Daniel Deronda* is the most moral of all of Eliot's works. Eliot's presentation of the "web of human things" is the summation of her faith in an encompassing larger purpose for each individual. However, the anonymous review in *The Saturday Review* of 16 September 1876 perceives the novel in an entirely different light and questions her contrasting presentation of Christian and Jewish themes. The reviewer finds the characters unsympathetic and the theme lost among Eliot's attempts to create "a religious novel without a religion." Eliot was aware of the controversy the novel caused as stated in her letter of 2 October 1876 to Mme. Eugene Bodichon. Referring to both Jewish and Christian reactions to her work, Eliot's letter to Harriet Beecher Stowe, on 29 October 1876, tells of her concern about the reading public's resistance to the novel, primarily because of Victorian religious prejudices. Eliot frowns on "the intellectual narrowness" of her culture, especially the lack of fellowship and knowledge of their own religious history.

R.R. Bowker, in an unsigned review in *International Review* (January 1877), proclaims that *Daniel Deronda*'s greatness lies in Eliot's presentation of the theme of humanity and the "conflict between character and circumstance." The double plot emphasizes the ongoing double histories of the characters as they develop because of their social circumstances. Bowker realizes the importance of Eliot's need to use the Jews in her novel because of their history and faithfulness to their principles of life.

Arlene M. Jackson's "*Daniel Deronda* and the Victorian Search for Identity," in *Studies in the Humanities* (October 1972), argues that in his search for identity, Deronda's association with a society, in this case the Jews, leads him away from the community and deeper into loneliness. Issues of separateness and communication confound Deronda's quest for identity within a larger identity. George Eliot puts forth an "answer through her concept of separate identity within a culture, diversity within the union of nations, and the diversity of thought--differing social relations, economic approaches, philosophic concepts --within a society which commonly accepts as its uniting bond the belief in the free will and dignity and, therefore, the *humanity* of man."

"The Rhetoric of Magic in *Daniel Deronda*" by James Caron, in *Studies in the Novel* (Spring 1983), studies how Eliot's technique supports her theme-- "an ideal of brotherhood and ecumenical history which seeks to minimize political and religious boundaries so that people might apprehend the truth of one fact--humanity's essential unity." The rhetoric of magic uses elements from romance, i.e., evil, witches, sorcery and divination to fuse ideas and actions, both sociological and parapsychological, into the grand scheme of the brotherhood of man.

Themes of sympathy, human charity, and humanism speak to Eliot's readers then and today. Abundant fellow-feeling, or the lack of it, determines the personae of the selves which determine the identity of the community. The universality of the theme of interconnectedness combines to create the social, psychological, and religious worlds of Eliot's fictional communities.

GENERAL RESPONSE
TO THE NOVELS

THE CONTEMPORARY REVIEW

August 1872

EDWARD DOWDEN

. . .The scientific observation of man, and in particular the study of the mutual relations of the individual and society, come to reinforce the self-renouncing dictates of the heart. To understand any individual apart from the whole life of the race is impossible. We are the heirs intellectual and moral of the past; there is no such thing as naked manhood; the heart of each of us wears livery which it cannot throw off. Our very bodies differ from those of primeval savages--differ, it may be, from those of extinct apes only by the gradual gains of successive generations of ancestors. Our instincts, physical and mental, our habits of thought and feeling, the main tendency of our activity, these are assigned to us by the common life which has preceded and which surrounds our own. 'There is no private life,' writes George Eliot in *Felix Holt,* 'which has not been determined by a wider public life, from the time when the primeval milkmaid had to wander with the wanderings of her clan, because the cow she milked was one of a herd which had made the pastures bare.'

If this be so, any attempt to render our individual life independent of the general life of the past and present, any attempt to erect a system of thought and conduct out of merely personal convictions and personal desires must be a piece of slight, idealistic fatuity. The worship of the Goddess of Reason and the constitution of the year one, are the illusions of revolutionary idealism, and may fitly be transferred from this Old World which has a history to the rising philosophers and politicians of Cloudcuckoo-town. Not Reason alone, but Reason and Tradition in harmonious action guide our path to the discovery of truth:--

We had not walked
But for Tradition; we walk evermore
To higher paths by brightening Reason's lamp.

Do we desire to be strong? We shall be so upon one condition--that we resolve to draw for strength upon the common fund of thought and feeling and instinct stored up, within us and without us, by the race. We enter upon our heritage as soon as we consent to throw in our lot with that of our fellow-men, those who have gone before us, who are now around us, who follow after us, continuing our lives and works. War waged against the powers by which we are encompassed leads to inevitable defeat; our safety, our honour, our greatness lie in an unconditional surrender.

It will be readily seen how this way of thinking abolishes rights, and substitutes duties in their place. Of rights of man, or rights of woman, we never hear speech from George Eliot. But we hear much of the duties of each. The claim asserted by the individual on behalf of this or that disappears, because the individual surrenders his independence to collective humanity, of which he is a part. And it is another consequence of this way of thinking that the leadings of duty are most often looked for, not within, in the promptings of the heart, but without, in the relations of external life, which connect us with our fellow-men. Our great English novelist does not preach as her favourite doctrine the indefeasible right of love to gratify itself at the expense of law; with the correlative right, equally indefeasible, to cast away the marriage bond as soon as it has become a painful incumbrance. She regards the formal contract, even when its spirit has long since died, as sacred and of binding force. Why? Because it is a formal contract. 'The light abandonment of ties, whether inherited or voluntary, because they had ceased to be pleasant, would be the uprooting of social and personal virtue.' Law is sacred. Rebellion, it is true, may be sacred also. There are moments of life 'when the soul must dare to act upon its own warrant, not only without external law to appeal to, but in the face of a law which is not unarmed with Divine lightnings--lightnings that may yet fall if the warrant has been false.' These moments, however, are of rare occurence, and arise only in extreme necessity. When Maggie and Stephen Guest are together and alone in the Mudport Inn, and Maggie has announced her determination to accompany him no farther, Stephen pleads:--'"We have proved that it was impossible to keep our resolutions. We have proved that the feeling which draws us to each other is too strong to be overcome: that natural law surmounts every other; we can't help what it clashes with." "It is not so, Stephen. I'm quite sure that is wrong. I have tried to think it again and again; but I see, if we judged in that way, there would be a warrant for all treachery and cruelty. We should justify breaking the most sacred ties that can ever be formed on earth. If the past is not to bind us, where can duty lie? We should have no law but the inclination of the moment."' Maggie returns to St. Oggs: Fedalma and Don Silva part: Romola goes back to her husband's house. We can imagine how unintelligible such moral situations, and such moral solutions, would appear to a great female novelist in France. The Saint Clotilda of Positivism had partly written a large work intended to refute the attacks upon marriage contained in the writings of George Sand, 'to whom,' adds her worshipping colleague, 'she was intellectually no less than morally superior.' Perhaps we may more composedly take on trust the excellence of Madame Clotilde de Vaux's refutation, inasmuch as the same object has been indirectly accomplished by the great female novelist of England, who for her own part has not been insensible to anything that was precious in the influence of Comte.

'If the past is not to bind us, where can duty lie?' As the life of the race lying behind our individual life points out the direction in which alone it can move with dignity and strength, so our own past months and years lying behind the present hour and minute deliver over to these a heritage and a tradition which it is their wisdom joyfully to accept when that is possible. There are moments, indeed, which are the beginning of a new life; when, under a greater influence than that of the irreversible Past, the current of our life takes an unexpected course; when a single act transforms the whole aspect of the world in which we move; when contact with a higher nature than our own suddenly discovers to us some heroic quality of our heart of the existence of which we had not been aware. Such is the virtue of confession of evil deeds or desires to a fellow-man, it restores us to an attitude of noble simplicity; we are rescued from the necessity of joining hands with our baser self. . . .

. . .This is the life we mortals live. And beyond life lies death. *Now* it is not hard to face it. We have already given ourselves up to the large life of our race. We have already died as individual men and women. And we see how the short space of joy, of suffering, and of activity allotted to each of us urges to helpful toil, and makes impossible for us the 'glad idlesse' of the immortal denizen of earth. . . .

THE FORTNIGHTLY REVIEW

1 November 1876

SIDNEY COLVIN

. . .Every problem in conduct, every human action and situation, involves some issue or other between personal cravings and instincts and the laws that make for the common good. Most writers of fiction have looked at life, and described its actions and situations from the point of view of the individual, and his feelings and experiences under trial; they have written in sympathy with their own characters in the struggle with the inexorable. George Eliot has changed the point of view; she has a sterner sense of the consequences and responsibilities of human action; she is severe upon her characters, and in sympathy, so to speak, with the inexorable. That a writer of fiction should have arisen who takes this new view of life's meaning, is a thing which marks an epoch; in finding room for these enlarged considerations, the art of fiction has taken a new departure. But the artist should be impartial, exhibiting all the phases of the conflict between desire and duty, what we would like and what we may have, but not taking a side too avowedly. . . .

. . .The art of fiction has reached its highest point in the hands of two women in our time. One of them has just been taken away, and as we read the work of the other who is left, it is natural that we should have hers also in our mind. Their excellences are in few things the same. The flow of George Eliot's writing, we have felt, is apt to be impeded with excess of thought, while of writing which does flow, and in flowing carry the reader delightfully along, George Sand is an incomparable mistress. But this is only the sign of deeper differences. George Sand excels in the poetical part of her art. George Eliot excels in the philosophical. Each is equally mistress of human nature and its secrets, but the one more by instinct, the other more by reflection. In everything which is properly matter of the intellect, the English writer is the superior of the French by far. She stands on different and firmer philosophical ground. George Sand had known and shared two great intellectual fevers of her time in France-- the social fever of those who hoped to end the unequal reign of wealth and privilege, and by remodelled institutions to make human brotherhood a reality; and the religious fever of those who, breaking with churches and abandoning the incredible, yet sought an anchorage for the individual soul in communion with a deity above the definition of dogma. Much of George Sand's work has in it the ferment of these doctrines--socialism and theism--but without, perhaps, gaining from the admixture. The quality of her speculative reflections is not on a level with the quality of her creations; she imagines much better than she thinks. On the other hand, it is not only that George Eliot is of a different genius, and thinks at least as well as she imagines; it is that she belongs to a school with which most of us to-day are more in sympathy, and which, whether we hold its principles final or not, at any rate stands on solid ground, and tells us things fruitful in practice and luminous as far as they reach. She is penetrated with the scientific spirit, and the conclusions of the scientific spirit, in their most comprehensive, most ardent, most generous shape, form the moral and intellectual foundation of her art. Only, such is the nature of art, that when it too much lays bare its own moral and intellectual foundations, it produces less effect than when it conceals them. . . .

SOCIAL ANALYSIS IN THE NOVELS OF GEORGE ELIOT

English Literary History, 1951

CLAUDE T. BISSELL

If we were to limit our examination of George Eliot's powers of social analysis to those novels where she is concerned with expounding a political thesis, we would be forced to conclusions no less dispiriting to the historian of political and social ideas than to the literary critic. Fortunately, however, we should have scant material to work upon. *Felix Holt*, a conscientious attempt to write a didactic political novel, would be the major document. According to one of the conventions of the genre, this novel has as its hero a young, incorruptible man of the people who has pledged himself to a career of selfless devotion to a programme of reform. The action springs out of a political situation and follows the vagaries of party allegiance. George Eliot is striving to depict the turmoil and dislocation that arise even in the backwater of a small rural settlement in the days following the passing of the first Reform Bill, and, at the same time, she is pointing out and heavily underlining the moral inadequacies of philosophical radicalism. But even in *Felix Holt* this elaborate attempt to write a political novel cannot overcome the pull of other interests. Felix Holt's admirable sentiments, an amalgam of Carlyle, Comte and the Victorian conscience, are swamped by the intricacy of the plot and, more acceptably, by the firm and compassionate handling of the relationship between a mother and her estranged son.

Only once again was George Eliot led astray by her enthusiasm for a political programme. The results this time are even more disastrous to her art, although fortunately they are apparent in only one section of the novel. The hero of *Daniel Deronda* is, like Felix Holt, a young and incorruptible reformer. This time, however, he emerges from a vague and mysterious background and he moves darkly toward a vague and mysterious goal. The goal becomes palpable when Daniel learns that he is a Jew and that circumstances have made him a messianic leader who will summon his race to a political destiny of "separateness with communication." The political situation from which Felix Holt emerged was, at least, specific and real, but the hapless Daniel moves in a mist of sentimental idealism in which at times one can vaguely recognize sympathy for nationalistic aspirations, belief in the power of heredity and in racial solidarity and tempered interest in the programme of Zionism. The political section of the novel provides a catalogue of almost all the vices to which the novelist can succumb: the prose is wooden, with much reliance on abstractions and heavy, over-stuffed phrases; the characters are puppets in a dull charade, unfortunately endowed by their manipulator with the gift of endless speech. But, as I have suggested, George Eliot did not in this novel follow false lights unswervingly. Set aside the 'Daniel Deronda' section, and the novel is George Eliot at her strongest and best, working in a social setting that she thoroughly understands and exploring a complicated network of motives with assurance and precision.

This inability to turn a political gospel into acceptable fiction does not mean that George Eliot was ill equipped to deal with social problems. Rather it serves to mark off sharply and to illuminate by contrast the area of social analysis in which she was most at home. It is the area that, it seems to me, properly belongs to the novelist whose imagination is kindled by the spectacle of man in society, who is concerned about the inter-relationship between the individual and the social groups and institutions of which he is a part. For such a novelist any exclusive concern with a particular programme is bound to be narrowing and may well be stultifying. George Eliot's role was to be that of recorder and reflective observer of man in society, and few English novelists have been better qualified to play it.[1]

On the basis of this scope of knowledge and depth of intellectual curiosity George Eliot's qualifications for this role are unquestioned. I suppose that one must leap ahead to Mr. Aldous Huxley before one meets a novelist of such commanding erudition, although Mr. Huxley wears his learning a good deal less gracefully than the Victorian Sibyl. Regarded as a speculative thinker, she, it is true, marked limitations. Her mind is not bold and adventurous; she is not impelled, as Meredith and Hardy were, towards the creation of metaphysics. She is at home only in those areas of thought where there is a solid basis in human experience--in the biological sciences, in religious and cultural history, in what today might be called sociology. But if this is a weakness for a philosopher, it may well be a strength for a novelist. She is inclined to be modest and tentative in her handling of knowledge, more prepared to examine the past carefully than to speculate about the future. Although she is skilled in analysis, in the uncovering of hidden causes and obscure motivations, she is free of the intellectual arrogance that often afflicts the Victorian agnostic. She fully realizes that this is an untidy and irrational world, that morals, manners and social institutions bear with them the superstitions and the prejudices as well as the enlightenments of the past. All these qualities then,--breadth of knowledge, intellectual curiosity, patience and skill in analysis, wisdom and compassion in judgment--at first precociously displayed in her early essays are transferred in subtler form to her work as a novelist.

Intellectual qualities such as these, admirable in themselves, do not, of course, ensure success in the writing of fiction. Indeed they may betray their possessor into writing novels that are merely historical documentaries or journalistic reports diluted with human interest. If George Eliot never sinks to this level, she does occasionally respond to a downward pull. The research worker and the novelist battle throughout *Romola* and there are not wanting uncharitable critics who award the victory to the former. But outside of this novel such a critical question does not seriously arise. What, I think, enables George Eliot to avoid the quality of the documentary in most of her novels is the fact that her material is bound to her by actual experience or by personal association and is transformed by memory and reflection. She is not simply stating facts that might be culled from a government report or recording the accurate impressions of the person who was there. She is giving her vision of a way of life that, although it is rooted in the past, continues to exist powerfully in her imagination.[2] This quality is most apparent in those passages where the autobiographical element is strong, in the opening chapters of *The Mill on the Floss*, for instance, where a brooding memory of her own childhood only gradually dissolves into the figure of an imaginary heroine.[3] This quest for a lost happiness is, however, a minor note. The appeal to the past is usually more impersonal and generalized, linking small recollections with broad historical events and forces. Here is such a passage, in which George Eliot summons up the memory of provincial society as it existed in the little town of St. Oggs in the late twenties of the nineteenth century:

Everywhere the brick houses have a mellow look, and in Mrs. Glegg's day there was no incongruous new-fashioned smartness, no plate-glass in shop windows, no fresh stucco-facing or other fallacious attempt to make fine old red St. Ogg's wear the air of a town that sprang up yesterday. The shop windows were small and unpretending; for the farmers' wives and daughters who came to do their shopping on market-days were not to be withdrawn from their regular, well-known shops; and the tradesmen had no wares intended for customers who would go on their way and be seen no more. Ah! even Mrs. Glegg's day seems far back in the past now, separated from us by changes that widen the years. War and the rumour of war had then died out from the minds of men, and if they were ever thought of by the farmers in drab greatcoats, who shook the grain out of their sample bags and buzzed over it in the full market-place, it was as a state of things that belonged to a past golden age, when prices were high. Surely the time was gone for ever when the broad river could bring up unwelcome ships: Russia was only the place where the linseed came from--the more the better-- making grist for the great vertical millstones with their scythe-like arms, roaring and grinding and carefully sweeping as if an informing soul were in them. The Catholics, bad harvests, and the mysterious fluctuations of trade, were the three evils mankind had to fear: even the floods had not been great of late years.[4]

Here past experience is not seen so much with the inward eye. The mood is one of clear-sighted objectivity in which past and present cast on each other an ironical glow.

The quality of objectivity that we have noted in this passage from *The Mill on the Floss* characterizes George Eliot's treatment of all her social material. It is present not only in her depiction of a historical era where, as we have seen, she is betrayed neither into a sentimental idealization of the past nor into a brash glorification of the present. It is at the heart of her analysis of various social classes. Here, an examination of her own happy relationship to the class structure of Victorian England will help us to understand why she can maintain this objective point of view. Recall the principal facts of her career. She grew up in the Warwickshire countryside. Her father was a workman of superior abilities

who, like Caleb Garth in *Middlemarch*, was entrusted with a position of
responsibility as the agent for a large country estate. Her family was on easy
terms with the tenant farmers and agricultural labourers, and at the same time,
enjoyed access to the homes of the gentry. Then, in the early forties, she and her
father moved to Coventry, and she finds herself a member of a little middleclass
group presided over by a successful industrialist with advanced views on a wide
range of topics. Some ten years later, there is an even more dramatic shift. She
is ushered abruptly into the London world of literature and journalism. After a
painful false start, she quickly adjusts herself to new challenges and responsibilities. Within a short time, the provincial girl with an impressive but unbalanced
intellectual background is the assistant editor of the most influential radical
journal of the time and the friend and confidante of philosophers, scientists, and
men of letters. Her union with George Henry Lewes in 1854 cuts her off for a
short time from English society, both from the provincial society of her early
years and the urban literary society she had known in London. But with her
growing fame as a novelist in the sixties and seventies, suspicion and disapproval
turn to acceptance and adulation. To respectability and fame has been added the
grace of wealth. The most vivid picture we have of her in the final years is that
given by young aspirants to a literary career like Henry James who gain
admission to her celebrated London receptions where a spirit of gentility and
reverence presides against a background of bric à brac.[5]

Even such a bald narration of facts provides material for a number of
diverting biographical interpretations. For my present purpose, it will be
sufficient to mention only one. Notice how George Eliot, by the strength of her
personality and the happy alliance of circumstances, was never closely identified
for any length of time with any one social group or any one class. She is, as it
were, removed from the world of petty aspirations and petty conflicts that dog
the author whose social status is a cause for personal concern. Not that she is
unaware of these aspirations and conflicts. They are often the very stuff of her
novels, but they are viewed with irony and detachment, never with the bitterness
that springs from personal spleen. She is never tormented, as one suspects
Thackeray and Meredith were, by the feeling that she doesn't quite belong to the
elite.

This release from a class point of view makes, then, for objectivity. This
objectivity is not to be confused, however, with aloofness and arid detachment.
No other Victorian novelist moves more firmly and confidently through almost
the entire range of nineteenth-century society. There are gaps, of course, but the
total picture is a tribute to her catholicity of vision. Her success with rural types
and with the world of middle-class commercialism is well known. Not so well
known, perhaps, is her success with a more sophisticated and aristocratic society,
the kind of society Dickens entered at his peril. I do not refer here to those
sketches of the amiable rural aristocracy that occur in *Felix Holt* and *Middlemarch*. These people do not constitute a world of their own; they are on the

fringe of the provincial society with which in these novels George Eliot was primarily concerned. But in her last novel, *Daniel Deronda*, she made an upper class world the centre of her vision. It is in many respects the same world as the one Henry James chose for his spiritual home, seen less plastically and less loving, but with a surer grasp, one suspects, of actualities and a sharper perception of social distinctions. Here is the kind of society in which the career of the heroine, Gwendolen Harleth, evolves toward its pathetic conclusion.

> A various party had been invited to meet the new couple: the old aristocracy was represented by Lord and Lady Pentreath; the old gentry by young Mr. and Mrs. Fitzadam of the Worcestershire branch of the Fitzadams; politics and the public good, as specialised in the cider interest, by Mr. Fenn, member for West Orchards, accompanied by his two daughters; Lady Mallinger's family, by her brother, Mr. Raymond, and his wife; the useful bachelor element by Mr. Sinker, the eminent counsel, and by Mr. Vandernoddt, whose acquaintance Sir Hugo had found pleasant enough at Leubronn to be adopted in England.[6]

George Eliot's insight into this cosmopolitan upper-class society is sharpened by her selection of a heroine who, lacking the pedigree of wealth and family name, can offer only beauty and a haughty temperament. But beauty and a haughty temperament can, if properly used, lead to the miracle of an aristocratic marriage. And to Gwendolen's relatives and friends such a marriage is an act of deep social piety. Her uncle, the local rector, reflects as follows on the opportunity this presented to his niece:

> This match with Grandcourt presented itself to him as a sort of public affair; perhaps there were ways in which it might even strengthen the Establishment. To the Rector, whose father (nobody would have suspected it, and nobody was told) had risen to be a provincial corn-dealer, aristocratic heirship resembled regal heirship in excepting its possessor from the ordinary standard of moral judgments. Grandcourt, the almost certain baronet, the probable peer, was to be ranged with public personages, and was a match to be accepted on broad general grounds national and ecclesiastical.[7]

Of course Gwendolen marries the young aristocrat. Her marriage swiftly and cruelly teaches her much about the moral reality that may underlie the charm and easy manners and the prestige of wide estates. Grandcourt, her husband, is a masterful analysis of what we might call the "infernal aristocrat" beside whom Lord Steyne is a genial and attractive Don Juan. I do not think that George Eliot wants us to look upon Grandcourt as a symbol of aristocratic decay; she was not given to symbolism and besides she was not naive enough to suggest that moral qualities are simply the product of social background. Still, as the following passage shows, there is no doubt that she saw a relationship between Grandcourt's supercilious amorality and his general view of society.

> Grandcourt's importance as a subject of this realm was of the grandly passive kind which consists in the inheritance of land. Political and social movements touched him only through the wire of his rental, and his most careful biographer need not have read up on Schleswig-Holstein, the policy of Bismarck, trade-unions, household suffrage, or even the last commercial panic. He glanced over

the best newspaper columns of these topics, and his views on them can hardly be said to have wanted breadth, since he embraced all Germans, all commercial men, and all voters liable to use the wrong kind of soap, under the general epithet of "brutes"; but he took no action on these much agitated questions beyond looking from under his eyelids at any man who mentioned them, and retaining a silence which served to shake the opinions of timid thinkers.[8]

Although the aristocratic world of *Daniel Deronda* is sharply observed and vividly recreated, it is true, none the less, that it lies outside the range of George Eliot's normal vision. In the novels on which her reputation chiefly depends she concentrates on rural and provincial England. And whereas *Daniel Deronda* is the novel in which she came closest to writing about her immediately contemporary world--it is set in the England of the sixties--she works most easily in an era that belongs to her own youth or to the youth of the preceding generation. She has, as it were, two historical centres towards which her imagination is strongly attracted. The first, and the less important, is the England of the turn of the century, an England that she thinks of as innocent of industrialism, as yet undisturbed by religious schism and social cleavage. This is the world of *Adam Bede* and *Silas Marner*. The second is the world that she recalls with all the warmth and immediacy with which she thinks of her own youth. It is the England of the late twenties and early thirties, of Catholic Emancipation and the first Reform Bill, an England moving quickly toward a new dispensation, an England where religion has hardened into habit or has split into sect, where the old social structure is feeling the pull of industrialism and new political faiths. This is the England of *The Mill on the Floss*, *Felix*, and *Middlemarch*.

What I propose to do now is to examine in some detail the kind of social analysis and the function it plays in three of these novels--in *Adam Bede*, in *The Mill on the Floss* and in *Middlemarch*.

Adam Bede, as we have seen, takes us back to the opening years of the century, to an era that George Eliot did not, of course, know at first hand, but whose flavour was communicated to her by stories and reminiscences heard during her youth. As George Eliot's first extended work in fiction, it is relatively simple and uncomplicated in action, and the characters follow bold and obvious lines. Although George Eliot transposes it in a philosophical key, we immediately recognize the familiar story of the handsome, carefree squire who seduces the pretty, unsophisticated peasant girl and shatters what might have been an idyllic pastoral romance. As befits such a story and such a caste of characters, the society of *Adam Bede* harks back to a preceding age. It is paternalistic and feudalistic, with the squire at the top of the hierarchy, and with tenant farmers, independent artisans, and agricultural labourers arranged carefully in descending order. There is nothing harsh and oppressive about this society. Indeed, on a casual social level, a spirit of camaraderie prevails. But what enables this camaraderie between classes to flourish is not, of course, any spirit of egalitarian democracy, but simply an unquestioning acceptance of the need and of the justice of rigid class distinctions. In this best of all possible worlds there is no place for protest and no need of escape. For such old-world Toryism George Eliot has a slightly wistful admiration. It finds its most shining embodiment in her hero, the strong and incorruptible workman, Adam Bede:

> Adam was very susceptible to the influence of rank, and quite ready to give an extra amount of respect to every one who had more advantages than himself, not being a philosopher, or a proletaire with democratic ideas, but simply a stout-limbed clever carpenter with a large fund of reverence in his nature, which inclined him to admit all established claims unless he saw very clear grounds for questioning them. He had no theories about setting the world to rights, but he saw there was a great deal of damage done by building with ill-seasoned timber--by ignorant men in fine clothes making plans for outhouses and workshops and the like, without knowing the bearings of things--by slovenly joiners' work, and by hasty contracts that could never be fulfilled without ruining somebody; and he resolved, for his part, to set his face against such doings. On these points he would have maintained his opinion against the largest landed proprietor in Loamshire or Stonyshire either; but he felt that beyond these it would be better for him to defer to people who were more knowing than himself.[9]

The society of *Adam Bede* is thus simple in structure and apparently self-contained and impervious to change.

A completely static world, however is not any more possible in fiction than it is in life. The rural centre of Hayslope is disturbed not merely by the fatal conjunction of a handsome and genially indiscreet young squire and a pretty, light-headed milk-maid, but by the belated arrival from the world outside of a mildly revolutionary force known as Methodism. But Methodism is more an alien curiosity in this setting than a conquering gospel. Into the mouth of Dinah, the Methodist preacher, George Eliot puts an analysis of the social background of Methodism, all the more effective because the speaker is not conscious of the full implications of her comments.

> But I've noticed, that in these villages where the people lead a quiet life among the green pastures and the still waters, tilling the ground and tending the cattle, there's a strange deadness to the Word, as different as can be from the great towns, like Leeds, where I once went to visit a holy woman who preaches there. It's wonderful how rich is the harvest of souls up those high-walled streets, where you seemed to walk as in a prison-yard, and the ear is deafened with the sounds of worldly toil. I think maybe it is because the promise is sweeter when this life is so dark and weary, and the soul gets more hungry when the body is ill at ease.[10]

Dinah, it is to be noted, transcends the religious movement of which she is the spokesman. As the novel progresses, we think of her less as a methodist and more as a practical saint divorced from sectarianism, as a warmly human embodiment of the essence of Christianity.

Although the social structure of *Adam Bede* is firmly and clearly indicated, it operates more as background than as an integral part of the problem posed by the action. Hetty's plight and Arthur's predicament are not given a social setting, outside of the fact, of course, that the wide separation in social status makes marriage impossible. If Hetty had been given more durable charms, if her aspirations to be a member of the great world had had a more realistic foundation, then we might have had a theme for social tragedy, not a study in the pathos of moral consequences. But that would be to ask for a level of sophistication that George Eliot at this time was not interested in achieving. *Adam Bede* is a folk story, given a realistic social setting and told in the light of advanced theories about the nature of human conduct.

Completely absent from *Adam Bede* are the sense of struggle, the grasping for security and social status, the frank acceptance of material values, the occasional note of protest that characterize the increasingly middle-class society of Victorian England. *The Mill on the Floss* ushers us immediately into such a world. It is, in some respects, George Eliot's most sustained analysis of English philistinism. The benevolent paternalism of *Adam Bede* is succeeded by a society where a certain measure of equality is within the grasp of all, provided one has a comfortable balance in the bank and the assurance of a good return on investments. With a few exceptions, the good citizens of St. Oggs--independent farmers, merchants, professional men--subscribe to the gospel of success whose characteristic virtues are diligence, frugality, and, if circumstances permit, honesty.

Since the characters in *The Mill on the Floss* have been partially released from a system of rigid class segregation, they are more sensitive to social status, more exposed to impersonal economic forces that were those in *Adam Bede*. We are now in a world that is dominated by the pursuit of financial security, a world that is to become increasingly familiar to us in English fiction. The passion for money runs through the story like a repulsive disease; the history of the Tulliver family, for instance, is charted in a series of financial crises. Beneath the casual pleasantries of social life lies a bedrock of economic necessity. It is a cause for wonder that no diligent Marxian critic, as far as I know, has extracted the following passage from *The Mill on the Floss* for appropriate comment:

> In writing the history of unfashionable families, one is apt to fall into a tone of emphasis which is very far from being the tone of good society, where principles and beliefs are not of an extremely moderate kind, but are always presupposed, no subjects being eligible but such as can be touched with a light and graceful irony. But then, good society has its claret and its velvet carpets, its dinner engagements six weeks deep, its opera and its faery ballrooms; rides off its ennui on thoroughbred horses, lounges at the club, has to keep clear of crinoline vortices, gets its science done by Faraday, and its religion by the superior clergy who are to be met in the best houses: how should it have time or need for belief and emphasis? But good society, floated on gossamer wings of light irony, is of very expensive production; requiring nothing less than a wide and arduous national life condensed in unfragrant, deafening factories, cramping itself in mines, sweating at furnaces, grinding, hammering, weaving under more or less oppression of carbonic acid--or else, spread over sheepwalks, and scattered in lonely houses and huts on the clayey or chalky corn-lands, where the rainy days look dreary. This wide national life is based entirely on emphasis--the emphasis of want, which urges it into all the activities necessary for the maintenance of good society and light irony: it spends its heavy years often in a chill, uncarpeted fashion, amidst family discord unsoftened by long corridors.[11]

A society such as this demands an approach radically different from that employed by George Eliot in *Adam Bede*. George Eliot is no longer the kindly romanticist describing a way of life whose disappearance she half regrets. She is now unsparingly analytical; she describes the solemn rites and customs of the Dodson family in the spirit almost of the anthropologist recording the peculiarities of a native tribe. And her tone is appropriately objective, enlivened by an irony that ranges from the playful to the mordantly serious. It is significant that Henry James--one of George Eliot's most discerning critics and a disciple, with qualifications--observed about *The Mill on the Floss* that "The portions of the story which bear upon the Dodson family are in their way not unworthy of Balzac. . . .We are reminded of him by the attempt to classify the Dodsons socially in a scientific manner, and to accumulate small examples of their idiosyncracies."[12]

The picture of this sordid, materialistic world is not, of course, the whole story of *The Mill on the Floss*. I have referred already to the passages of poetic recollection where George Eliot sees her own childhood and youth in the childhood and youth of Maggie Tulliver. And Maggie's whole life is, you might say, a persistent attempt to escape from the cramping environment of St. Oggs. She is an early Dorothea, emotional, idealistic, striving to encompass certain vaguely benevolent ends. True, Maggie falls short of the heroic; her infatuation for one of George Eliot's schoolgirlish sketches of masculine charm might seem to be a pathetic climax to life that, so we are told, "was full of eager, passionate longings for all that was beautiful and glad." Possibly the love affair between Maggie and Stephen is meant to be a crowning irony, George Eliot's final comment in the novel on the fragility of ideals in a materialistic society. But the problem is more complex than that. At the moment of her greatest weakness and, even more, at the moment of her greatest humiliation, George Eliot wants us to look upon Maggie as inherently noble. We may be sure that she is not arguing romantically that Maggie merits our sympathy and praise because she turns back to face the uncomprehending wrath of society at the call of a moral principle--a society, moreover, that is blind to spiritual subtleties and would have acquiesced in the easier solution of her problem. Maggie's action thus becomes a symbolic denial of the validity of utilitarian ethics. If she had obeyed her natural desires and married Stephen, she would not, it is true, have brought the greatest happiness to the greatest number of people, but at least she would have brought the least pain to the least number of people. But Maggie scorns this compromise. She resolves on a course that can bring no approval from the community and only a troubled peace to her own conscience. The dilemma is too great for Maggie Tulliver and, one suspects, for George Eliot. The flood waters of the Floss provide a convenient solution.

What I want to emphasize, then, about social analysis in *The Mill on the Floss* is, first, that it is more complex and more pervasive than social analysis in *Adam Bede* and, consequently, bulks more significantly in the novel. In the second place, the analysis of social forces is here bound up closely with the working out of the theme. Whereas in *Adam Bede* society is simply framework or background, in *The Mill on the Floss* it is an active agent. Not merely must the heroine subdue the tumult in her own soul; she must fight against the collective prejudices of a society for which the greatest good can be reckoned only in terms of material success. Yet, in charting George Eliot's use of social analysis, *The Mill on the Floss* is only, as it were, a half-way house. She is still dealing with a relatively simple and undifferentiated society, one, moreover, that is innocent of ideas and is quarantined from the larger world outside. To demonstrate fully her power of social analysis, she needed a society more complex in its structure and more deeply implicated in the world of thought and controversy. In *Middlemarch*, the greatest of her novels, she created just such a society.

On the surface, *Middlemarch* seems to be merely a bulkier and more detailed examination of the same material that George Eliot had used in *The Mill on the Floss*--the provincial English town and the surrounding countryside of which it is the economic and cultural capital. But in reality the range of observation has become greater and the point of view has shifted notably. St. Oggs is one particular provincial town, clearly seen and vividly recreated; *Middlemarch* is English provincial society in the days just before the first Reform Bill. At the heart of this society, increasingly assertive and self-confident, is the prosperous middle-class, deriving wealth and prestige from commerce and banking and occasionally from a profession--the Vincys, the Bulstrodes and the Lydgates. From this centre we move upward into the squierarchy and the local families of established position--the Brookes and the Casaubons, and touch finally upon the life of the lesser, rural aristocracy. As we move downward from this same centre, we remain longest with a family like the Garths, honest and industrious folk who have not yet learned the catechism of success; we pause briefly to observe the repulsive entourage that gather around the expiring Featherstone--small, independent farmers of some means; and we listen from time to time to the voice of the tenant farmer and the agricultural labourer, raised bitterly and sometimes drunkenly against the ills of his lot. In this rural, midland society George Eliot had, of course, no place for the industrialized working class or for the artisans and colliers who appear in *Felix Holt*. Perhaps this is just as well. Like most of the Victorian novelists, she did not know the working man; she saw him at a distance, and at this remove he appeared less as an individual and more as a vague and disturbing element in society.

To this diversity of social class George Eliot in *Middlemarch* has added diversity of occupation and profession, so that social analysis is conducted from a multiple point of view. Thus, Casaubon is a study in the pathos of an arid and unimaginative scholarship. Lydgate, in his way, is a village Huxley who has dedicated his life to the ideals of disinterestedness and uncompromising veracity.

Mr. Brooke is a politician, although inept in method and muddled in theory. Will Ladislaw is a free-lance intellectual, with an extensive if unorganized repertory of ideas. Even Dorothea, denied a profession and a rational education by the dictates of the age, tries to carve out a career as humanitarian and philanthropist.

It is, of course, typical of George Eliot's art that, given characters such as these, she should try to relate them to their appropriate background. Casaubon and Lydgate emerge to the accompaniment of random observations on and brief sketches of the state of contemporary scholarship and medical science. The political material is even more prominent and often operates as a sort of central reference point for George Eliot's multiple approach. The livelier minds of the community look beyond the immediate and the personal and reflect on the political problems of the day. Whereas St. Oggs had groped its way into political consciousness only on the issue of Catholic emancipation--not so much a realistic problem as a momentary return to the passions and prejudices of the past--*Middlemarch* is awake in a wide-eyed and eagerly naive fashion to the great issues of reform.

The increased scope and allusiveness of George Eliot's social analysis enables her to examine more fully than before the counterpoint of class and social distinction. In *Adam Bede* wholly, and in *The Mill on the Floss* mainly, the characters were placed against an unchanging social and political back-ground; here, however, we are in the midst of flux, in a world of rapid change that has swallowed many of the old taboos and standards and is busily creating new ones. If rural gentry and aristocracy mix more easily with solid middle-class families, the solid middle-class families are more sensitive to distinctions within their own group. The vice of snobbery, unknown in *Adam Bede* and incipient in *The Mill on the Floss*, has now emerged and taken on cruel refinements. The Vincys, for instance, look down upon the Garths because Mrs. Garth has taken in pupils and Mr. Garth is financially unsound.

This is a world, moreover, where ideas, no less than economic status and social position, can divide or unite. The reform movement cuts boldly across class divisions and gathers in a diverse brood of adherents. Enlisted under its banner are Bulstrode, wealthy banker and pious dissenter, Farebrother, tolerant, this-worldly church of England clergyman, Vincy, prosperous merchant and genial man of the world, and Will Ladislaw, bohemian and intellectual. The number of malcontents, of those who try to burst out of their social mould, has, in this novel, greatly increased. St. Oggs could throw up only a Maggie and a Philip, but most of the leading characters in *Middlemarch* are jarred into dissatisfaction and sometimes even into active rebellion. Usually, of course, the rebellion is abortive; circumstances twine about the idealist and bind him securely to the commonplace and the respectable. But still rebellion exists, and escape is not impossible.

Middlemarch might be described as a picture of a society where two opposed principles struggle for dominance. The one we might call the rigid or the static. It is embodied in the class structure, in the prejudices and customs that make for division and segregation, in the materialism that discourages thought and strangles aspiration. The other we might call the flexible or the dynamic. It is embodied in the social and intellectual movements that disdain the niceties of class division and in the personal vision that sets at nought the things of this world. In George Eliot's reading of life, it was the former principle that more often than not triumphed, but not without a struggle.

I have tried to show the different roles that social analysis plays in three novels: how in *Adam Bede* it has a minor, background role; how in *The Mill on the Floss* it bulks much more significantly and strengthens and clarifies the theme; how finally in *Middlemarch* it helps to determine the choice of material, gives added depth to characterization, and provides one of the ideas by which a diverse and complex world takes on form and meaning. Yet I do not want to suggest that in *Middlemarch* the reader is being constantly reminded of the existence of a social context. If George Eliot has more powerfully than any other English novelist the social vision--the ability to embrace a diversity of social material: economic status, class division, professional characteristics, political divergences, she has at the same time, the power to fuse this material unobtrusively with her analysis of private motives. In *Middlemarch*, for instance, notice the way the political issue remains in the background, coming forward only to add colour and excitement to a scene or to sharpen conflicts that have already been established. I select as an example of this a scene in the novel that would appear to have a heavy political emphasis.[13] Lydgate and Ladislaw argue about electoral reform. A familiar antithesis is sharply and economically set forth in the exchange between the two men: Lydgate protests against "crying up a measure as if it were a universal cure, and crying up men who are part of the very disease that wants curing"; Ladislaw cheerfully admits that electoral reform is no cure-all and that reform candidates are often corrupt and ignorant, but argues that, after all, "your cure must begin somewhere." Now this dialogue is no doubt politically illuminating, but its real function in the novel lies elsewhere. The conversation takes place in the Lydgate drawing-room in the presence of Lydgate's wife, Rosamond, who looks upon it as a boring and vexatious interruption of the pleasant inanities of social life. As he talks, Lydgate is aware not only that his wife is bored but that she derives a pleasure from Ladislaw's innocent attentions that his own presence and conversation can no longer give. These disturbing thoughts force a more acrimonious note into his speech, which becomes stronger as he realizes the ironic cross-reference between his own relations with the hypocritical Bulstrode and his spirited protest against the linking of high, political goals with narrow measures and inferior men. This scene, then, emerges naturally from a private situation and illuminates character and content. Social analysis is the handmaiden, not the mistress, of George Eliot's art.

There are, it seems to me, two principal dangers to which the novelist deeply interested in the ways of society is exposed. One of these dangers is described by Mr. Edwin Muir in a comment he makes about the novels of H.G. Wells and John Galsworthy. "To Mr. Wells and Mr. Galsworthy," he writes, "society is essentially an abstract conception, not an imaginative reality; they do not recreate society, therefore, in their novels, they merely illustrate it, or rather their ideas about it. . . .To them society is there full grown as an idea at the beginning; it is not created by the characters, rather it creates them; but at the same time it is always beyond them, exists as a thing in itself, and cannot be adumbrated completely except by employing the arts of exposition."[14] The other danger is illustrated in the novels of Thackeray. Here there is no question of an abstract conception of society and of characters who are merely deduced from that conception. As Mr. Muir further observes, "Thackeray sets his characters going, he exhibits them continuously in a present not verbal but psychological, and at the end a picture of society has sprung up before our eyes."[15] But one should add that at the end of the Thackeray novel the characters he has so magnificently created tend to lose their identity and to disappear into the limbo of Vanity Fair. George Eliot, not the least accomplished of the Victorians in the art of compromise, avoids these two extremes. In *Middlemarch*, for instance, her vision of society and her vision of the individual never split asunder. They are bound together by an interlocking of the particular and the general, of the concrete and the theoretical, by a method of social analysis that has been refined into a subtle and complex art.

NOTES

1. This, I take it, is largely what Mr. F.R. Leavis has in mind when he refers to George Eliot's "Tolstoyan depth and reality." The whole passage from Mr. Leavis is worth quoting if only as an indication of the extent to which he will go in his effort at the critical rehabilitation of George Eliot. One regrets that his brilliant and perceptive critical analysis should be marred by a kind of literary Darwinism that marks out one novelist for survival in a ruthless struggle for existence: "I. . .affirm my conviction that by the side of George Eliot--and the comparison shouldn't be necessary--Meredith appears as a shallow exhibitionist (his famous 'intelligence' a laboured and vulgar brilliance) and Hardy, decent as he is, as a provincial manufacturer of gauche and heavy fictions that sometimes have corresponding value. For a positive indication of her place and quality I think of a Russian, not Turgenev, but a far greater. Tolstoy--who, we all know, is pre-eminent in getting 'the spirit of life itself.' George Eliot, of course, is not as transcendentally great as Tolstoy, but she *is* great, and great in the same way. . . .Of George Eliot it can be said that her best work has a Tolstoyan depth and reality." (F.R. Leavis. *The Great Tradition* [London, 1948], pp. 124-5.)

2. In the light of these comments, we can overcome the slight sense of shock occasioned by the critical juxtaposition of George Eliot and Proust. It is not merely a question of a somewhat similar use of memory. Proust knew the novels of George Eliot well and deeply admired them. For a discussion of the relationship between George Eliot and Proust see Franklin Gary, "In Search of George Eliot. An approach through Marcel Proust." *Symposium*, IV (1933), pp. 182-206; L.A. Bisson, "Proust, Bergson and George Eliot," *Modern Language Review*, XL (1945), pp. 104-14.

3. Gary (*op. cit.*, p. 184) quotes from a Proust letter: "Mais deux pages du *Moulin sur la Floss* me fait pleurer."

4. *The Mill on the Floss* (Everyman edition), Book 1, Ch. 12, p. 108.

5. Henry James writes in a letter to William James, May 1, 1878: "The Leweses were very urbane and friendly, and I think that I shall have the right *dorénavant* to consider myself a Sunday *habitué*. The great George Eliot is both sweet and superior, and has a delightful expression in her large, long, pale, equine face. I had my turn at sitting beside her and being conversed with in a low, but most harmonious tone; and bating a tendency to *aborder* only the highest themes I have no fault to find with her." *The Letters of Henry James*, ed. Percy Lubbock, (New York, 1920) i, 61.

6. *Daniel Deronda* (Library Edition) Book V, Ch. 35, pp. 291-2.

7. *Ibid*, Book II, Ch. 13, pp. 99-100.

8. *Ibid*, Book VI, Ch. 84, p. 423.

9. *Adam Bede* (Everyman edition) Ch. 16, p. 160.

10. *Adam Bede*, Ch. 8, p. 91.

11. *The Mill on the Floss* (Everyman edition) Book IV, Ch. 3, pp. 272-3.

12. Henry James, "The Novels of George Eliot" in *Views and Reviews*, (Boston, 1908), pp. 31-32. The question of specific influences is a difficult one in considering a writer like George Eliot whose reading in the novel, as in most other fields of literature, was so extensive. Still it is significant that she had been reading and reflecting on the novels of Balzac just when she was beginning her career as fiction writer. On July 21, 1855, there appeared an article by her in *The Leader*, "The Morality of Wilhelm Meister," in which she referred to Balzac as "perhaps the most wonderful writer of fiction the world has ever seen." She goes on, however, to say that Balzac has overstepped the limit of permissible realism and that "he drags us by his magic force through scene after scene of unmitigated vice, till the effect of walking among this human carrion is a moral nausea." The essay is reprinted in *Essays and Collected Papers* (Boston, 1909), pp. 305-09.

13. *Middlemarch* (Everyman edition), Book V, Ch. 46.

14. Edwin Muir, *The Structure of the Novel* (London, 1928), p. 122.

15. *Ibid*.

GEORGE ELIOT'S LOCATION OF VALUE IN HISTORY

Renascence, 1980

SARA MOORE PUTZELL

In an age of vanishing certainties and a disappearing God, the Victorians looked to science, to philosophy, to the emerging disciplines of sociology and psychology--even to fiction--to provide new, more secure sources of value for human activity, particularly for the progress of human civilization of which they were so conscious. One of the most important answers to their search came from George Eliot, whom they knew to be conversant with the most advanced ideas of the day and whom they respected for having "in the midst of great perplexities. . .brought great intellectual powers to setting before us a lofty moral ideal."[1] That ideal as summarized in Eliot's famous poetic credo, "O May I Join the Choir Invisible," is to

join the choir invisible
Of those immortal dead who live again
In minds made better by their presence.

Eliot taught her readers to aspire to meliorate present human suffering and to contribute to the moral evolution of the species. It is a commonplace of Eliot criticism that such ennobling action arises in her fiction from sympathy, an imaginative fellow feeling that coincides with thought to form, as Norman Feltes demonstrates, a higher, "unified sensibility."[2]

Variously described as Wordsworthian, Feuerbachian, and intuitionist, Eliot's faith in individual feeling as moral guide suggests a corollary faith in free will, yet her novels portray the subordination of individual wills to the communal in a context of inexorable causality. Consequently, while to some readers Eliot seems simply to have secularized Christian ethics, to others--most notably George Levine--she seems a determinist for whom man's will is not free, but conditioned by experience.[3] A major obstacle to critical agreement concerning the unity of Eliot's faith in feeling with her belief in causal law has been a confusion of the function of feeling with its object; that is, feeling has been regarded as both a guide to moral action and as a locus of value. Locating value in feeling results in the kind of contradiction that Ian Milner finds in Bernard J. Paris's study of Eliot's values, *Experiments in Life*, which attributes to her the view that man is "the helpless pawn" of "blind forces" and on the same page asserts that she believed in "a class of moral doctrines which have nothing to do with the cosmic order of things," but "derive their sanction. . .from the personal consciousness of human beings."[4] Individual feeling cannot logically be the locus of value in a world in which society and nature shape character, yet to regard any law external to the individual--whether it be natural, social, or supernatural-- as the locus of value for Eliot is to ignore the tension between her protagonists and their societies as well as her comments on the failure of universal laws to cover individual cases.[5] Logic indicates that the locus of value is the point of intersection of individual lives with the larger life of the world, which is history.

In *George Eliot's Early Novels*, U.C. Knoepflmacher analyzes history as a possible locus of value for Eliot. After placing her "conflicting impulses" toward realism and idealism in the context of Carlyle's advice to "Examine History" for a new basis for faith, Knoepflmacher argues that, while Eliot felt the importance of temporal laws and made the perception of the individual's relation to historical forces a condition of heroism in her novels, history did not yield for her "Carlyle's subjective belief in the operations of a mystical *Geist*." Although Eliot follows "the lead of post-Hegelians like Feuerbach" in locating man's salvation in the temporal world, Knoepflmacher finds that she resists the transcendence of actual existence Hegel's philosophy implies until in her later novels, particularly *Daniel Deronda*, she creates from history "a power corresponding to the exacting Miltonic God which she had rejected"; even so, Knoepflmacher says, "the split between artistic and historical truth would still remain."[6] For several reasons, history as Hegel understands it should be reconsidered as a locus of value in what Knoepflmacher calls Eliot's "Morality of Experience."[7] First, as the translator of Feuerbach and Strauss and the admirer of Comte, Eliot is the intellectual granddaughter of Hegel, and, as Jerome B. Schneewind points out, her integration of intuitionism and determinism in *Daniel Deronda* is comparable to that of post-Hegelian British idealists.[8] Second, Hegel's transcendent Absolute or *Geist* comes to be only in and by actual existence, much as Eliot's sympathetic imagination and the transhuman life it allows is inseparable from actual existence. Finally, like Hegel, Eliot describes individuals and cultures as part of an evolving world soul such that history is a locus of moral value.

The birth of thought is the birth of civilization for Eliot, who pictures the "young race" as "Dividing towards sublimer union" under the influence of an "omnipresent Energy" that

Clove sense & image subtilly in twain,
Then wedded them, till heavenly Thought was born.[9]

The mind of man, which is the world's soul, then evolves through "that partition of mankind into races and nations, resulting in various national points of view or varieties of national genius, which has been the means of enriching and rendering more and more complete man's knowledge of the inner and outer world."[10] Through the interaction of peoples arise the cultural forms that are the embodiment or life of the world soul: "that treasure of knowledge, science, poetry, refinement of thought, feeling, and manners, great memories and the

interpretation of great records, which is carried on from the minds of one
generation to the minds of another" and is only accumulated through "the slow
stupendous teaching of the world's events" (*Essays*, 425, 429). Eliot's last novel,
Daniel Deronda (1876), constitutes her fullest exposition of this concept of
evolving cultural or world consciousness, for the hero's development is one of
recognizing his importance as a repository of the idea of Jewish national unity
and thus of contributing to the life of his people and to a kind of Hegelian
Weltgeist. Deronda learns that "The world grows, and its frame is knit together
by the growing soul" that evolves through peoples and individuals: "The life of
a people grows. . .it absorbs the thought of other nations into its own forms, and
gives back the thought as new wealth to the world," and it does so through the
mind and life of the individual "who feels the life of his people stirring within
his own" and thus makes "a new pathway for events."[11]

Deronda's recognition that his duty as a self-conscious Jew is to work
for the cause of Jewish nationalism typifies the relation between individual and
world history in Eliot's fiction. Individuals contribute to the evolution of the
world soul by the actions--the work--in which they realize their identities. This
work may be a kind of physical labor that makes all civilization possible,
according to Eliot's eulogy of one of her model workmen in *Middlemarch*:

Wise in his daily work was he:
  To fruits of diligence,
And not to faiths or polity,
  He plied his utmost sense,
These perfect in their little parts,
  Whose work is all their prize--
Without them how could laws, or arts,
  Or towered cities rise? (IV, xl, 190)

This work may also be a more intellectual kind of labor, such as Ladislaw's
editing a reform newspaper in *Middlemarch*, work that he defends against a
charge of inadequacy by pointing out that a "cure must begin somewhere, and.
. .a thousand things which debase a population can never be reformed without
this particular reform to begin with" (V, xlvi, 292). The work may be spiritual
or artistic, for religion embodies man's "conscientious effort to *know*," and Eliot
says, "The fundamental principles of all just thought and beautiful action or
creation are the same, and in making clear to ourselves what is best and noblest
in art, we are making clear to ourselves what is best and noblest in morals."[12]

Through their individual works men create civilization, which acts as a
kind of intellectual mold that determines the basic mental level of those born into
a culture. Thus, that the generality of mankind is not more primitive, more
superstitious and cruel, is not due to their individual natures, Eliot explains, so
much as to their being

pressed upon and held up by what we may call an external Reason--the sum of conditions resulting from the laws of material growth, from changes produced by great historical collisions shattering the structures of ages and making new highways for events and ideas, and from the activities of higher minds no longer existing merely as opinions and teaching, but as institutions and organisations with which the interests, the affections, and the habits of the multitude are inextricably interwoven. (*Essays*, 402)

Comparable to the objective mind or life of Hegel's *Geist*, this external Reason appears in Eliot's novels most obviously in such elements as the growing shipping industry to which Tom Tulliver's trading contributes in *The Mill on the Floss*, the spreading railroads that change English society in general and the life of Fred Vincy in particular in *Middlemarch*, and the conflicting political groups that shape the lives of Felix Holt, Will Ladislaw, and Tito Melema. To the extent that this external Reason is still in evolution, it serves as a limitation on such "later-born Theresas" as Dorothea Brooke, whose attempts "to shape their thought and deed in noble agreement" may seem "mere inconsistency and formlessness" if "helped by no coherent social faith and order which could perform the function of knowledge for the ardently willing soul" (*Middlemarch*, Prelude, 2). However shapeless an individual's life may seem, "there is no private life which has not been determined by a wider public life" (*Felix Holt*, iii, 72).

As "external Reason," that public life implies an internal reason, a subjective mind in Hegel's terms, which is also transmitted from generation to generation. In *The Spanish Gypsy*, Fedalma feels the presence of such an internal reason when the revelation of her gypsy heritage comes to her like "a part" of her, "a wakened thought/That, rising like a giant,. . ./. . .grows into a doom" (161). Deronda feels it when the revelation of his Jewish heritage reveals immediately to him the purpose and the work for which he has instinctively longed. Of the transmission of such feeling, Eliot says, "Our sentiments may be called organised traditions; and a large part of our actions gather all their justification, all their attraction and aroma, from the memory of the life lived, of the actions done, before we were born" (*Essays*, 409). Thus, while individuals create history, history shapes individuals, for they are born out of and live in specific historical contexts.

Eliot stresses the historicity of individual human nature in describing the character of Maggie Tulliver in *The Mill on the Floss*. Maggie is "not her characteristics, but her history, which is a thing hardly to be predicted even from the completest knowledge of characteristics" (VI, vi, 210). As a "history," rather than a set of fixed qualities, Maggie is describable as a sequence of actions in response to her inherited idea of herself, the historical society in which she lives, and the new relations to that idea and society created by her actions. Consequently, to understand her and other "young natures in many generations, that in the onward tendency of human things have risen above the mental level of the generation before them," we must feel, says Eliot, the "oppressive narrowness" of the families and societies against which they struggle to distinguish their individual selves and "to which they have been nevertheless tied by the strongest fibres of their hearts" (IV, i, 6). Through her struggle to harmonize her individuality with the customs of her family and culture, Maggie realizes a superior identity, discovers a basis for moral action, and contributes to the "growing good" of the world.

Maggie develops through experiencing and reflecting on the contradictions between her feeling that as a dutiful daughter she should join her family and society in "revering whatever was customary and respectable" and her acting as an individual whose unique experiences result in deeds that separate her from her family. As a child, she tries to dissociate her idea of herself from the objective reality of her deeds; she tells her brother, for example, that she "couldn't help it" that the rabbits she had promised to feed starved to death. As an adult, however, she learns to connect her idea of herself with the historical person her acts create. This lesson comes through her personal suffering, which enables her to imagine the suffering her historical self must cause others. Having suffered throughout her adolescence from the feeling that she must deny herself all that gives her most pleasure--books, music, friendship--Maggie suffers most when she relaxes her resistance and drifts into an elopement with Stephen Guest, her cousin Lucy's accepted suitor. This expression of her individual passion brings her into immediate conflict with herself as a member of her family and society, giving her pain over what she has done and over what this historical action means for others: "I should never have failed towards Lucy and Philip [Maggie's suitor]," she says, "if I had not been weak, selfish, and hard--able to think of their pain without a pain to myself that would have destroyed all temptation" (VI, xiv, 330). In thinking about how her action affects these two, Maggie attains a fuller idea of herself as not only her ideas and her acts but also the relations to others that her acts make. In feeling how the elopement that epitomizes her separate individuality injures others and, in fact, implicates her further in their lives, Maggie brings together her hitherto abstract idea of herself as a dutiful member of her family and community with her knowledge of herself as a sequence of concrete and often calamitous acts.

Maggie's recognition that her ties to others are part of a historical identity that she has forged by her deeds gives her a basis for moral decision. When Stephen argues that their romance has "proved" that "natural law surmounts every other," Maggie rejects her individual desire as "but the inclination of the moment" and affirms her *entire* history, which is both individual and social, as her law: "If the past is not to bind us," she asks, "where can duty lie?" (VI, xiv, 329). What Maggie feels bound by is not her family's idea of duty nor any categorical imperative, but her own concrete, historical experience. In contrast to "the men of maxims," whom Eliot criticizes for being "guided in their moral judgment solely by general rules, thinking that these will lead them to justice by a ready-made patent method, without the trouble of exerting patience, discrimination, impartiality--without any care to assure themselves whether they have the insight that comes from a hardly-earned estimate of temptation, or from a life vivid and intense enough to have created a wide fellow-feeling with all that is human" (*Mill*, VII, ii, 363), Maggie makes her decision to renounce Stephen on the basis of her memory of her own unhappy history and of the unhappiness that must be part of her present self if she marries him.

Maggie's basing her decision on her knowledge of suffering represents no adherence to an abstract value, but a reliance on actual, lived history, as Felix Holt's explanation of his own morality makes clear. Much as Maggie rejects Stephen's vision of a future when "their life together must be heaven" because she cannot bear to continue causing "misery to those whom the course of [their] lives has made dependent on [them]" (VI, xiii, 318; xiv, 329), Felix refuses to join "the push and the scramble for money and position" because he cannot accept a potentially pleasant future as justification for contributing to the world's present misery (*Felix Holt*, xxvii, 36). "Any man is at liberty to call me a fool, and say that mankind are benefited by the push and the scramble in the long-run," says Felix. "But I care for the people who live now and will not be living when the long-run comes" (XXVII, 36). Among these people is Felix himself. Like Maggie, he has an idea of himself, derived from his heritage and experience, that he cannot contradict without pain. "It all depends," he explains,

on what a man gets into his consciousness--what life thrusts into his mind, so that it becomes present to him as remorse is present to the guilty, or a mechanical problem to an inventive genius. There are two things I've got present in that way: one of them is the picture of what I should hate to be. I'm determined never to go about making my face simpering or solemn, and telling professional lies for profit; or to get tangled in affairs where I must wink at dishonesty and pocket the proceeds, and justify that knavery as part of a system that I can't alter. If I once went into that sort of struggle for success, I should want to win--I should defend the wrong that I had once identified myself with. I should become everything that I see now beforehand to be detestable. (xxvii, 37)

In contrast to Lydgate and Bulstrode in *Middlemarch*, who virtually conspire to conceal murder in order to preserve their ideas of themselves as potential saviors of humanity, Felix looks to no abstract "long-run" to justify his acts; rather, he looks to the historical identity that his acts have created and are now creating. The consequences of his acts for himself are thus present to him not as future ends, but as the present experience in which he knows himself.

Eliot's location of value in history can be seen negatively in her portrayal of Mrs. Transome in *Felix Holt*. Eliot presents Mrs. Transome's mercenary marriage and subsequent adultery as regrettable in terms not of laws or customs, but of the miserable human being they create. Her history destroys her one hope for happiness--her son's love--when he discovers his true paternity and recoils from her. Eliot's terse comment on her misery is taken from Aeschylus:

'Tis law as steadfast as the throne of Zeus--Our days are heritors of days gone by. (xlviii,329)

Similarly, in *Romola* Eliot shows the evil of Tito Melema as lying not so much in his breaking any law as in his consciously acting on "a choice which he would have been ashamed to avow to others" and thereby condemning himself to a life of "baseness rather than that the precise facts of his conduct should not remain for ever concealed" (I, ix, 153-54).

Because we must live with the selves that our historical choices create, from Eliot's perspective "Our finest hope is finest memory" (*Felix Holt*, Epilogue, 357). In thus emphasizing the past and the consequences of our deeds not as they will be felt but as they are actually felt in the present, Eliot avoids the charge--often falsely lodged against Hegel--of calling whatever contributes to world history right and of condoning suffering and evil in the name of progress. She deals with this problem explicitly in her first novel, *Adam Bede*, in which Adam's exposure to the sufferings of his fiancée and friend is in large part responsible for his own spiritual development. "That is a base and selfish, even a blasphemous, spirit," says Eliot, "which rejoices and is thankful over the past evil that has blighted or crushed another, because it has been made a source of unforeseen good to ourselves." Such baseness represents an epistemological error, for the reality of events is not to be altered by moral labels, as she points out when she imagines Adam's saying, "Evil's evil, and sorrow's sorrow, and you can't alter its nature by wrapping it up in other words. Other folks were not created for my sake, that I should think all square when things turn out well for me" (VI, liv, 364-65). Hetty's pregnancy and trial for infanticide, Arthur's self-imposed exile from his beloved home, Adam's loss of his first love--these are historical events, continuing to have effect in the world, but in themselves unchangeable, irrevocable. Such suffering may be an inevitable result of the laws of progress, but to sanction or to contribute to it on that ground is, writes Eliot, to make of the idea of progress "as bad a superstition or false god as any that has been set up without the ceremonies of philosophising" (*Deronda*, VI, xlii, 378).

To make moral judgments on the basis of an abstract idea of the laws of progress is to ignore the fact that the world progresses--or does not progress--because men choose to act. In *Daniel Deronda*, a member of "The Philosophers" club asks, "Is all change in the direction of progress? if not, how shall we discern which change is progress and which not?. . .how far and in what ways can we act upon the course of change so as to promote it where it is beneficial, and divert it where it is injurious?" (VI, xliii, 377). After another member begs the question by arguing that change takes place according to the "laws of development" and is thus "necessarily progressive," Deronda and his mentor, Eliot's spokesmen, counter this blind necessitarianism by arguing for the importance of individual choice. Whatever the "laws of development," Deronda points out, "There will still remain the degrees of inevitableness in relation to our own will and acts, and the degrees of wisdom in hastening or retarding; there will still remain the danger of mistaking a tendency which should be resisted for an inevitable law that we must adjust ourselves to" (VI, xlii, 377-78). If man relies on faith in laws of progress external to himself, he thinks like a pagan without any rational conception that these things exist only as men actually think about and act on them. Tendencies become inevitabilities because men choose to act, not because laws operate outside of human action. As Mordecai explains,

the strongest principle of growth lies in human choice. The sons of Judah have to choose that God may again choose them. The Messianic time is the time when Israel shall will the planting of the national ensign. The Nile overflowed and rushed onward: the Egyptian could not choose the overflow, but he chose to work and make channels for the fructifying waters, and Egypt became the land of corn. Shall man, whose soul is set in the royalty of discernment and resolve, deny his rank and say, I am an onlooker, ask no choice or purpose of me? That is the blasphemy of this time. The divine principle of our race is action, choice, resolved memory. Let us contradict the blasphemy, and help to will our own better future and the better future of the world. . . .(VI, xlii, 396)

Not only individual history, then, but national and world history are inseparable from "action, choice, resolved memory"--the past man makes for himself through the deeds in which he actualizes his idea of himself. Because it is a historical self and a historical world that we create, the locus of value for Eliot is finally history itself.

NOTES

1. Leslie Stephen, "George Eliot," *Cornhill Magazine*, 43 (February 1881), rpt. in *George Eliot: The Critical Heritage*, ed. David Carroll (New York: Barnes & Noble, 1971), p. 484.

2. N.N. Feltes, "George Eliot and the Unified Sensibility," *PMLA*, 79 (1964), 130-36.

3. See Thomas Pinney, "George Eliot's Reading of Wordsworth: The Record," *Victorian Newsletter*, No. 24 (Fall 1963), pp. 20-22 and "The Authority of the Past in George Eliot's Novels," *Nineteenth Century Fiction*, 21 (1966), 131-47. Bernard J. Paris emphasizes Eliot's debt to Feuerbach in *Experiments in Life: George Eliot's Quest for Values* (Detroit: Wayne State Univ. Press, 1965); cf. Neil Roberts, *George Eliot: Her Beliefs and Her Art* (Pittsburgh: Univ. of Pittsburgh Press, 1975), which accepts Comte, Feuerbach, Evangelicalism, and evolutionary theory as major influences. Regarding Eliot's intuitionism, see David Carroll, "*Middlemarch* and the Externality of Fact," in *This Particular Web: Essays on "Middlemarch"*, ed. Ian Adam (Toronto: Univ. of Toronto Press, 1975), pp. 73-90. On Eliot's Christian ethics, see C.B. Cox, "George Eliot: The Conservative-Reformer," in *The Free Spirit: A Study of Liberal Humanism in the Novels of George Eliot, Henry James, E.M. Forster, Virginia Woolf, Angus Wilson* (London: Oxford Univ. Press, 1963), pp. 13-37, and Margaret Maison, *The Victorian Vision: Studies in the Religious Novel* (New York: Sheed and Ward, 1961). Arguments for Eliot's determinism include George Levine, "Determinism and Responsiblity in the Works of George Eliot," *PMLA*, 77 (1962), 268-79, and Felicia Bonaparte, *Will and Destiny: Morality and Tragedy in George Eliot's Novels* (New York: New York Univ. Press, 1975).

4. Paris, *Experiments*, p. 245. Milner points out the contradiction in *The Structure of Values in George Eliot* (Prague: Universita Karlova, 1968), pp. 3-4.

5. Milner describes a tension between individual and bourgeois values and between idealism and determinism in *The Structure of Values in George Eliot*.

6. *George Eliot's Early Novels: The Limits of Realism* (Berkeley: Univ. of California Press, 1968), pp. 19, 20, 23, 30, 34. Knoepflmacher discusses Eliot's growing idealism in depth in Part IV of *Religious Humanism and the Victorian Novel: George Eliot, Walter Pater, and Samuel Butler* (Princeton: Princeton Univ. Press, 1965).

7. Knoepflmacher, *Religious Humanism*, p. 96.

8. "Moral Problems and Moral Philosophy in the Victorian Period," *Victorian Studies*, 9, supplement (1965), 29-46.

9. "Ex Oriente Lux," quoted in Bernard J. Paris, "George Eliot's Unpublished Poetry," *Studies in Philology*, 56 (1959), 542-43.

10. George Eliot, "A Word for the Germans," *Pall Mall Gazette*, 7 March 1865, rpt. in *Essays of George Eliot*, ed. Thomas Pinney (New York: Columbia Univ. Press, and London: Routledge and Kegan Paul, 1963), p. 388. All further references to Eliot's essays are to this edition and appear parenthetically in the text.

11. *Daniel Deronda*, Cabinet Edition (Edinburgh and London: William Blackwood, 1878), Bk. V, Ch. xl, p. 341, and Bk. VI, Ch. xlii, p. 378. All further references to Eliot's novels are to the Cabinet Edition and appear parenthetically in the text.

12. *The George Eliot Letters*, ed. Gordon S. Haight (New Haven: Yale Univ. Press, and London: Oxford Univ. Press, 1956), IV, 385; and "Art and Belles Lettres," *Westminster Review*, 65 (April 1856), 343.

CRITICAL RESPONSE TO
ADAM BEDE

BLACKWOOD'S EDINBURGH MAGAZINE

April 1859

W.L. COLLINS

. . .The great merit of *Adam Bede* consists in the singular grace and skill
with which the characteristic detail of country life are rendered. To say of such
a book that it does not depend for its main attraction on the development of a
carefully-constructed plot, is little more than saying that it is a novel of character
rather than action. With one great exception, the masters of fiction of our own
day--and among these Mr. Eliot has incontestably made good his place--either
fail in the constructive power, or will not condescend to write a story. They
throw all their force into the delineation of character, and the enunciation of their
own favourite philosophy by the actors whom they place upon the stage. This
Mr. Eliot has done, and done it admirably. The story itself is simple enough, and
the interest of a very quiet order, until the commencement of the third volume,
when it is worked up with great power of detail, and becomes even painfully
absorbing. The whole account of Hetty Sorrell's night-wandering in the fields is
as strong an instance of the author's power in vivid melodramatic description,
as the lighter parts of the book are of genuine humour and truth. . . .
. . .One of the most real things in these volumes, which will at once
strike all those who have had any experience of its truth, is the picture they give
of the state of religious feeling in country villages--as it was fifty years ago, and
as it is now, for there has been little change.
Adam Bede is not "a religious novel." It would hardly be recommended
without reservation to that large class of readers who take Miss Yonge and Miss
Sewell for their high-priestesses; and will run some risk of being placed in the
index expurgatorius of the Evangelicalism. The author has a presentiment that
to some minds the Rector of Broxton will seem "little better than a pagan." Yet

for both parties it would be a very wholesome change to lay aside for an hour or two the publications of their own favourite school, and to read Mr. Eliot's story. For its religious principle is a large-hearted charity. And this, after all, is surely the right ground on which to treat religious questions in a work of fiction. . . .The author of *Adam Bede* is not one of those who, in the eloquent words of a late preacher, "have restricted God's love, and narrowed the path to heaven." No one handles Scripture more reverently; none with better effect; because it is not as a weapon against opponents, but as armour of proof.

It is very cheering too, setting the religious question apart, to read a book in which the writer has the courage to say that "by living a great deal among people more or less commonplace and vulgar," he "has come to the conclusion that human nature is lovable"--and has the ability to maintain his thesis. He does not conceal or palliate the weaknesses of humanity; there is no attempt to paint rural life as an Arcadia of innocence; we have Hetty's silly vanity, and young Donnithorne's weakness of principle, and Lisbeth's petulance, all truthfully set before us; and even Adam, the hero, has quite enough of his old namesake about him to be far from perfect; yet we part from all of them at last with an honest sympathy, or, at the worst, a mild and tearful pity. It is encouraging, as it is unfortunately rare, in fiction, to find ourselves watching the operations of a skilful anatomist, as he lays bare the secrets of our quivering frame, and to feel that the hand is not only sure and steady, but gentle as a woman's. It is pleasant to find, combined with all the power of the satirist, the kindly warmth of human charity, and to mark the light which it throws upon human failings; not concealing them, but softening the harsher outlines, mellowing the glaring tones, and bringing out beauties of which we were before unconscious. We have here no morbid dwelling upon evil, nor yet an unreal optimism which dresses out life in hues of rose-colour; but a hearty manly sympathy with weakness, not inconsistent with a hatred of vice. The "common, coarse people" shame us sometimes, as they do in actual life, by the delicacy of their moral organization; the outwardly gentle and refined shame us no less by their coarse selfishness. It is no small praise to Mr. Eliot, that he has described to us the attractions of sense without allowing them to influence our judgment.

THE TIMES

12 April 1859

E.S. DALLAS

There can be no mistake about *Adam Bede*. It is a first-rate novel and its author takes rank at once among the masters of the art. Hitherto known but as the writer of certain tales to which he gave the modest title of 'Scenes,' and which displayed only the buds of what we have here in full blossom, he has produced a work which, after making every allowance for certain crudities of execution, impresses us with a sense of the novelist's maturity of thought and feeling. Very seldom are so much freshness of style and warmth of emotion seen combined with so much solid sense and ripened observation. We have a pleasant feeling of security in either laughing or crying with such a companion. Our laughter shall not be trifling, and our tears shall not be maudlin. We need not fear to yield ourselves entirely to all the enchantments of the wizard whose first article of belief is the truism which very few of us comprehend until it has been knocked into us by years of experience--that we are all alike--that the human heart is one. All the novelists and all the dramatists that have ever lived have set themselves to exhibit the differences between man and man. Here, they seem to say, are circumstances precisely similar, and yet mark how various are the characters which grow out of these circumstances. The Pharisee in the Temple felt that he was different from other men, thanking his God for it; and which of us, in the immaturity of experience, is not forced chiefly to consider the differences between ourselves and other men, often utterly forgetting the grand fact of an underlying unity? Here we see monsters, and there we see angels, alien faces and inaccessible natures. It is only after much beating about, long intercourse with society, and many strange discoveries and detections, that the truism which we never doubted becomes a great reality to us, and we feel that man is like to man even as face answers to face in a glass. . . .With regard to which philosophy two things are to be noted,--the first that, whether true or false, it is the reverse of uncharitable; it is the expression of a warm human sympathy. In point of fact, it is but a secular rendering of the deepest sentiment of Christianity--the sense of personal unworthiness in the presence of God, which teaches us the weakness of our nature and how near the very best of us are of kin to the chief of sinners and the most degraded of beings. The second, that a novelist, writing in accordance with this philosophy, has a most difficult task to perform. It is comparatively easy to draw a character so long as we dwell mainly on points of difference and contrast. But when the object is to touch lightly on mere peculiarities, and to dwell mainly on those traits which we have all in

common, and, which, therefore, are anything but salient, the difficulty of the task
is enormously increased.

We do not mean for one moment to detract from Mr. George Elliot's
[*sic*] originality when we say that after his own fashion he follows this difficult
path in which Mr. Thackeray leads the way. He has fully reached that idea which
is so easy to confess in words, but so hard to admit into the secret heart, that we
are all alike, that our natures are the same, and that there is not the mighty
difference which is usually assumed between high and low, rich and poor, the
fool and the sage, the best of us and the worst of us. In general, it is only
matured minds that reach this state of feeling--minds that have gone through a
good deal and have seen through a good deal; and our author has precisely this
broad sympathy and large tolerance, combined with ripe reflection and finished
style, which we admire in Mr. Thackeray. Here the comparison ends. Mr. Elliot
[*sic*] differs so widely from Mr. Thackeray in his mode of working out the
philosophy which is common to both that some of our readers may wonder how
we could ever see a resemblance between him and the great painter of human
vanities and weaknesses. Whereas Mr. Thackeray is, to the great disgust of many
young ladies, continually asserting that we have all got an evil corner in our
hearts, and little deceitful ways of working, Mr. Elliot [*sic*] is good enough to
tell us that we have all a remnant of Eden in us, that people are not so bad as is
commonly supposed, and that every one has affectionate fibres in his nature--
fine, loveable traits, in his character. The novel before us is crowded with
characters, but they are loveable. It is true that one individual is guilty of
seduction, that another is guilty of murder, and that a third is a greedy old miser,
but the author finds good in them all and lets them off easy, not only with
pardon, but in the two former cases loaded with affectionate sympathy. If in this
way he has gone to an extreme, it is a fault which most persons will readily
forgive, since it enables them to think better of poor fallen human nature. . . .We
might quote a long passage to a similar effect from the first chapter of the
second volume, but it will be sufficient to give one sentence in which the author
represents human affection as triumphing over every obstacle of mental
deficiency and personal appearance. After mentioning the ugly fellows with squat
figures, ill-shapen nostrils, and dingy complexions, whose miniatures are kissed
in secret by motherly lips, he says:--'And I believe there have been plenty of
young heroes, of middle stature and feeble beards, who have felt quite sure they
could never love anything more insignificant than a Diana, and yet have found
themselves in middle life happily settled with a wife who waddles'. . . .

It will be evident that in order to establish the identity of man with man
an author must travel a good deal into the region of latent thoughts, and
unconscious or but semi-conscious feelings. There is infinite variety in what we
express; there is a wonderful monotony in that great world of life which never
comes into the light, but moves within us like the beating of the heart and the
breathing of the lungs--a constant, though unobserved influence. It is in this

twilight of the human soul that our novelist most delights to make his observations. Old Lisbeth Bede says of her son Adam, who is continually visiting the Poysers with the object (unknown even to himself) of seeing Dinah Morris:--'Eh, donna tell me what thee't sure on; thee know'st nought about it. What's he allays going to the Poysers' for, if he didna want t' see her? He goes twice where he used t' go once. Happen he knows na as he wants t' see her; *he* knows na as I put salt in's broth, but he'd miss it pretty quick if it warna there.' It is to the world of thoughts indicated in Mrs. Bede's very homely remark that the author has turned his chief attention. Like Mr. Thackeray, he takes a peculiar pleasure in showing the contrariety between thought and speech, the heart within and the mask without, which we call a face. He is always showing that we are better than we seem, greater than we know, nearer to each other than, perhaps, we would wish. . . .

ELIOT TO FRANCOIS D'ALBERT-DURADE

The George Eliot Letters, 1978

6 DECEMBER 1859

. . .I have no longer any antagonism towards any faith in which human sorrow and human longing for purity have expressed themselves; on the contrary, I have a sympathy with it that predominates over all argumentative tendencies. I have not returned to dogmatic Christianity--to the acceptance of any set of doctrines as a creed, and a superhuman revelation of the Unseen--but I see in it the highest expression of the religious sentiment that has yet found its place in the history of mankind, and I have the profoundest interest in the inward life of sincere Christians in all ages. . . .On that question of our future existence, to which you allude, I have undergone the sort of change I have just indicated, although my most rooted conviction in, that the immediate object and the proper sphere of all our highest emotions are our struggling fellowmen and this earthly existence. . . .

ADAM BEDE: SOCIETY IN FLUX

Unisa English Studies, 1973

BRIAN D. BEYERS

George Eliot indulges neither in sentimental idealization of the past, nor in unwarranted glorification of contemporary society. In *Adam Bede* (1859), she describes the modes of living of various social classes in a pre-industrial age-- modes familiar to her as a child, before religious schism, social change, and industrialization came to disturb the prevailing tranquility of rural England.

It is essential to see the lives, and actions of her characters in *Adam Bede* against this traditional social background. George Eliot acquaints us with all social strata, from artisans and labourers to rectors and squires, and we become familiar with the established rhythm of village life at Hayslope. The full effect of the novel's central tragedy depends on the particular relationship that exists between Adam Bede, Arthur Donnithorne, and Hetty Sorrel on the one hand, and this traditional background on the other. Hayslope is situated in Loamshire, a sheltered and fertile region:[1]

That rich undulating district of Loamshire to which Hayslope belonged, lies close to a grim outskirt of Stonyshire, overlooked by its barren hills as a pretty blooming sister may sometimes be seen linked in the arm of a rugged, tall, swarthy brother. . . .(pp.18-19)

Though poverty is rare in Hayslope, its close proximity to prosperity and fertility is revealed by George Eliot's juxtaposition of 'rich undulating' and 'barren', 'blooming' and 'swarthy', in a single sentence. We are made aware that an abundance of luxuries does not necessarily preclude the possibility of future destitution: present stability does not guarantee future security. George Eliot continues her description of Loamshire in the following terms:

High up against the horizon were the hugh conical masses of hill, like giant mounds intended to fortify this region of corn and grass against the keen and hungry winds of the north; not distant enough to be clothed in purple mystery, but with sombre greenish sides visibly specked with sheep, whose motion was only revealed by memory, not detected by sight; wooed from day to day by the changing hours, but responding with no change in themselves--left for ever grim and sullen after the flush of morning, the winged gleams of the April noonday, the parting-crimson glory of the ripening summer sun. (p.19)

George Eliot proceeds systematically to describe the 'more advanced line of hanging woods, divided by bright patches of pasture or furrowed crops' directly below the hills, and then the valley with its thicker woods. The whole scene stresses the order and continuity of nature, and of a rural community: we are transported into an era of stability and serenity, where even the motion of the sheep is 'only revealed by memory'. But a sense of imminent change is suggested in 'the keen and hungry winds of the north', a phrase which points to the pressing needs of the people living in the industrial towns. The magnitude and urgency of their demands for alleviation are indicated by the size ('huge', 'giant') of the barriers required to separate them from the 'rich undulating district of Loamshire'. George Eliot's use of 'like' and 'intended', however, conveys the impression that such protection will ultimately be of no avail, especially when we recall that Loamshire is 'overlooked' by the barren hills of Stonyshire. Furthermore, she indicated the reason why life in Loamshire must inevitably be altered: the hills, touched only superficially by the course of the sun, and 'wooed from day to day by the changing hours, but responding with no change in themselves', reveal not only stability and endurance, but what could in human terms be regarded as excessive rigidity and narrowness. It is a refusal to adapt to changing circumstances that George Eliot implies will prove to be the cause of the downfall of a traditional way of life. Human beings who have never known privation and suffering, are unable to understand or sympathize with the dire needs of others. A spiritual hardness that will contribute towards its downfall can, therefore, be detected beneath the material prosperity of Loamshire.

Like its natural surroundings, the social structure of Hayslope is apparently simple, self-contained, and impervious to change. Adam Bede, who is presented as a carpenter of ability and integrity, typifies the general outlook of his contemporaries: traditional class distinctions are still more important to him than abstract philosophy or unproven theories for the reconstruction of society. The impression that different classes of society can continue to co-exist in harmony is strengthened by George Eliot's former description of the successive levels of natural vegetation, and by Adam's rationalization of society in natural terms:

Adam, I confess, was very susceptible to the influence of rank, and quite ready to give an extra amount of respect to every one who had more advantages than himself, not being a philosopher, or a proletaire with democratic ideas, but simply a a stout-limbed clever carpenter with a large fund of reverence in his nature, which inclined him to admit all established claims unless he saw very clear grounds for questioning them. He had no theories about setting the world to rights, but he saw there was a great deal of damage done by building with ill-seasoned timber. . . .(pp. 159-60)

Despite George Eliot's denial that Adam has any definite social theories, the accumulation of superlatives in this passage--'very', 'extra', 'every', 'large'-- indicates Adam's supreme confidence, strengthened by his innate mastery of his craft, in his powers to determine what is right in society. The passage also conveys the impression that, once Adam has decided on a course of action, he is rigid and unbending in his attitude. Thus, when the mildly revolutionary influence of Methodism threatens to disrupt the settled order of life at Hayslope, he tends to elevate the dignity of labour above spiritual values:

And there's such a thing as being over-speritial; we must have something beside Gospel i' this world. Look at the canals, an' th' aqueducs, an' the' coalpit engines, and Arkwright's mills there at Cromford; a man must learn summat beside Gospel to them things, I reckon.' (p.11)

Ironically, Adam is here championing inanimate forces that are even more inflexible than those in his own nature: industrialization ignores, and eventually tends to destroy, all human and spiritual values. Adam, however, shares a common humanity with his contemporaries, and George Eliot shows how he is later profoundly altered by events, the moral complexity of which he had confidently believed he understood. Adam's incorporation of varied aspects of the industrial scene into his reasoning in the above passage, for example, reveals a conviction in his ability to control his own life. He has foreseen the consequences of industrialization on traditional society, but this prevents him from identifying himself with the human lot:

Whenever Adam was strongly convinced of any proposition, it took the form of a principle in his mind: it was knowledge to be acted on, as much as the knowledge that damp will cause rust. Perhaps here lay the secret of the hardness he had accused himself of: he had too little fellow-feeling with the weakness that errs in spite of foreseen consequences. (p.204)

Abstract principles and practical knowledge, which later effectively dominate the industrial scene, replace in Adam any tendency to 'patience and charity towards [his] stumbling, falling companions in the long and changeful journey' (p.204). His self-confidence makes him intolerant even of his father's failings, until the drowned body of old Thias Bede forces an awareness of the immediacy of future suffering on Adam's consciousness. His rectitude is shaken for the first time, but he still has much to learn before he eventually discovers that it is his own self-righteousness that mars his relationship with others. His suffering is the result of his unimaginative rigidity. George Eliot clearly reveals how emotional involvement in the lives of other human beings results in an increased self-awareness for Adam:

And there is but one way in which a strong determined soul can learn it--by getting his heart-strings bound round the weak and erring, so that he must share not only the outward consequences of their error, but their inward suffering. That is a long and hard lesson, and Adam had at present only learned the alphabet of it in his father's sudden death. . . .(p.204)

Here George Eliot distinctly indicates the need for Adam's sensibility and imagination to be educated beyond his initial egoism; the disillusionment leading to his fight with Arthur Donnithorne marks the next stage in his education, and awakens in him a sense of personal weakness. Adam's inborn susceptibility to the influence of rank, inclines him 'to admit all established claims', and, despite his acceptance of and respect for industrial development, he still places high value on the feudal hierarchy with its rigid class distinctions. The following passage--even though it hints at the later striving after security and social status mainly amongst the rising middle classes--stresses Adam's acceptance of such a state of society, and his veneration of the upper classes:

The word 'gentleman' had a spell for Adam, and, as he often said, he 'couldn't abide a fellow who thought he made himself fine by being coxy to's betters'. . . .Towards the young squire this instinctive reverence of Adam's was assisted by boyish memories and personal regard; so you may imagine that he thought far more of Arthur's good qualities, and attached far more value to very slight actions of his, than if they had been the qualities and actions of a common workman like himself; (p.160)

The repetition of 'far more' points to the basic weakness of the entire social system as it then existed; undue importance was attached to 'very slight' actions just because they were performed by the aristocracy.[2] Such an attitude tends to create the situation where Arthur Donnithorne, for example, comes to see himself as his tenants see him: the approbation of others feeds his egoism, he becomes irresponsible, and, in deluding himself, betrays his order. Like Adam, therefore, Arthur is primarily a victim of his own nature. His belief that he has earned the approbation of his social inferiors, and his considerable reliance on his own virtues, lead him candidly to accept the existence of a few personal failings, especially when his social position is taken into account:

But he had an aggreable confidence that his faults were all of a generous kind--impetuous, warm-blooded, leonine, never crawling, crafty, reptilian. It was not possible for Arthur Donnithorne to do anything mean, dastardly, or cruel. 'No! I'm a devil of a fellow for getting myself into a hobble, but I always take care the load shall fall on my own shoulders.' (p.121)

Arthur's self-deception is based on his failure to distinguish between what he is, and what he appears to be: his social position, and ability always to pay for his requirements, give him the confidence to pursue his every desire. The casual, colloquial tone of the above passage hides a basic dishonesty and lack of self-restraint. His failure to uphold the dignity of his social status, leads to his flirtation with Hetty Sorrel, and to his subsequent fight with Adam in the wood. Passionately denouncing the young squire, Adam is right when he says,

Why, then, instead of acting like th' upright, honourable man we've all believed you to be, you've been acting the part of a selfish, lightminded scoundrel. You know, as well as I do, what it's to lead to, when a gentleman like you kisses and makes love to a young woman like Hetty, and gives her presents as she's frightened for other folks to see.' (p.288)

The intensity of Adam's feeling can be gauged when we consider the barrier of custom and deference he must overcome to be able to deliver this tirade: it is only the sense of outrage to one whom he has long loved in secret that enables him to discover the 'selfish, light-minded scoundrel' beneath 'th' upright, honourable man'. Arthur is confused, irritated, and alarmed by this attitude, since he considers 'that a man to whom he had shown so much favour as to Adam, was not in a position to criticise his conduct' (p.287). His initial impulse to assert his rights as a feudal landlord subsides, however, when he discovers the relationship between Adam and Hetty:

The discovery that Adam loved Hetty was a shock which made him for the moment see himself in the light of Adam's indignation, and regard Adam's suffering as not merely a consequence, but an element of his error. (p.290)

Arthur, accustomed to seeing himself as others see him, is now compelled to view his action in an unfavourable light: the repeated reference to Adam in the above passage suggests the deepening impression that the human rights of another individual make, perhaps for the first time, on his sensibility. Although genuinely unaware of Adam's love for Hetty, he has quite knowingly betrayed the very principles upon which his social status relies, and we recall his own former evaluation of the whole affair:

To flirt with Hetty was a very different affair from flirting with a pretty girl of his own station: that was understood to be an amusement on both sides; or, if it became serious, there was no obstacle to marriage. But this little thing would be spoken ill of directly, if she happened to be seen walking with him; and then those excellent people, the Poysers, to whom a good name was as precious as if they had the best blood in the land in their veins--he should hate himself if he made a scandal of that sort, on the estate that was to be his own some day, and among tenants by whom he liked, above all, to be respected. (p.135)

The whole concept of traditional society is embodied in this passage. The use of 'as if' demonstrates that, although the Poysers are a highly respectable family, they belong to a lower social order, and there can be no thought of a union between a member of their family and the squire of the estate. Arthur's seduction of Hetty is, therefore, an unnatural act, morally and socially; it effectively destroys both Hetty's dream of becoming a fine lady (she believed that marriage to Arthur would rapidly and automatically elevate her social and material status), and Arthur's real desire to become a good squire. The facts that Hetty accepts presents she is 'frightened for other folks to see', and that Arthur knows it would be wrong for her 'to be seen walking with him', stress the continual need for secrecy--a need entirely alien to both their natures. The discovery of their affair, therefore, leaves them defenceless: Arthur has to face the 'tenants by whom he liked, above all, to be respected', and Hetty is compelled by the very standards of conduct and morality which prevail in the stable social background provided by the Poysers, and upon which, as a foundling, she is more dependent than most other individuals, to take flight before her baby is born. Hetty's 'crime', consequently, transcends the bounds of a purely personal tragedy: it disturbs the settled life of the whole village, violating the bonds of family and friendship. Adam has to reconsider his former confident belief in an ordered world, and the fight between him and Arthur becomes symbolic of ensuing social disruption that marks the transition away from the feudal relationship in society.

NOTES

1. All quotations are from the Dent edition of *Adam Bede*, London, 1966.
2. Nevertheless, material values were beginning to prevail, and Henry James, writing in the *Atlantic Monthly* of October 1866, recognized this tendency. He found, especially in *Silas Marner*, 'a deep impression of the grossly material life of agricultural England in the last days of the old regime,--the days of full-orbed Toryism, of Trafalgar and of Waterloo, when the invasive spirit of French domination threw England back upon a sense of her own insular solidity, and made her for the time doubly, brutally, morbidly English'. G.S. Haight (ed.): *A Century of George Eliot Criticism*, Methuen, London, 1965, p. 46.

BIBLIOGRAPHY

Carroll, D. (ed.) *George Eliot: The Critical Heritage*, Routledge and Kegan Paul, London, 1971.

Cooper, L. *George Eliot*, Longmans, London, 1960.

Creeger, G.R. (ed.) *George Eliot: A Collection of Critical Essays*, Prentice-Hall, New Jersey, 1970.

Gardner, C. *The Inner Life of George Eliot*, Pitman, London, 1912.

Haight, G.S. (ed.) *A Century of George Eliot Criticism*, Methuen, London, 1965.

Haight, G.S. *George Eliot: A Biography*, Oxford, New York, 1969.

Haldane, E.S. *George Eliot and Her Times: A Victorian Study*, Appleton, London, 1927.

Hardy, B. *The Novels of George Eliot*, Athlone, London, 1963.

Harvey, W.J. *The Art of George Eliot*, Chatto and Windus, London, 1963.

Jones, R.T. *George Eliot*, Cambridge, London, 1970.

Jones, R.T. *George Eliot: Adam Bede*, Macmillan, London, 1968.

Speaight, R. *George Eliot*, Barker, London, 1954.

Stephen, L. *George Eliot*, Macmillan, London, 1902.

Thale, J. *The Novels of George Eliot*, Columbia, New York, 1959.

Viner, A.E.S. *George Eliot*, Oliver and Boyd, Edinburgh, 1971.

Williams, B.C. *George Eliot: A Biography*, Macmillan, New York, 1936.

INFANTICIDE AND RESPECTABILITY: HETTY SORREL AS ABANDONED CHILD IN *ADAM BEDE*

English Studies in Canada, 1983

MASON HARRIS

Adam Bede has usually been enjoyed and interpreted as a celebration of pastoral community, a loving backward look at a long-vanished rural world. Yet much of this novel's interest, especially for the modern reader, lies in its combination of nostalgic retrospect with "modern" problems not usually found in a pastoral. In particular, Hetty Sorrel's unwed pregnancy, desperate flight, abandonment of her child, and trial for its murder, seems to many readers the most striking episode in the novel. Eliot's vivid depiction of Hetty's flight has attracted some excellent criticism: both Barbara Hardy and Ian Adam analyze the remarkable way in which the narrator merges with Hetty's consciousness to bring us the immediate experience of a confused and inarticulate character.[1]

Our admiration for Eliot's achievement here, however, has tended to raise questions about Hetty's relation to the novel as a whole. The modern reader is likely to be put off by an apparent harshness in Eliot's commentary on Hetty throughout much of the novel--a harshness which seems oddly in contrast to her sympathy during the flight episode; some have seen Hetty's fate as a severe punishment for sexual love. Most serious, because most threatening to the novel's integrity, is the influential view that the realism of Hetty's "Journey in Despair" simply does not belong to the rest of the novel. In his well-known essay, "The Two Worlds of *Adam Bede*," Ian Gregor argues that most of the novel is old-fashioned pastoral, while Hetty's flight represents the intrusion of a modern "fiction of moral and philosophical inquiry" incompatible with the pastoral tradition.[2] If we accept this conclusion then we must consider the character at the centre of the plot and the modern reader's interest an inspired accident, and relegate the rest of the novel to a charming but obsolete literary genre. The vital issues raised by Hetty's disaster become irrelevant to Eliot's depiction of the world of Hayslope, and her fall seems a matter of private sin played off against a background of "immemorial" rustic virtue.[3]

The real question lies not in the rather abstract matter of genre but in the novel's sense of community, especially in the opposition between Hetty and her aunt and uncle Poyser, who represent the best aspects of the respectable tenant farmers of Hayslope. Despite the fine studies of Hetty's flight, surprisingly little criticism has been directed to her relation to the Poysers, and this is the area we must explore if we are to get beyond the inhibiting view of her as a separate case. Only if she belongs to the Poysers can she be shown to belong to the novel as a whole.

In his convincing interpretation--published a quarter of a century ago and still one of the most important essays on *Adam Bede*--J.R. Creeger takes the novel out of the realm of "pastoral" (in the simple sense intended by Ian Gregor) when he demonstrates that Eliot's admiration for the Poysers is not unqualified, and that Dinah's Methodism provides a critical perspective on the world of Hayslope.[4] Hetty is usually seen as quite different from the apparently warm-hearted Poysers, but in emphasizing the difference between their values and Dinah's Creeger suggests that Hetty does indeed belong to Hayslope: she is "a perfect representative of the Loamshire-Hayslope world: she has its fertility, and she has its beauty, which nevertheless conceals an essential hardness."[5] He argues that the effect of her "ordeal is to externalize the hardness which has hitherto been concealed." Although the inhabitants of Hayslope refuse to forgive her crime and thus cannot help her, "they are implicated in her condition."[6]

Perhaps Creeger's insights have not been followed up in any clear way because of the confusing effect of Eliot's ambivalence both towards the Poysers, who are presented so warmly early in the novel but who later repudiate their erring niece, and Hetty, whom the narrator frequently disparages and yet depicts as sympathetic despite her undeniable crime. Finally, Eliot's affection for the Poysers triumphs in a happy ending which gets rid of Hetty and seems designed to make us forget the shortcomings of Hayslope.

Despite these difficulties, Hetty's role deserves further consideration. She is one of the most convincing depictions of a fallen woman in Victorian literature; as we shall see, she is also a crucial instance of the problems of the relation between individual and community in Eliot's fiction. Criticism has had difficulty in recognizing her full significance because of the mistaken assumption that Eliot intends a complete moral polarity between the novel's community and its main character. If the Poysers are seen to represent an ideal familial togetherness which stands for their whole community, then in her lack of family feeling and her most unfamilial crime Hetty can only be seen as an alien threat which tests the coherence of the community. Since Hetty accomplishes this through sexual indiscretion she can also be seen as the heroine of an erotic idyll set in total contrast to the Puritan virtues of the Poysers, and cruelly punished by an equally Puritan author.[7]

The view of Hetty as a sinful intruder on pastoral innocence involves a misunderstanding of her nature as a character--a misunderstanding which in turn obscures her most obvious link with the Poysers. If we look beneath Eliot's sometimes annoying commentary we will discover that she presents Hetty not as an adult sinner but as a confused child, and that it is through her role as child that her relation to her community can best be understood.

Hetty devastates the traditional family life of the Poysers by killing her child; because of this crime we tend to forget that she is herself an orphaned child for whom they have a parental responsibility. Their unthinking adherence to tradition may have something to do with her failure to grow up, and certainly provides the values which motivate her disastrous flight. In her blind respectability she rejects all possibility of rescue, hiding her child in a forest in a compulsive attempt to recover her position as the Poyser's child. As we shall see, the state of mind in which she commits the "murder" reveals a young child's inability to handle inner conflict. Childishly dependent on the values of her community, she remains trapped in a world which cannot recognize the isolated individual; yet her anguished confusion provides the novel's most intense portrayal of individual experience. As lost child, Hetty also acquires a central, if difficult, role in Eliot's preoccupation with moral education through experience, a concern which itself arises out of the breakdown of community.

In attempting a comprehensive study of Hetty's role, we encounter an interesting problem which may help to explain why such a fragmented picture of her is to be found in criticism. There may be some difficulties in perspective in approaching a character who is thematically at the centre of the novel, but psychologically isolated by her narcissism from all the other characters: to understand her as a character we must study her in relation to her own very narrow world, but to understand the full significance of her role in the novel we must see her in relation to a much larger world of which she has no comprehension--a problem made more difficult by her abrupt disappearance from the story after her confession to Dinah.

To accomodate this dual aspect of Hetty, my essay will move through two stages. I will first concentrate on her relation to the Poysers and her psychological motivation, viewing her abandonment of her child and subsequent mental collapse as a comment on the limitations of the communal world she shares with her foster parents. Then, taking a larger perspective, I will consider her in relation to other characters and the main themes of the novel, finally asking why the author herself abandons the pathetic child for whom she has won so much sympathy. A fuller understanding of the psychological and social aspects of Hetty's role will reveal that Eliot's shift from "pastoral" to "realism" is not a break in the novel's continuity but a result of its natural development. Only in the happy ending do we find a pastoral incompatible with Eliot's realism.

II

We first encounter Hetty as a very self-centred and naive girl competently performing her tasks at the Poysers' farm, but without affection for her foster parents or their way of life. It is the editorial commentary here which offends the modern reader; many have assumed that Hetty is being presented as a monster of egotism, especially in Chapter Fifteen, where she is seen in contrast to her Methodist cousin Dinah, who works in a factory and ministers to the poor in industrial Stonyshire, and occasionally visits the Hall Farm, but refuses to live there because she cannot accept the Poysers'complacent prosperity.

In terms of the novel's Wordsworthian values, Hetty does seem rather unwholesome. The narrator tells us that she hates young animals and children, especially those belonging to the Poysers. We should note, however, that the way the narrator describes Hetty suggests that her problem lies in extreme immaturity rather than in wickedness. Despite her distaste for babies and the natural world she is frequently compared to small and young animals: she has a "beauty like that of kittens, or very small downy ducks. . .or babies just beginning to toddle and to engage in conscious mischief--a beauty with which you can never be angry, but that you feel ready to crush for inability to comprehend the state of mind into which it throws you"; here Hetty seems just at the infantile beginning of consciousness.[8] "She was like a kitten, and had the same distractingly pretty looks, that meant nothing, for everybody that came near her" (xix,213). Hetty's "look" can mean nothing because it has no recognition of the subjective reality of others. Both her admirers seem attracted by her resemblance to small animals: Adam observes her bad temper with "a sort of amused pity, as if he had seen a kitten setting up its back, or a little bird with its feathers ruffled. . .the prettiest thing in the world" (xxiii,269), and, when she weeps, Arthur finds her irresistibly like "a bright-eyed spaniel with a thorn in its foot" (xiii,138).

Before condemning Eliot for moral intolerance towards Hetty, we must remember the problem Eliot faced in retaining the sympathy of a Victorian audience for this character. By criticizing Hetty early in the novel Eliot expresses beforehand the disapproval her audience might be expected to feel later, and also, by the very nature of her criticism, implies that Hetty's problem is really psychological, more deserving of sympathy than harsh judgement. Mentally she is a child, a case of arrested development, not responsible for her actions, and thus a victim no matter what she may finally do. Dinah foreshadows the "Journey in Despair" when she compares Hetty facing a woman's destiny to a "child hugging its toys in the beginning of a long toilsome journey, in which it will have to bear hunger and cold and unsheltered darkness" (xv,160). Later, Adam repeatedly excuses Hetty on the grounds that "'She's all but a child'" (xxviii,308). Clearly we are invited to do the same; the more Eliot emphasizes Hetty's childishness the better case she has for sympathy later on.

In considering the Poysers' role as Hetty's foster parents, we should remember that despite Eliot's nostalgia for Hayslope she had a sharp critical understanding of the class to which they belong. As prosperous English yeomen, the Poysers represent the very best of the peasant class Eliot describes in her sociological essay, "The Natural History of German Life," but their world-view reveals that predominance of tradition over individual consciousness which she finds characteristic of the peasantry: with the peasant, "Custom holds the place of sentiment. . . .The peasant never questions the obligation of family ties--he questions no custom [but] with him general custom holds the place of individual feeling."[9] Mr. Poyser habitually displays a "predominant after-supper expression of hearty good-nature" (xxv,285), but towards a man of whose farming methods he does not approve he is "as hard and implacable as the north-east wind" (xiv,145). Mrs. Poyser constantly criticizes the housekeeping of neighbouring wives, and her frequent tirades against Hetty and the servants are associated with that compulsive cleanliness which Eliot finds less of a virtue when inflicted on Maggie by the Dodson aunts in *The Mill on the Floss*. Mrs. Poyser berates Molly, the all-purpose maid, for having been hired "without a bit o' character" and kept despite her filthy ways (vi,73-74 and xx,231-32). It would seem that in her first novel Eliot made humour out of certain characteristics of the respectable peasantry (the origins of her own family) towards which she actually felt ambivalent--if we are to judge by her next novel.

Some bitter remarks by "old Martin," Mr. Poyser's father and Hetty's grandfather, reveal that before Hetty's parents died they disgraced themselves through improvident farming. The senior Poyser has never forgiven his daughter, Hetty's mother, for marrying a poor man against his will; he retains "a long unextinguished resentment, which always made [him] more indifferent to Hetty than to his son's children. Her mother's fortune had been spent by that good-for-nought Sorrel, and Hetty had Sorrel's blood in her veins" (xxxi,344). The Poysers scrupulously acknowledge their obligation to take care of their niece, but their rigid values might well have a stunting effect on a girl dispossessed at the age of ten when her parents died in poverty. Mrs. Poyser means well towards Hetty, but often berates her along with the servants; it would not occur to her to treat the orphan niece as an equal to her own children. Though they wish the best for Hetty in marriage, the Poysers do not see her as "a daughter of their own," but as a "penniless niece. For what could Hetty have been but a servant elsewhere, if her uncle had not taken her in and brought her up as a domestic help to her aunt?" (ix,98). Hetty occupies an ambiguous position below the Poysers' children, yet partaking of the Poyser respectability, and thus above the more easygoing world of the servants and farmhands.[10] Despite the contrast between the Poysers' good intentions and Hetty's narcissism, she can be seen as a product of their world--a possible outcome of the narrowness and complacency of their values along with their somewhat impersonal attitude towards her as a "domestic help."

Hetty's state of mind can be consistently interpreted as a case of childhood narcissism accompanied by intense sibling rivalry: having lost her own position as daughter she hates the Poysers' children as rivals and does not care much for the parents who produced them. Chapter Fifteen provides a comprehensive account of Hetty's attitude towards the Poysers' family life. She has no "loving thought of her second parents--of the children she had helped to tend--of any youthful companion, any pet animal, any relic of her own childhood even" and "did not understand how anybody could be very fond of middle-aged people. And as for those tiresome children. . .Hetty would have been glad to hear that she should never see a child again." She also hates "the nasty little lambs" brought in for special care, but at least the lambs, unlike the Poysers' children, "*were* gotten rid of sooner or later." This seems a death-wish; Mrs. Poyser complains that she showed no feeling when the infant Totty was missing and assumed drowned. Hetty's attitude towards young animals suggests repulsion towards anything suggestive of birth or the maternal: "Hetty would have hated the very word 'hatching' if her aunt had not bribed her to attend the young poultry" (xv,156-58). She resembles the four-year-old Totty in preoccupation with clothing, in her interest in getting presents, and in being compared to young animals by the narrator. We shall see that, despite her lack of affection, Hetty is actually very dependent on her family.

While Mrs. Poyser rails at Hetty and the servants she constantly coddles Totty: she admits, Totty is "spoiled shameful. . .being the youngest, and th' *only* gell" (vii,87, italics mine). Hetty particularly dislikes this child, who was born after she came to the Poysers. The absence of any attachment to the present or fondness for the past suggests a disturbance associated with that past; Hetty's fantasies deny the existence of time. As we have seen, she hates the thought of birth and babies of any species. When Eliot compares her to young animals she implies that babies do not like other babies, and that a woman who has remained a child is not likely to be a sympathetic mother. Hetty's gentlemen admirers are quite mistaken when they imagine, "How she will dote on her children! She is almost a child herself, and the little pink round things will hang about her like florets round the central flower" (xv,154).[11]

In her obsession with costume, Hetty is not a temptress but a little girl. She projects her childhood interest in clothes and rivalry into adult relationships, thinking of marriage as an occasion "when she would have a silk gown and a great many clothes all at once" (xxxi,342). She is preoccupied with dressing better than Mary Burge, daughter of the owner of the local timber yard. Her main interest in both Mary and Adam seems to derive from the fact that Mary likes Adam, while Adam has eyes only for herself: "she felt nothing when his eyes rested on her, but the cold triumph of knowing that he loved her, and would not look at Mary Burge" (ix,99). At the height of her affair with Arthur she still pauses to give Adam one of her "brightest smiles" because "she knew Mary Burge was looking at them" (xxii,256).

Hetty's feeling for Arthur is just a Cinderella-fantasy in which he plays a god-like handsome prince who will magically elevate her above all rivals, especially Mary Burge. The extent to which her fantasies about Arthur involve infantile dressing up should dispel any belief that sensual love or romantic passion is involved here. As she parades "with a pigeon-like stateliness" before her bedroom mirror, she dreams of Captain Donnithorne, who thought her "prettier than anybody in Hayslope. . .and prettier than Miss Bacon, the miller's daughter, who was called the beauty of Treddleston. . .he would like to see her in nice clothes, and in thin shoes and white stockings, perhaps with silk clocks to them. . .of every picture she is the central figure in fine clothes. . .and everybody else is admiring and envying her" (xv,152-56). Critics are mistaken who assume that Eliot attacks sensual love in having this affair end in disaster; Hetty is infantile from the beginning, and Arthur likes her that way. Hetty's problem is not sin but a regressive narcissism which, with its concomitant naiveté, sets her up as Arthur's victim and then, given the bad luck of his transfer to Ireland, becomes, along with her intense respectability, the driving force behind her crime. In her case criminal justice seems both cruel and irrelevant.

As we have seen, Hetty projects her feeling of dispossession into very naive fairy-tale aspirations; despite her hostility to her family and longing to rise above it she cannot perceive any reality outside her family life. Thus, when she runs away to hide her shame, her dark journey does not represent an advance in experience of the outside world, but a blind, regressive drive to reassert the respectability she possessed when she lived with the Poysers. In this state of mind she acts out a grim parody of their values.

An important comment on Hetty's motivation links her narcissism with the Poysers' sense of respectability. After reading Arthur's letter putting an end to the affair, she resolves that "nobody should find out how miserable she was. . .They would think her conduct shameful; and shame was torture. That was poor little Hetty's conscience" (xxxi,343). The full force of her narcissism is focussed on being seen by others in terms of the respectable standards of her community: "Hetty had a certain strength in her vain little nature: she would have borne anything rather than be laughed at, or pointed to with any other feeling than admiration" (xviii,202).

The emphasis on being "laughed at" or "pointed to" reveals shame-culture at its most basic. Hetty's obsession with maintaining her respectability is related to the distinction, important to both Eliot and G.H. Lewes, between shame and the sympathetic imagination as the basis of morality--also a distinction between primitive and civilized world-views.[12] The Poysers and their community are still mainly at the level of shame-culture, manifested in extreme form in Hetty's case, while Dinah, the self-denying Methodist from industrial Stoniton, combines the sympathetic imagination with an Evangelical disregard for social status, and thus is able to "save" Hetty when the community condemns her. The parallel Eliot suggests between Mr. Poyser's rejection of his niece and Hetty's child-murder indicates the need for a more conscious morality than that of tradition-bound Hayslope.

Early in her flight Hetty displays a social attitude characteristic of the Poysers' world: "she was most of all afraid of. . .becoming so destitute that she would have to ask for people's charity; for Hetty had the pride not only of a proud nature but of a proud class--the class that pays the most poor-rates, and most shudders at the idea of profiting by a poor rate" (xxxvi,379). Later she is quick to assure the innkeeper that "I belong to respectable folks" (xxxvii,389).

At the beginning of the "Journey in Despair," Eliot describes Hetty's dread of shame as a class-attitude in a passage which brings some central themes together:

She thought of a young woman who had been found against the church wall at Hayslope one Sunday, nearly dead with cold and hunger--a tiny infant in her arms; the woman was rescued and taken to the parish. "The parish!" You can perhaps hardly understand the effect of that word on a mind like Hetty's, brought up among people who were somewhat hard in their feelings even towards poverty, who lived among the fields and had little pity for want and rags as a cruel inevitable fate such as they sometimes seem in cities, but held them a mark of idleness and vice--and it was idleness and vice that brought burthens on the parish. To Hetty the "parish" was next to the prison in obloquy; and to ask anything of strangers--to beg--lay in the same far-off hideous region of intolerable shame that Hetty had all her life thought it impossible she could ever come near. (xxxvii,386)

Here Hetty partakes of the conviction, already enunciated by Mrs. Poyser in her criticism of Methodists (viii,94), that if you're poor it's your own fault--"idleness and vice" are the leading qualities of those who choose to live at the ratepayers' expense. With the Poysers this attitude is natural because they "live among the fields" where Dinah finds "a strange deadness to the Word" (viii,92). As Dinah admits, her religion flourishes only in cities; it is through contact with the industrial poor that she has been able to develop her democratic vision of poverty as a "cruel inevitable fate" rather than a comment on one's moral character (viii,92). For Hetty and her class, people who are not respectable, and thus have no place in the social order, cease to exist morally. "Charity" denotes not Christian love but something so degrading that those who receive it have lost all claim to be considered human. No significant distinction can be made between being on the "parish" and imprisonment for a crime.

When worried about possible eviction by the old Squire, the Poysers think of moving twenty miles away to the next parish as a kind of death: "we shall. . .die o' broken hearts among strange folks" (xxxviii,359). After Hetty's disaster this move seems necessitated by a loss of status felt quite literally as worse than death. Repeatedly insisting on the Old Testament view that their children and grandchildren must suffer for Hetty's disgrace, the Poyser father and son play the role of Pharisee, while the lost sinner can only be saved by Dinah, whose religion emphasizes forgiveness and universal suffering represented by Christ as the "Man of Sorrows":

the Hall Farm was a house of mourning for a misfortune felt to be worse than death. The sense of family dishonour was too keen even in the kind-hearted Martin Poyser the younger, to leave any room for compassion towards Hetty. . . .Hetty had brought disgrace on them all--disgrace that could never be wiped out. That was the all-conquering feeling in the mind of both father and son--the scorching sense of disgrace, which neutralized all other sensibility; Mr. Irwine was struck with surprise to observe that Mrs. Poyser was less severe than her husband. We are often startled with the severity of mild people on exceptional occasions; the reason is, that mild people are most liable to be under the yoke of traditional impressions. (xl,423)

The intensity of feeling which Mrs. Poyser manifests in her role as sharp-tongued defender of Hayslope morality can also grant her a certain independence from that morality: though she thinks on conventional lines she can sometimes experience as an individual. If Martin is more tradition-bound because he has less feeling, then we can conclude that Hetty, who has no feeling for others, is the most likely to be "under the yoke of traditional impressions." With his sensibility "neutralized," Mr. Poyser temporarily enters a state of mind which is permanent with Hetty. Weeping "hard tears" he says that he will pay for her defence at the trial, but "I'll not go nigh her, nor ever see her again, by my own will. She's made our bread bitter to us for all our lives to come, an' we shall ne'er hold up our heads i' this parish nor i' any other" (xl,423). Mr. Poyser's attitude here is more excusable than Hetty's crime, but both repudiate a child because they equate disgrace with death.

Dinah's implied criticism of Hayslope is dramatized by Hetty's flight. Hetty enjoys fantasies of rising above the Poysers, but her behaviour in the flight reveals that she is childishly dependent on her environment and thus blindly follows its values; she possesses no inner consciousness to oppose the compulsion of respectability. Alienated from family life and isolated by her narcissism, she reproduces the Poysers' values without their feeling for kin and community. Of course, this is a distortion of their world-view, but the analogy between her abandonment of her child and her uncle's attitude towards her implies a repudiation of the human on both sides.

Despite Hetty's "resolute air of self-reliance," her actions during the "Flight in Despair" are completely irrational; like a young child, she can only express conflicting drives in contradictory behaviour. She flees from Hayslope to escape "discovery and scorn" before "familiar eyes," but refuses all offers of help on the journey because she takes the outside world as an extension of her community. She seeks a pool in which to drown herself--a pool deep enough so that her body will not be discovered until summer, by which time no one will be able to recognize her. Yet as she searches for such a pool she maintains a respectable appearance, takes care with her money, and travels back towards home.

When she finds a pool she postpones suicide to eat "eagerly" and fall asleep, awakening terrified in "cold, and darkness, and solitude--out of all human reach" (xxxvii,395). By contrast she thinks of the Hall Farm: "The bright hearth and the voices of home--the secure uprising and lying down,--the familiar fields, the familiar people" (xxxvii,395). This antithesis between lethal solitude, the outcome of her flight from human vision, and home perceived in terms of light, heat, the sound of voices--the impersonality of unvarying routine and "familiar people"--presents an extreme form of communal identification. She seeks to return to no particular relationship, but to merge into a total pattern which will be static and therefore absolute.

After recovering from her panic, she feels "exultation" at still being alive and, in an uncharacteristic display of emotion, kisses "her arms with passionate love of life" (xxxvii,395). Yet this inherent vitality, evoked by her rejection of suicide, cannot extend to a sense of the value of life in general, not even that of the child to which she will soon give birth. The next morning her "passionate joy in life" (xxxvii,397) succumbs to a moralistic peasant who calls her a "wild woman," renewing her sense of disgrace so that "she felt that she was like a beggar already" (xxxvii,395-97).

Hetty passionately loves her own flesh, yet passes sentence of death on her pregnant body. She can resolve this dilemma once the child is born by killing it in order to return to the only life she can imagine--unquestioned acceptance in the community. Hetty resists with her whole being the disruption of her infantile dependence on her kin by the child to which she has given birth; there is only room for one infant in her world and that is herself. Later she tells Dinah of her plan to drown the baby so that she could be once more "safe at home": "I thought I'd find a pool, if I could, like that other. . . .I thought I should get rid of all my misery, and go back home, and never let 'em know why I ran away. . . .I longed so to be safe at home. . . .I seemed to hate the baby--it was like a heavy weight hanging round my neck" (xlv,462-63). Yet as Hetty resolutely takes the baby into the woods she experiences for the first time a counter-movement of feeling for it. This can only find expression in tactile terms: "the baby was warm against me. . .its crying went through me, and I daredn't look at its little face and hands" (xlv,463). Instead of experiencing the baby only as a "heavy weight" she recognizes the existence of a face by refusing to look at it.

The child is not saved by this feeling, but Hetty's longing to express it will prompt the confession which returns her to humanity.[13] At present the impulse to kill the child still dominates; rather than weighing alternatives Hetty commits the act, but does it in a way that expresses her ambivalence (xlv,463-64). By covering up the baby in a hole under a bush in the woods Hetty leaves to almost certain death by exposure, and signifies her lethal intentions by describing the hole as a "grave"; the child is so well hidden that, as we learn at the trial, a man who searched the spot after hearing it cry couldn't find it (xliii,444-45). Yet by also leaving an opening for it to breathe she expresses the wish that it "wouldn't die." She thinks only now of abandoning the child so that it might live; yet she had a good opportunity to do this earlier after giving birth in the house of a sympathetic woman. At that time, however, when she was actually in contact with another person, her flight from shame demanded a lonely murder in the woods. By burying the child, but not completely, Hetty tries both to kill it and to let it live, and of course the result is death.

Only after she abandons the child does her feeling for it begin to get the upper hand. At this point most Victorian novelists would have presented a scene of melodramatic remorse, but Eliot is too good a psychologist to let Hetty depart from character. Since her consciousness cannot accomodate conflict, her maternal feeling finds expression in auditory hallucination and a compulsive return to the scene of the crime. Miles away she hears the baby crying, a literal expression of the wish that it might still be alive. The "crying" finally overcomes her flight from shame, forcing her to return to the place where she hid the baby: "I'd left off thinking about going home--it had gone out o'my mind" (xlv,464). Hetty could never have made this confession had she not finally been able to forget her drive to return home.

Since she has no inner consciousness, this feeling appears only after the fulfilment of her drive towards isolation and murder, and then only as hallucination, paralysis of the will, and psychic fragmentation--she never rejects her original goal but only notes later that it had "gone out" of her mind. It seems that she can experience feelings that conflict with her narcissism only as external forces compelling action against her will. Ironically, her belated feeling for the child brings about her arrest and a disgrace worse than unwed motherhood. Unable to face real suicide, she responds with psychotic withdrawal from humanity. During the "Journey in Despair" her features have already become petrified and petrifying "like that wondrous Medusa face, with the passionate, passionless lips" (xxxvii,393);[14] now her whole being follows suit: "My heart went like a stone: I couldn't wish or try for anything; it seemed like as if I should stay there for ever, and nothing 'ud ever change. But they came and took me away" (xlv,465). Here "heart" and time freeze in a repudiation of life-processes.

Her psychic suicide seems another parallel to her uncle's attitude towards her. He casts her out of the family, while she "will not confess her name or where she comes from" (xxxix,418)--in Hetty's kinship-oriented world to have neither place nor name is to be dead. Mr. Poyser will act as though he never had a niece while Hetty "denies that she has had a child" (xl,427). Killing one's own child, whether in metaphor or fact, is an extreme way of denying the narrator's assertion that we should "help each other the more" because "we are children of a large family" (xxvii,298).

We have seen that the experience of abandoning the child opens, for the first time, a breach in Hetty's narcissistic world; confession of this experience to Dinah is a step outside herself which earlier would have been impossible. Dinah attributes this change to divine grace but it really arises from the therapeutic value of confession itself.[15] Hetty cannot conceptualize her experience, but in the course of the confession the persistent "crying" and her return to the child change from hallucination and compulsion to an image of guilt linking the present to the past. In tribute to the honesty of Eliot's characterization, however, we must note that Hetty's account of her new feelings is limited to very concrete terms: "that crying and the place in the wood," which she hopes God will "take away" as though it were a physical pain (xlv,564). Her confession can only be seen as the beginning of consciousness.

III

Hetty's confession is the emotional climax of the novel; nowhere else do we approach such intense involvement with any of the characters. Yet the confession is also the focal point of our problems with the novel, for we are never to see Hetty again, and thus all the questions raised by this climactic scene remain unanswered. Eliot first turns away from Hetty to concentrate on the sympathetic concern felt for her by other characters, and then, having rescued her from the gallows and shipped her off as a transported convict, forgets her altogether--except for a few cold references in the final Book of the novel, where the sole purpose of the narrative is to celebrate the Poysers' harvest supper and lead towards the happy marriage of Adam and Dinah.

The difficulty presented by Hetty's exile can be seen more clearly by comparison to the easier time Eliot has with her fellow sinner, Arthur. Since both Arthur and Hetty have fallen from the rustic community, any sense of reconcilia-tion on their part must come from self-understanding and a sense of reconcilia-tion with humanity in general. Arthur achieves this in Chapter Forty-Eight, where he reestablishes his friendship with Adam, declares his intent to sacrifice himself by leaving for India so that no one else need leave town, and makes Adam promise to persuade the Poysers to stay. His exile is a healing of his relation with the community: he accepts his guilt, does the best thing for others, and thus prepares for his happier return seven years later.

Arthur's capacity for self-understanding, and his resources as officer, gentleman, and landlord, provide the basis for a conventional expiation. Hetty's exile, however, is not a matter of choice; while we trust she has made a beginning we have yet to see how she will deal with guilt and shame, especially as a transported convict.[16] In this context, Eliot's refusal to say anything at all about Hetty's further development seems unforgivable. When, after Arthur has been welcomed back in "The Epilogue," Dinah rather glibly remarks that "the death of the poor wanderer, when she was coming back to us, has been sorrow upon sorrow" (549), we can only take this as a rather cheap way for the author to fudge unfinished business; it would seem that death is after all the only permissable fate for the fallen woman.

Fortunately, this failure occurs too late to inflict fatal damage on the novel. Despite the incompleteness of her story, Hetty stands out, in the very difficulties she creates, as one of Eliot's great heroines. Her flight from Hayslope brings together the problems of community and individual development, and pushes them to the limits of Eliot's realism. The crime led up to by her journey, coldly investigated at her trial, and finally explained in her confession, is the true centre of the novel because its social and psychological causes include so much of the novel's reality. I will show how the main themes of the novel move towards a climax in her flight and confession, and then are defused by her exile.

The nostalgic affection with which Eliot regards the Poysers, especially on our first tour of the Hall Farm, has blinded many readers to the fact that this novel deals with two problems characteristic of her fiction: the difficulties of growing from confused adolescence to moral maturity, and the virtues and limitations of a tradition-bound community. These concerns are closely related because it is a breach in the community which necessitates individual development, and to learn to think for oneself one must transcend the limitations of one's community.

Although Eliot lovingly depicts the tranquil life of the older generation, represented by the Poysers and their Anglican shepherd Mr. Irwine, the novel is really about the problems of three confused children: Arthur and Hetty, both orphans living with relatives, and Adam, a virtual orphan who assumes responsibility for a drunken father and a foolish, querulous mother. In each case, the moral deficiencies of the child are related to an absence of parental guidance and to feelings of resentment towards inadequate parent-figures: Adam responds to his father's disgrace by incorporating Hayslope's "hardness" into his moral independence, while Arthur compensates for his grandfather's hostility and greed by dreaming how, upon inheriting the estate, he will become an ideal Squire, paternally bestowing largesse on his tenants and beloved by them in return. Both must achieve maturity by learning to see beyond the limitations of their class, Arthur much more painfully than Adam. (Dinah is also an orphan, but we are never shown the experience through which she achieves her sympathetic vision. If she seems too good to be true, this may be because Eliot has not confronted the psychological problems in her ascetic religion--as she does later with Maggie Tulliver and Dorothea Brooke.)

Hetty becomes the most interesting of the orphaned children because she presents the most serious threat to the respectable community and the most extreme case of the difficulties of growing up. Eliot's failure to complete Hetty's story indicates that these problems have not been resolved in the novel. With Maggie Tulliver, the heroine of her next novel, Eliot presents a more explicit version of conflict with family and community, but Maggie's sympathy and intelligence also make it easier for Eliot to develop and analyze this conflict within the moral context of the novel.[17] Never again does Eliot give such a central role to so intractable a character as Hetty.

On the psychological level, Hetty is an effective portrayal of a dark aspect of childhood experience; she seems both attractive and alarming because we recognize in her a stage through which we all have passed. Her tragedy reveals the consequences of failure to grow out of childhood, thus incidentally commenting on masculine idealization of childishness in women. The fact that Hetty represents childhood experience is relevant both to the defensive criticism of her early in the novel, and to Eliot's ability to identify with her in the flight. As we leave Hetty on the road at the end of Chapter Thirty-Seven we abruptly return to the sympathetic distance of mature adult vision--"My heart bleeds for her as I see her toiling along weary feet" (xxxvii,397)--but parental concern on the part of the narrator, Dinah, and Adam is not in itself an adequate way to deal with the character who emerges from the "journey" and the confession.

Adam provides the moral of the story when he overcomes his own version of Hayslopian hardness and agrees to accompany Bartle Massey to Hetty's trial: "I'll stand by her--I'll own her. . . .They oughtn't to cast her off-- their own flesh and blood. We hand folks over to God's mercy and show none ourselves. . . .I'll never be hard again" (xlii,439). Since Hetty's anguish is, however, more interesting than Adam's, most readers are unwilling to view her fall primarily as payment for his education; whatever the quality of his insights, we really want to know the outcome of her experience. Adam's moral improve- ment can be taken for granted; the most interesting problem at the end of the novel is how a character as regressive as Hetty can develop at all--a problem made all the more interesting by the fact that her confession does suggest the possibility of change. Eliot's religion of humanity depends on the replacement of Christian revelation with moral education through experience, and it is the confused Hetty, not the clear-headed Adam, who provides the real test case for this. Despite Hetty's lack of sympathy and intelligence, we respond more to the nightmare confusion of her aimless journey than to the morally lucid experience of Adam and Dinah.

While Hetty presents an unanswered challenge to Eliot's moral psychology, she also leads us to the most complex aspects of the novel's social vision. Both the classes which dominate the novel, landowning aristocracy and respectable tenant farmers, are implicated in her crime. The first of these is easier for Eliot to deal with than the second; the indolent young Squire and his miserly grandfather threaten the rustic community from the outside, reinforcing its values by way of contrast, while Hetty, the embarassing product of this community, threatens it from within. We need not invoke the pastoral tradition to explain Eliot's fondness for Hayslope, for she was here describing the origins of her own family.[18] As the daughter of a man who, like Adam, rose from carpenter to estate-agent, she might well admire hardworking artisans and farmers while feeling a certain hostility towards lazy landlords (of whom we see more in *Silas Marner*). Yet Dinah's rejection of Hayslope implies a reservation about the Poysers, and this expands as the novel develops; as we have seen, the shortcom- ings of Hayslope become a major theme after Hetty takes over from Arthur as leading character.

Mrs. Poyser complains that the tenant farmers must sweat on fields which others own (xxxii,353), but we discover that they in turn are "hard" towards the dispossessed proletariat to which Dinah ministers and into which Hetty falls, sinking all the deeper through her compulsive respectability. Her flight puts her community in a colder perspective; the Poysers are now seen as members of a "proud class," which despises those who "profit" by the poor-rates. Though still sympathetic characters, they are no longer protected by their virtuous role in the enclosing world of Hayslope; after Hetty's flight we see them in ambiguous relation to a larger reality. If Hetty is a case of arrested psychological development, it is also true that the class to which she belongs displays a primitive social vision, in contrast to Dinah, whose moral maturity includes a sympathetic understanding of the industrial poor, and social outcasts in general.

We have seen that a conflict between self and community is implicit in Eliot's portrayal of Hetty (a conflict more clearly developed in her later fiction, but always rendered difficult by her nostalgia for community). In *Adam Bede*, one manifestation of this conflict appears in the difference in realism between the early chapters and Hetty's flight--a problem fatally oversimplified by Gregor and others. Ian Adam has demonstrated that this novel contains a variety of "realisms" (see note 1). I would add that there is a logical transition between the very different "realisms" of our first visit to the Hall Farm and of Hetty's anguish and flight, and that the contrast between these is an important aspect of the thematic structure of the novel.

The pleasant pastoral of our first visit to the Hall Farm in Chapters Six and Seven is mainly the result of narrative distance; both narrator and reader are assumed to be tourists from the city enjoying a visit to a rural world remote in time and space: "The dairy was certainly worth looking at: it was a scene to sicken for with a sort of calenture in hot and dusty streets" (vii,82). At this point we can appreciate the cozy sense of community because we are not threatened with personal involvement.

Eliot encourages us to enjoy the "pastoral" as an entrance to the novel, but does not allow us to remain permanently in a mood which depends on not identifying too closely with the feelings of any one character. As we settle down in the world of the novel, we become aware of something slightly oppressive about the Poysers' way of judging everyone by kin, cleanliness, and farming methods. Adam seems more independent than they, but then he moralizes excessively at his fellow workmen, feels little sympathy for his father, and consoles himself for the latter's death by meditating on the accuracy of arithmetic: "the nature o' things doesn't change. . . .The square o' four is sixteen" (xi,116). The impersonal, collective quality of the novel gradually becomes less our way of enjoying the characters and more a potentially confining manifestation of the Hayslope world-view.[19] In this clearly illuminated, orderly landscape there is no place for the subjective self. The external quality of this world becomes not only the narrator's way of looking at it, but the confines of the world itself, out of which the narrative now seeks to emerge.

In the imagery of dream, vision, and moonlit darkness associated with Dinah in Chapter Fifteen, Eliot suggests an imagination founded on Wordsworthian feeling, but the subjective self becomes located inside Hayslope only through Dinah's moral opposite, Hetty, who, as the literal-minded product of her community, has no imagination at all (in the Wordsworthian sense). Hetty is no longer seen as an alien in the rural world, but, by the beginning of her flight, as a human reality concealed beneath it: "a human heart beating heavily with anguish. . .hidden behind the apple-blossoms, or among the golden corn" (xxiv,371).

By undergoing inner conflict with no sense of an inner self, Hetty reveals the deficiencies of the Poysers' world, while the literalness with which she takes everything on her journey parodies their unquestioning common sense. Her flight is not a break in the novel's reality but a meaningful shift in perspective; the community we once saw from the outside as an organic whole is now experienced subjectively from the inside by a character with whom the narrator temporarily merges in unqualified identification. In Hetty's confession the objective world which seemed so solid dissolves into conflicting fragments and hallucination--a borderline madness which is also her truest way of seeing. Since Hetty acts out in extreme form problems we have all experienced, she becomes the novel's most impressive representative of the subjective self--a fact to which the narrator's intense identification with her has already attested.

The communal world, which has so far provided the novel's objective reality, now becomes a prison in which the self is condemned to death, and we feel the need for an inner transformation which will free Hetty from her past and reveal, to her as well as to the reader, a larger world of human possibility.[20] Eliot gives this experience instead to Adam, who has always had an unquestioned place in the community. Paradoxically, Hetty disappears into the outside world, while Eliot, through Adam's happy marriage, invites us to take as the repository of human values a community which has never acknowledged anything outside itself.

We have seen what an important role Dinah's independence of Hayslope plays in the thematic structure of the novel. Now our consolation for Hetty's exile is to see her virtuous cousin inherit her position as Adam's fiancée and the Poysers' niece, along with that trousseau of linen Mrs. Poyser has been laying up for Hetty's marriage. When Dinah gives up preaching to merge with Adam's prospering career and the Poysers' respectability, the values of Hayslope become, for the first time, the unchallenged standard of the novel. Yet the gradual but persistent development of the novel has been away from warm pastoral towards a vision of the limitations of Hayslope and of the need for a more comprehensive sense of humanity. Thus the reconstructed, Hetty-less pastoral of the ending seems to refute the whole process of the novel.[21]

When Adam finally becomes the main character, his enlightened patriarchal authority encourages us to forget the problems of fallen women and the class divisions of Hayslope. In his rather idealized nobility, the mature Adam seems entirely removed from Hetty in character and situation. Eliot's emphasis on his regenerative suffering is not an effective way to incorporate the burden of her experience into the novel, especially when we consider that her fall saves him from the worse suffering of marriage to her and clears the way for an ideal "second love."[22] Adam, unlike both Hetty and George Eliot, can grow up without leaving home, while the girl who has to leave is never heard from again--except for a brief obituary. Yet we know that despite the title, our main character is not the hero but the heroine. In the dark wood of Hetty's ambivalence we find the living centre of the novel, and the problems which point beyond the false pastoral of the ending. Eliot's first novel has many virtues, but owes both its unity and its enduring interest to the mystery of Hetty Sorrel.

NOTES

1. Barbara Hardy, *The Novels of George Eliot* (London: Athlone Press, 1963), pp. 25-27, and Ian Adam, "The Structure of Realisms in *Adam Bede*," *NCF*, 30 (September 1975), 141-48. Since Hardy and Adam have discussed Eliot's technique in depicting Hetty's flight, I will concentrate on Hetty's psychological motivation.

2. Ian Gregor and Brian Nicholas, *The Moral and the Story* (London: Faber and Faber, 1962), p.29. Jerome Thale sees Hetty's flight as "the most compelling thing in *Adam Bede* and one of the high points of nineteenth-century fiction," but argues that it is a twentieth-century addition to a Wordsworthian pastoral (*The Novels of George Eliot* [New York: Columbia University Press, 1959], pp.30-33).

3. Neil Roberts argues that "In *Adam Bede* George Eliot creates the illusion of a stable and immemorial rural world" where Hetty's fall becomes a "static moral drama" (*George Eliot: Her Beliefs and Her Art* [Pittsburgh: University of Pittsburgh Press, 1975], pp.63-67). I have disputed this view in an article previously published--"Arthur's Misuse of the Imagination: Sentimental Benevolence and Wordsworthian Realism in *Adam Bede*," *English Studies in Canada*, 4 (Spring 1978), 41-59.

4. George R. Creeger, "An Interpretation of *Adam Bede*," *ELH*, 23 (1956), 218-38.

5. Creeger, p.266.

6. Creeger, p.230.

7. Critics who assume that Eliot is making a Puritan attack on sensual love--David Cecil, *Victorian Novelists* (Chicago: University of Chicago Press, 1958)--or that this affair is a genuine pastoral idyll-- Ian Gregor (see note 2) or Michael Squires, *The Pastoral Novel: Studies in George Eliot, Thomas Hardy, and D.H. Lawrence* (Charlottesville: University Press of Virginia, 1974)--make the mistake of taking Arthur's high-flown view of Hetty at face value. I have discussed this problem in an article previously published (see note 3). The most recent view of Eliot as Puritan moralist is Nina Auerbach's "The Rise of the Fallen Woman," *NCF*, 35 (1980), 29-52. Auerbach says that "George Eliot seems to condemn Hetty Sorrel's ambitious sexuality with unyielding austerity" (p.40). Auerbach sees Hetty as "lush and sensuous" (p.40), but also remarks that "for all her sexuality. . .Hetty is oddly devoid of erotic life. George Eliot reminds us constantly that she is ambitious, not passionate" (p.49). Much difficulty about Hetty's "sexuality," and the author's attitude towards her, arises from the assumption that she has both the feelings and the moral responsibility of an adult. In my view Hetty becomes "subversive" to her community not by achieving the status of a rebel, but by acting out a naive version of its values. I will argue that her pathetic social aspirations are akin to childhood rivalry, and that her "sensuality" is self-directed narcissism.

8. George Eliot, *Adam Bede*, ed. Gordon S. Haight (New York: Holt, Rinehart and Winston, 1948), Chapter vii, p.83. All subsequent references will be from this edition. Hetty's dream-world is described in water-imagery combining a womblike absence of weight with self-reflection and plantlike passivity, which also suggests a regressive narcissism.

9. George Eliot, *Essays of George Eliot*, ed. Thomas Pinney (New York: Columbia University Press, 1963), pp.279-80.

10. Eliot compares Hetty to two girls of lower social status: Molly, the housemaid, whom the children always "called on for her ready sympathy" (xviii,195), and the "unsoaped" Bessy Cranage, the blacksmith's daughter, who is Hetty's equal in trivial vanity but has the advantage of her "in the matter of feeling" (xxv,281). Neither has to maintain the Poysers' pretensions to respectability.

11. In this rather bitter editorial aside Eliot accusses both Arthur and Adam of idealizing Hetty's childishness, and implies that Adam wants his wife to be his intellectual inferior (xv,154). Eliot does not pursue this theme, insisting instead on the nobility of Adam's misplaced love. Hetty's seduction could be seen as a fortunate fall which saves him from the much worse fate of marriage to her. In *Middlemarch* Lydgate takes a view of Rosamond very similar to that suggested in the above-mentioned paragraph, and discovers his error through marriage.

12. See G.H. Lewes, *The Study of Psychology: Its Object, Scope, and Method* (Boston, 1879), p.150. I discuss this concept in "Arthur's Misuse of the Imagination: Sentimental Benevolence and Wordsworthian Realism in *Adam Bede*," *English Studies in Canada*, 4 (Spring 1978), 54.

13. Ian Adam is the only critic to note how the events of the journey prepare Hetty for confession to Dinah--in addition to the essay cited in note 1, see Adam's "Restoration Through Feeling in George Eliot's Fiction: A New Look at Hetty Sorrel," *Victorian Newsletter*, 22 (Fall 1962), 9-12. I agree with Adam that Hetty is intended to fit into Eliot's concept of moral regeneration, but differ in my view of her actual impact on the novel.

14. In Greek art Medusa was traditionally portrayed as a hideous demon, but Hellenistic artists gave her a pathetic beauty. Eliot shows that she is aware of the dual nature of the Medusa when she remarks, in her review of Adolf Stahr's *Torso. Kunst, Künstler und Kunstwerk der Alten* (Brunswick, 1854), that in an early sculpture "the Medusa is a hideous caricature; how far from the terrible beauty of the Medusa Rondanini!" (*Saturday Analyst and Leader*, 6 [17 March 1855], 257). The Medusa Rondanini is a sculpture fragment representing Medusa's head, in a museum in Munich. During the composition of *Adam Bede* Eliot transcribed in her notebook a paragraph from Stahr's book giving two accounts of Medusa's transformation into a Gorgon: "Medusa. . .dared to compare herself in beauty to Athena, and the goddess, thereby enraged, changed the girl into a horrible monster. According to another version of the story. . .Medusa's fate was yet more undeserved. . . .Poseidon raped the incomparably beautiful princess in Athena's temple. . . .Athena's punishment. . .fell on the innocent victim, because she was powerless to punish the guilty god." See Joseph Wiesenfarth, "George Eliot's Notes for *Adam Bede*," *NCF*, 32 (September 1977), 148-49 (Wiesenfarth's translation). Both the punishment for rivalry, and the unjust punishment which should have fallen on the male, seem relevant to Hetty's case. Hetty turns herself to stone, but her uncle also reveals the "hardness" of Hayslope in his response to her crime.

15. In his analysis of the secular meaning of religious experience, Ludwig Feuerbach gives special importance to the psychological benefits of Confession (*The Essence of Christianity*, trans. George Eliot [New York: Harper, 1957], pp.78-79 and 122-24).

16. Hetty would certainly be exposed to temptation in a situation where prostitution was taken for granted and also offered escape from heavy labour in appalling conditions. When the female convicts arrived, the officers, soldiers, and farmers (the latter released male convicts) chose the prettiest women as "servants"; also the peculiarly unpleasant life of those not chosen was hardly conducive to virtue--see Margaret Wiedenhofer, *The Convict Years: Transportation and the Penal System, 1788-1868* (Melbourne: Lansdowne Press, 1973), pp.74-77 and 93-96. Despite Eliot's emphasis on realism, her imagination does not follow Hetty to Australia.

17. The heroine of *The Mill on the Floss* combines the hostility towards family life, the Evangelical religion, and the struggle for moral maturity which are here divided between Hetty, Dinah, and Adam; she also winds up in the painful position of having a moral sensibility like Dinah's while being in disgrace like Hetty. Though Maggie is less of a threat to Eliot's values than Hetty, the flood does seem an abrupt end to her moral education. Perhaps Eliot also had difficulty in imagining Maggie's maturity.

18. See Eliot's account of the novel's origins in "History of 'Adam Bede,'" *The George Eliot Letters*, ed. Gordon S. Haight (New Haven: Yale University Press, 1954-55), iii, 502-04. Marghanita

Laski discusses the relation of the novel, in locale and characters, to Eliot's family in *George Eliot and Her World* (London: Thames and Hudson, 1973), pp.64-66.

19. Raymond Williams complains that in *Adam Bede* Eliot presents the rustic characters collectively "as a landscape. . .a kind of chorus" which "can emerge into personal consciousness only through externally formulated attitudes and ideas" (*The Country and the City* [London: Chatto and Windus, 1973], p.206). I argue here that this collective quality is not a defect in Eliot's vision, but an attempt to recreate the world-view of Hayslope and enable us to experience both the pleasant and confining aspects of living there.

20. My discussion of Eliot's realism is indebted to Peter Rees's suggestive argument, in an essay constituting part of an unpublished thesis, that the novel's conclusion requires, but fails to provide, a transformation in Eliot's social vision. Peter Rees, in "The Defective Mirror of *Adam Bede*: The Hall Farm and George Eliot's Unnatural History of English Life" (Simon Fraser University, 1980), agrees with Williams that Eliot's pastoral springs from a defective vision of the Poysers' class.

21. Only at this point does Eliot's ambivalence towards community produce a break in the novel's reality. In an essay relevant to all of Eliot's fiction, Carole L. Robinson has noted that in *Romola* "there is no recognition, much less reconciliation, of the disparity between the idealization of 'community' and the more realistic appraisal of the community itself. (At the heart of the failure in *The Mill on the Floss* is a not dissimilar contradicition)" ("*Romola*: A Reading of the Novel," *VS*, 6 [1962-63], 35). The ending of *Adam Bede* is an example of the same problem, though I would add that the failure of an ending is by no means to be considered the failure of the novel as a whole; otherwise there would be few successes in Victorian fiction.

22. For a more favourable view of the capacity of Adam's crisis and the novel's conclusion to assimilate Hetty's suffering, see Jay Clayton's suggestive essay, "Visionary Power and Narrative Form: Wordsworth and *Adam Bede*," *ELH*, 46 (1979), 645-72. Clayton sees a transformation, beginning with Hetty's confession, from a narrative driven by grim consequences to a Wordsworthian visionary mode governed by sympathy rather than cause and effect. This essay provides important insights into Eliot's relation to Wordsworth but does not resolve the question as to whether such a conclusion would be appropriate to the novel; a sudden shift in reality could be taken as evasion in a novel so committed to psychological realism. In my view the grimness of Hetty's story arises not from the narrator's values, but from Hetty's consciousness and the values of her community, and can only be dealt with in terms of its source.

CRITICAL RESPONSE TO
THE MILL ON THE FLOSS

THE GUARDIAN

25 April 1860

UNSIGNED REVIEW

. . .Two faults strike us at once in this remarkable work. One is of structure. Nobody who reads it can, we should think, avoid the feeling that in the last volume he passes into a new book. There is a clear dislocation in the story, between Maggie's girlhood and Maggie's great temptation. It is perfectly true that it may be the same in real life. There was very likely a tranquil childhood previous to deeds or sufferings which have made the world ring. The commonplace trivialities and unmeaning events of life go on in their most unexciting course to the very eve and verge of the frightful catastrophe--the sudden death, the downfall of prosperity, the hopeless wreck of character and hope. But the course of human things is not necessarily the pattern for a work of art. . . .

Our other objection is a different one. Passion is one of the legitimate materials of the novelist. But he incurs deep responsibility by the way in which he treats it. And we cannot think that he does good service by bringing into clear and powerful light its perverted and unwholesome growths; by making seem probable a development of it which, on the data given us, is an improbable one. It goes against our sense of likelihood that Maggie, being what she is represented, could have been so fascinated by Stephen; certainly nothing is shown us in Stephen, except his own admiration for her, to account for it; and again, we must say that it is most improbable that if Maggie had strength to break her chain at the last and most difficult moment, she should not have had strength to break it before. Moral improbabilities are not atoned for by the power which softens them down and disguises them. But, however this be, the picture of passion gradually stealing like a frightful and incurable poison over not merely principle and self-respect, but even over the faith and honour to the unsuspecting and confiding which the very opinion of the world helps us to hold sacred--of the 'limed soul which, struggling to be free, is more engaged,' is one which had better never have been set before us with so much plainness. We will say at once that the writer never for an instant loses sight of the sin and the shame which she is describing. There may be a passage here and there which show how dangerous the subject is to meddle with. But there is nothing but warning in the result; the loss and the brave penitence, the incurable wound and the generous and humble acceptance of necessary chastisement, are more moving than many sermons. But fully allowing all this, we still hold that there are temptations which it is of itself a temptation to scrutinise too closely; conflicts in the conscience, which it only hardens us to contemplate, much more to do so in our idle hours--wrong doing and wrong feeling, which we are safer and happier in knowing only at a distance--

Non raggioniam di lor, ma guarda e passa.[1]

And in this story, the boldness and power with which ultimate victory and recovery are held up before us are, practically, not a compensation for the equal power and boldness with which, secure of the final triumph of good, the writer has displayed in all its strength the force of evil, changing itself into ever new shapes, penetrating into the most unexpected recesses of the heart, starting up afresh after it seemed conquered, and sweeping two helpless souls before it, like an irresistible fate, up to the last and most improbable moment of rescue.

NOTE

1. Virgil's advice to Dante: 'Let us not speak of them, but look and pass by' (*Inferno*, iii, 51).

THE TIMES

19 May 1860

E.S. DALLAS

'George Eliot' is as great as ever. She has produced a second novel, equal to her first in power, although not in interest. As far as interest is concerned, indeed, it would have been exceedingly difficult to repeat the triumph of *Adam Bede*, in which the author contrived to paint the lily and to gild refined gold by adding the charm of a delightful philosophy to the pleasure of a good story. The reader will at once remember that he could not help liking all the characters in that history. The general influence of the book was to reconcile us to human nature, to make us think better of our fellow men, to make us feel that in the weakest there is something to be admired, in the worst something to be loved, to draw us nearer to each other by showing how completely we are one, and so to give us not only the temporary delight of listening to a pleasant tale, but also the permanent good of an increased sympathy with our kind. It was comparatively easy to excite our interest in the doings of persons towards whom we were led to entertain such friendly feelings. We treasured all their sayings, we watched eagerly all their movements, we were curious as to all their thoughts. The author, apparently afraid of repeating herself, and determined to avoid the imputation of representing the world as too good and sugary, now introduces us to a very different set of personages. A majority of the characters brought together in these three volumes are unpleasant companions--prosaic, selfish, nasty. We are launched into a world of pride, vain-glory, and hypocrisy, envy, hatred and malice, and all uncharitableness. Everybody is quarrelling with everybody in a small mean way; and we have the petty gossip and malignant slander of village worthies painted to the life. . . .

The Dodson family are stingy, selfish wretches, who give no sympathy and require none, who would let a neighbour starve, and let a brother be bankrupt when a very little assistance would save him from the disgrace; but they would not touch a penny that is not theirs, there is no legal obligation which they would not discharge, they would scorn the approach of a lie. They would be truthful and honest, not as a social duty, but as a personal pride--because nobody should have it in his or her power to say that they were weak enough to neglect a manifest obligation. From the same source of self-satisfied strength comes pugnacity in all its forms of rivalry and contradiction, jealousies and criticisms, lawsuits, and slanders, and blows. Everybody in this tale is repelling everybody, and life is in the strictest sense a battle. . . .

This life of proud self-assertion that on the bad side presents itself in an incessant bickering, and on the best side appears as a devotion to justice and truth for selfish ends, may become interesting by being made heroic. . . . 'George Eliot' has attempted a more difficult task. She takes these characters as we find them in real life--in all their intrinsic littleness. She paints them as she finds them--snapping at each other over the tea-table; eyeing each other enviously at church; privately plotting how to astonish each other by some extraordinary display; putting the worst construction on every word and act; officiously proffering advice and predicting calamity; living with perfect content their sordid life of vulgar respectability. The first half of the novel is devoted to the exhibition of this degraded species of existence, which is dissected with a masterly hand. Although it is the least exciting part of the work, it is the part of which the reader will carry away the most vivid recollection. The Dodson family will live for ever, and they inspire the work. With a self-denial which we cannot but admire, the author has resolutely set herself the task of delineating, without exaggeration, without extenuation, with minute accuracy, the sort of life which thousands upon thousands of countrymen lead--a life that outwardly is most respectable, but inherently is most degraded--so degraded, indeed, that the very virtues which adorn it are scarcely to be distinguished from vices. . . .

THE MILL ON THE FLOSS AND THE CONTEMPORARY SOCIAL VALUES: TOM TULLIVER AND SAMUEL SMILES

Cahiers victoriens et edouardiens, 1987

DAVID MALCOLM

Critical tradition has tended to ignore contemporary, radical social issues in George Eliot's fiction. It is as a conservative chronicler of rural life or of the mainstream of middle-class intellectual experience that most critics--even the best--see her.[1] While there are important elements of truth in such critical attitudes, they ignore ways in which her novels are strongly relevant to the contemporary world, and adopt firmly hostile, if complex attitudes to the contemporary political and social status quo.[2]

Despite its ostensible time scheme (it is laid in the 1820s and 1830s) *The Mill on the Floss* is a text for the late 1850s and 1860s in its forceful attack on the materialism and inhumanity of the "Dodsons" and of St. Ogg's, and its recommendation of mutual responsibility and community (embodied sometimes in Maggie and Dr. Kenn) as a solution to social ills. Nowhere however is the novel more allusive to its contemporary social and ideological environment than in its critique of those corner-stones of mid-nineteenth century *laissez-faire* society, individualism and the success ethic. *The Mill on the Floss* is in part a reckoning with Samuel Smiles and the mid-century creed of success which he represents. It is an assault (albeit a complex one) on important aspects of the enabling ideology of mid-century capitalism.

There is no evidence that Eliot read Smiles's most famous work, *Self-Help* (1859), although it is chronologically possible that she did so while writing *The Mill on the Floss,* the second volume of which she did not complete until January 1860.[3] There is however evidence of her acquaintance with the long-running, current debate on the question of the value of individualism and the pursuit of material success: Craik, one of the early advocates of an individualist success ethic in the 1830s, was known to her and Lewes personally, and in 1857 she has read Smiles's newly-published *The Life of George Stephenson,* which rehearses the arguments and ethic of *Self-Help,* with "real profit and pleasure."[4] Her notebook has two separate entries recording material from it, and Wiesenfarth has pointed out its relevance to the composition of *Adam Bede.*[5] Furthermore, in a journal entry dated 10 November 1859 (while she was in the process of writing the second volume *The Mill on the Floss*) Eliot records a discussion at the Congreves' "about George Stephenson, religion etc.."[6]

Eliot's attentive reading of Smiles is evident in *The Mill on the Floss,* above all in the way in which Tom Tulliver is presented throughout as a type of the Smilesian hero. Smiles clearly sets forth the qualities which he most admires in men. "It happens," he writes in *Self-Help*, "that the men who have most moved the world, have not so much been men of genius, strictly so-called, as men of intense, mediocre abilities, untiring workers, persevering, self-reliant, and indefatigable."[7] All of what Smiles writes here of his hero in the abstract is anticipated in *The Life of George Stephenson*.

The life of George Stephenson will be found to furnish subject of interest as well as instruction. Strongly self-reliant, diligent in self-culture, and of indomitable perseverance, the characters of such men--happily numerous in England--are almost equivalent to institutions.[8]

He was a steady, sober, hardworking young man, and nothing more, according to the estimate of his fellow workmen. (*LGS*, p.11). The great secret of his success, however, was his cheerful perseverance. He was never cast down by obstacles, but seemed to take pleasure in grappling with them, and he always rose from each encounter a stronger as well as a wiser man. (*LGS*, p. 148).

Abstinence, self-reliance, tenacity in the face of life's trials, ordinary abilities made fruitful by application; these are the qualities of the Smilesian ideal both in *Self-Help* and in *The Life of George Stephenson*: indeed we are told that Stephenson shows "the spirit of self-help." These qualities are also those of Tom Tulliver, although in Eliot's eyes they are far from ideal attributes, in spite of all the complexity with which they are viewed.[9]

We see an identification of Tom with Smiles's railway engineer hero throughout the novel. For example, there are local echoes of the earlier work in Tom's experiences in the way in which Stephenson too keeps tame rabbits as a youth, and in which Smiles firmly identifies Stephenson's success with the major technological change of his time (*LGS*, p.9,64,465), as Mr. Deane does of Tom's rise in Guest and Company.[10] But more importantly the Smilesian echoes in Tom's character are even stronger. Eliot tells us explicitly of Tom's self-control and abstinence: "His practical shrewdness told him that the means to such achievements could only lie for him in present abstinence and self-denial" (II,66). And we see that a struggle against hard circumstances is the key to his whole career. "'You struggled with your feelings, you say.'" he tells Maggie. "'Yes! I have had feelings to struggle with; but I conquered them. I have had a harder life than you have had; but I have found *my* comfort in doing my duty'" (II,343). The author stresses his thoroughly average qualities and the tenacity and stern integrity which make a great deal of them (I,214-15,217-18; II,65,192), while self-reliance is one of the most prominent features of his character. For example, we are told that "There were no impulses in Tom that led him to expect what did not present itself to him as a right to be demanded" (I,353), and that "Tom had shown no disposition to rely on anyone but himself" (II,68).

In the later stages of the novel it is Tom's complete individualism that becomes more marked, and more harshly judged by the author. Tom makes it clear that it is he and no other who saves the family from dishonor (II,119), and when Maggie brings disgrace on his efforts, he is prepared to cut her off from himself and the family (II,341). We see him lonely and isolated (II,192), and his final, literal isolation, surrounded by flood waters, is fitting (II,398). Even the residual loyalty to others or to his family, which his "Dodson" kin maintain, has sometime since merged into an egoism (II,366-7).

In *Self-Help* Smiles emphasizes, much more than he does in *The Life of George Stephenson*, the individualist and *laissez-faire* aspects of his ethic (although these are implicit in the earlier book).

For the nation is only the aggregate of individual conditions, and civilization itself is but a question of personal improvement. (*SH*, p.50)

The success ethic becomes more and more unabashed.

All may rise equally, yet each, on the whole very much according to his deserts. . .Those who fail in life are very apt to assume the tone of injured innocence, and conclude too hastily that everyone excepting themselves has had a hand in their personal misfortunes. (*SH*, p.132)
It will generally be found that men who are constantly lamenting their ill luck are only reaping the consequences of their own neglect, mismanagement, improvidence, or want of application. . .Practical industry, wisely and vigorously applied, never fails of success. (*SH*, p.194)

Not just in Tom, but in her depiction of St. Ogg's and all it stands for, Eliot engages in a critical analysis of such ideas. The implied ideology of St. Ogg's is patently that of the nineteenth-century *laissez-faire* individualism, which Smiles so effectively embodies. Here the individual is alone in society, responsible only to himself, solely answerable for his success or failure in any sphere, and deserving blame, if he does fail in any way. This attitude also suggests that the individual accumulation of material wealth and social power is the only criterion of worth. Such an ideology of individualism is one with which Eliot has clearly little sympathy. Dr. Kenn surely speaks for the author in this matter.

I should often lose heart at observing the want of fellowship and sense of mutual responsibility among my own flock. At present everything seems tending towards the relaxation of ties--towards the substitution of wayward choice for the adherence to obligation which has its roots in the past. (II,358)

This quotation forms a key part of the novel's moral and social vision, and here moral and social complaint are one. In St. Ogg's, in Tom, and in the "Dodsons" Eliot depicts a society increasingly reluctant to recognize any duty toward fellow human beings. To highlight this the theme of charity, in a broad sense of practical human benevolence, and its neglect, runs throughout the novel.

The parables of the Prodigal Son and the Good Samaritan stand at the beginning and end of the novel (I,43; II,376), and the legend of St. Ogg's is one of practical, uncalculating benevolence (I,179-81). But modern St. Ogg's exemplifies the traditional British simile "as cold as charity" (I,184-8). The

"Dodsons" for example are disinclined to charitable actions in principle (even the genial Mr. Tulliver is at times), and only ever practice these within the small family group of "kin". Here where it is necessary, as in the Tullivers' case, it is coupled with harsh blame and punitive contempt (I,109,323-45; II,8-9). Tom is not charitable even in that limited sense: his harshly-enforced self-reliance, his severe self-discipline isolate him from any sense of his fellowship with others, while the blame of the "Dodsons" becomes in him a crushing success ethic. Even his sense of family is attenuated and becomes an individual egoism (II,366-7). These are the forces behind his treatment of Maggie in the final book of the novel--"'I wash my hand of you forever. You don't belong to me'" (II,341)-- treatment which Aunt Glegg's behavior in the closing stages of the work puts in a very damning perspective (II,364-6). Maggie's debate with Stephen in Mudport should be seen in the light of these concerns, for what Maggie asserts here is the importance of other human beings. She refuses to seek her own good at the expense of others and insists on the value of human fellowship in a society increasingly antipathetic to it. This antipathy is something which she experiences on a personal level in the treatment meted out to her when she returns to St. Ogg's (II,328-36,356).

In her development of the theme of charity in the novel Eliot traces a line of public, historical development manifested on a private, moral level. The "Dodsons" with their collective egoism appear to belong, as their financial habits often do (I,196), to an older, more primitive world than the novel's present, to an almost tribal world. Tom grows out of this towards a set of social attitudes--a punitive success ethic, a complete disdain of charity, a thorough-going individualism--which we associate with a large part of the capitalist nineteenth century. As well as being a group of credible individual portraits, the "Dodson" clan presents a movement of history in microcosm. It is here above all that the novel shows a close connection with its setting in the 1830s, for Tom and the "Dodsons" often speak in the tones of the apologists of the New Poor Law.[11]

What has been suggested above with regard to Tom also applies to the rest of St. Ogg's. The author makes it clear that many aspects of character and action are generally representative of the environment she is depicting, and although our experience of the town is limited (largely to Book VII), we know St. Ogg's fairly well by the middle of the novel. Here Eliot's stress on a general, unrelieved "emphasis of want" (Book IV, Chapter 3) obviously broadens the theme of charity considerably.[12]

If we follow the theme of charity in the novel, we see that Eliot is also taking a critical look at the ethic of success of St. Ogg's. Tom's standards are (as we have seen) those of a success ethic, and he draws such standards from his environment. For example, the "Dodsons" will help their needy kin, but will make sure that those who have failed feel the full weight of their disapproval (I,323-45), and Mr. Deane, with one foot in the "Dodson" camp and one in St. Ogg's proper, even more clearly represents such an attitude. "Mr. Deane," Tom reflects, "had succeeded by his own merit, and. . .what he had to say to young men in general was, that if they didn't succeed too, it was because of their own demerit" (II,201-2). The successful businessman considers in his domestic prosperity and happiness that it is his "merits" which have earned him them (II,240). From his childhood a part of such an ethic is implicit in Tom's character.

> Tom was only thirteen, and had no decided views in grammar and arithmetic, regarding them for the most part as open questions, but he was particularly clear and positive on one point--namely, that he would punish everyone who deserved it: why, he wouldn't have minded being punished himself, if he deserved it; but then he never *did* deserve it. (I,53)

The child's standards, like those of his adult relatives, are charitable, and Tom's struggle with the inhospitable world accentuates these qualities in him (II,66-7). He too sees material success as a result of his own merit. "'You never do wrong,' said Maggie tauntingly. 'Not if I know it,' answered Tom with proud sincerity" (II,117). He has no sympathy with those who fail or are in need in any way, and it is in his treatment of his sister at the end of the novel that we see this ethic and its limitations most clearly. It is worth noting here that Maggie's failure seems at first sight a moral one, but it is more importantly a social one. She has imperiled the family's social position (and above all Tom's), and her failure is the equivalent of her father's bankruptcy (I,384). Tom, in Book VII, cuts off the failed member of his family, and while the author allows us to understand his action, she also asks us to view it critically. Indeed, here she suggests that a success ethic is potentially hypocritical for St. Ogg's would have accepted Maggie had she married Stephen. And what would Tom's reaction have been if his sister--now Mrs. Guest--had no longer been a social disgrace to him? An ethic of success is, as Houghton suggests, fundamentally amoral (in spite of its roots in a tradition of Protestant thought).[13]

We know of Eliot's connected concerns of charity and individualism from elsewhere in her work. Indeed her condemnation of Tom's irresponsible individualism is part of her attack throughout her writing on our egoisms, social and individual. One of Amos Barton's most glaring faults is that he fails miserably in his charitable responsiblities in his parish (a failure reflected within his own family).[14] In the lesser works, *Romola* and *The Spanish Gypsy*, there are striking central moments in which characters must decide between their own individual concerns and a broader duty to others.[15] These are akin to the concern with charity in *The Mill on the Floss*. In *Daniel Deronda* one of the primary sources of Gwendolen's guilt is that she has "'thrust out others'", has "'made a gain out of their loss.'"[16] In *The Mill on the Floss*, in the "Dodsons", in Tom, and in what we know of St. Ogg's the author indicts a society for just the quality suggested by Gwendolen's words, for a lack of fellow-feeling, and for a concomitant egoistic individualism. (While in *The Mill on the Floss* she insists that "moral judgements" must be "checked and enlightened by perpetual reference to the special circumstances that mark the individual lot" (II,362), and in letters and elsewhere in her fiction she is chary of collectivist responses to social ills, Eliot continually points to irresponsible individualism at the root of moral, social, and personal corruption.)[17]

The principles of St. Ogg's and of Tom Tulliver outlined above have a long tradition, as does the debate about their value. Tawney suggests that their roots are to be found in the economic, social, and religious changes of the sixteenth and seventeenth centuries.[18] Carlyle sees them as among his society's besetting sins in *Past and Present* in 1843.[19] J.L. Winter has recently indicated in detail how the debate about the individualistic pursuit of wealth runs throughout the ninteenth century.[20] However, as Houghton shows, the mid-century marks a crucial turning-point in which the "creed of success" becomes at once "naked" and "eminently respectable."[21] Palmerston expresses it in scarcely disguised form throughout the 1850s and 1860s, and the two texts by Smiles, which this article has discussed, indicate the relevance of this debate in the late 1850s.[22] It continues on into the 1860s. Harrison in 1865, Mill in 1867, and (perhaps most celebratedly) Arnold in 1869 all take as their theme criticism of the unrestrained individualist emphasis of contemporary Britain with its orientation towards material success.[23] In Tom Tulliver and his echoing of Smilesian ethos we can see Eliot participating in this debate and, anticipating some of her illustrious contemporaries, delivering a critical thrust against an increasingly accepted aspect of contemporary social thinking.

NOTES

1. See: Leslie Stephen, "George Eliot", *Cornhill Magazine*, 43, (February 1881), 152-68--reprinted in *A Century of George Eliot Criticism*, ed. Gordon S. Haight (Boston, 1965; rpt. London: Methuen, 1966), pp.138-9; Frederic Harrison, "George Eliot's Place in Literature," *Forum* (September 1895), pp.66-78; F.R. Leavis, *The Great Tradition* (1948; rpt. Harmondsworth: Pelican, 1967), p.10,51; Neil Roberts, *George Eliot: Her Beliefs and Her Art*, Writers and Their World (London: Paul Elek, 1975), pp.9-20, 24; Gordon S. Haight, *George Eliot: A Biography* (Oxford: Oxford University Press, 1968), p.543. Raymond Williams's arguments are more complex, but still under-estimate the radical criticism of contemporary Britain in Eliot's novels (e.g. *Culture and Society, 1780-1950* (1958; rpt. Harmondsworth: Pelican, 1963), pp.112-19; *The English Novel from Dickens to Lawrence* (1970; rpt. St. Albans: Paladin, 1974), p.23. Notable exceptions to this tendency of neglect are: John Killham in his essay "Tennyson and Victorian Social Values", in *Tennyson*, ed. D.J. Palmer, Writers and Their Background (London: G. Bell and Sons, 1973), p.160; and Valentine Cunningham, *Everywhere Spoken Against: Dissent in the Victorian Novel* (Oxford: Oxford University Press, 1975), pp.178-88,99.

2. Early reviews of the novel show little sense of the historical distance of its setting; on the contrary they readily identify contemporary critical issues in the work. One hostile reviewer of *The Mill on the Floss* is constrained by the socially critical element in the novel to describe its author as "a sort of womanly Carlyle" (*Dublin University Magazine*, 57, (February 1861), 192-200--reprinted in *George Eliot: The Critical Heritage*, ed. David Carroll (London: Routledge and Kegan Paul, 1971), pp.145-53 (p.152)).

3. There is no reference to it in any of the following: *The George Eliot Letters*, ed. Gordon S. Haight, 7 vols. (London and New Haven: Oxford University Press and Yale University Press, 1954-

55); William Baker, *The George Eliot-George Henry Lewes Library: An Illustrated Catalogue of Their Books* at Dr. Williams' Library, London (New York and London: Garland, 1977); *George Eliot, A Writer's Notebook, 1854-79: and Uncollected Writings*, ed. Joseph Wiesenfarth (Charlottesville, Virginia: University of Virginia Press, 1981).

4. *The George Eliot Letters*, IV,469; II,369.

5. *A Writer's Notebook*, p.20,30,155,163.

6. *The George Eliot Letters*, IV, 11 (footnote 5). With regard to Eliot's comment on Smile's biography of Stephenson and her later casual remark to Caroline Bray that "Geo. Stephenson [sic] is one of my great heroes--has he not a dear old face," the argument of this article, that Eliot is adopting in *The Mill on the Floss* an attitude fundamentally critical of a Smilesian ethos, must appear odd. However in the light of Eliot's own complicated attitude to Tom and her tenacious commitment to complexity in general ("that complex, fragmentary doubt provoking knowledge we call truth" [*The Mill on the Floss*, Cabinet Edition, 21 vols. (Edinburgh and London: Blackwood, 1877-80), II,298]), such a mixed response to the world should not be too surprising.

7. Samuel Smiles, *Self-Help: With Illustrations of Character and Conduct* (London: John Murray, 1859), p.50. Hereafter this work is cited in the text as *SH*.

8. Samuel Smiles, *The Life of George Stephenson, Railway Engineer* (London: John Murray, 1857), p.50. Hereafter this work is cited in the text as *LGS*.

9. *Life of George Stephenson*, p.16,22,46; *Self-Help*, p.3,16,216. It should be noted however that Eliot was proud of how sympathetic she felt she had made Tom appear (*The George Eliot Letters*, III,397).

10. All references to the novels of George Eliot in this articles are to editions appearing in the Cabinet Edition, 21 vols. (Edinburgh and London: Blackwood, 1877-80).

11. See: R.H. Tawney, *Religion and the Rise of Capitalism* (1926: rpt. Harmondsworth: Pelican, 1938), Chapters 4-5; J.F.C. Harrisson, *Early Victorian Britain, 1835-51* (1971; rpt. Glasgow: Fontana, 1979), pp.106-112; *Contemporary Sources and Opinions in Modern British History*, ed. Lloyd Evans and Philip J. Pledger, 2 vols. (London and New York: Frederick Warne, 1967), I, 141-52.

12. See also: *The Mill on the Floss*, II,7,9-10,385. See in addition the analyses of Stelling in I, 208, and of Wakem in I, 394.

13. Walter E. Houghton, *The Victorian Frame of Mind, 1830-1870* (New Haven and London: Yale University Press, 1957), p.194.

14. *Scenes of Clerical Life*, I,35-42,97.

15. *Romola*, II, 99-101; *The Spanish Gypsy: A Poem*, p.156,161,163.

16. *Daniel Deronda*, II,264; III,225.

17. *The George Eliot Letters*, I,252-55; II,403; VI,99; *Felix Holt*, II,90.

18. Tawney, p.244,264.

19. Thomas Carlyle, *Past and Present*, Book III, Chapter 2--reprinted in Thomas Carlyle, *Selected Writings*, ed. Alan Shelston (Harmondsworth: Penguin, 1971), pp.276-7.

20. J.L. Winter, "Self-Helpers, and Self-Seekers: Some Changing Attitudes to Wealth, 1840-1910", *Victorian Newsletter*, no.60 (Fall 1981), pp.27-31.

21. Houghton, p.192,194-5.

22. The *Don Pacifico* speech (June 1850) and a speech given at the prizegiving of the South London Industrial Exhibition (April 1865)--quoted in Geoffrey Best, *Mid-Victorian Britain 1851-70* (1971; rpt. Glasgow: Fontana, 1979), pp.255-8.

23. Frederic Harrisson, "Limits of Political Economy" (1865), in *National and Social Problems* (London, 1908), pp.274-305 (p.277); J.S. Mill, "Inaugural Address at St. Andrews" (1867)--quoted in Houghton, pp.289-90; Matthew Arnold, *Culture and Anarchy*, ed. J. Dover Wilson (1932; rpt. Cambridge: Cambridge University Press, 1960), p.49.

ONTOGENY AND PHYLOGENY IN THE MILL ON THE FLOSS

Victorian Newsletter, 1988

PRESTON FAMBROUGH

The subject of George Eliot's fiction is man's moral experience; and as she chronicles moral triumph and failure in novel after novel, there emerges not only a consistent moral credo centered on faithfulness and responsibility but also a distinct physiology of moral behavior in human life. The twin derivation of this moral physiology from Wordsworth and Comte is well known.[1] In Wordsworth she found a valorization of feeling as the root of moral action, an idealization of childhood as the time of freshest and most intense feelings, and an ideal of adult life in which the individual's days would be bound each to each through memory and through successive reaffirmation of the natural piety of the child. In Comte and positivism she found the application of universal laws to human affairs and the conviction that "the past rules the present, lives in it, and we are but the growth and outcome of the past" (*Letters*, 3:320).

The view of society as an organism, an analogy which has figured in moral philosophy at least since the Stoics and which came to dominate nineteenth-century social thought, adds to the urgency of George Eliot's moral vision by revealing "the infinite issues belonging to everyday duties" (*MF* 150; bk.2, ch.4). Since human society is a living unity of interdependent parts, the slightest action of any of these human integers theoretically affects the whole and every part, not merely for the present but for all time. As Bourl'honne summarizes, "les consèquences de nos actes se propagent inèluctablement dans le temps et dans l'espace" (135-36).

George Eliot was especially struck by the corollary of nineteenth-century organicism holding that the life of an individual recapitulates the life of the species,[2] a theory she endorses most explicitly in *Romola* in asserting that our lives make a moral tradition for our individual selves, as the life of mankind at large makes a moral tradition for the race" (420; bk.7, ch.39). In George Eliot's fiction, Suzanne Graver explains, the process of development

applies to the individual no less than society, and the crucial correspondence between the two makes these connections the most vital of all for George Eliot. As a result the natural history of our social life finds its complement in what she later called a 'natural history of the mind,' with 'mind' signifying the psychological evolution of developing capacity for moral growth.(33)

Similarly, William Myers observes that for George Eliot, "the individual and society are constituted in each other's structures" (67).

The analogy between the individual's experience and the community's is most vividly manifest in *The Mill on the Floss*, George Eliot's one novel chronicling the moral-psychological development of its protagonist from childhood to adulthood against the background of a community whose moral history is powerfully if intermittently evoked.[3] In this *Bildungsroman* the heroine's experience closely parallels the experience of the community itself. In both the individual and the collective history, moral behavior is shown to depend on attentiveness and fidelity to memories of past acts of compassion: the response of the medieval St. Ogg to the heart's need of a suffering woman corresponds to Maggie's early movements of sympathy and love, while the moral failings of both heroine and community are shown to result from a similar fragmentation of experience, a repudiation or alienation of the past.

For George Eliot, the essence of moral experience lies in feelings of pity and affection, feelings without which, as we see from the example of Tom Tulliver, human beings are capable of nothing higher than a narrow, pharisaical form of justice. Like Wordsworth, George Eliot held these feelings of spontaneous compassion to be part of the "natural piety" of childhood. And these first affections, for the novelist as for the poet, are seen as "the fountain-light of all our day." The highest morality springs from a retention or recovery, through memory and sometimes conscious effort, of those childhood well-springs of affection. According to Ruby Redinger George Eliot considered her own childhood "the source of her power to love as a mature woman, for only love can beget love" (49). And Ernest Bevan reflects that "the memory which recalls youth helps return her characters to their better selves and strengthens those affections which generate the flow of sympathy" (66).

Like Wordsworth, George Eliot insists repeatedly in *The Mill* on the Edenic quality of childhood existence. Thus Maggie's promise to kiss Philip when they should meet again proves

void, like so many other sweet, illusory promises of childhood; void as promises made in Eden before the seasons were divided, and when the starry blossoms grew side by side with the ripening peach-- impossible to be fulfilled when the golden gates had been passed. (166; bk.2, ch.7)

And the chapter ends with the solemn refrain: "They had entered the thorny wilderness, and the golden gates of their childhood had forever closed behind them" (171; bk.2, ch.7).[4] Critics have long complained of an alleged incongruity between the narrator's idealization of childhood as paradise and the facts of the heroine's experience.[5] It is true that Maggie's is from the start a "troublous life" (44, bk.1, ch.6) and that those with whom she shares "those first affections"-- Tom and her father--cannot fully reciprocate her love (though Knoepflmacher certainly exaggerates the deficiency of Tom's early affection for her [216-17]). But the real point of the narrator's insistence on the Edenic nature of Maggie's childhood lies elsewhere, not in its "delight and liberty" or even in the greater reciprocity of her affections encounter at this period in Tom and her father, but rather in the quality of *her own* first affections. As in "Intimations of Immortality," we understand that the "glory" (used in the poem in its religious sense of a halo, an aura of heavenly light) described as lying about the child in infancy and steadily fading as it grows older, actually inheres in the child as a state of mind, a vestige of prenatal paradise in which the individual soul is *at one* with creation. Maggie's childhood is seen as a paradise because, as the period when her primary affections are strongest and purest, it is a lifelong source of her natural piety. As in "Intimations," the memory of childhood constitutes a memory of a memory of paradise. Thus her childhood home is always for Maggie a "sanctuary where sacred relics lay" (420; bk.16, ch.14), and the leitmotif of "sacredness" recurs throughout the book linking childhood and paradise.[6] The moral vision stemming in the novel from George Eliot's idealization of childhood, her clear endorsement of Maggie's choices of renunciation of present happiness in favor of ties to the past, has mystified many readers and repelled others. Her repudiation of an incipient friendship with Philip in deference to her father's and brother's animosity seems wholly unreasonable. And the reader's difficulty is compounded by the novelist's intellectual and artistic honesty in developing with great cogency a point of view opposed to her own. Philip's argument that Maggie's renunciation is but a "narrow self-delusive fanaticism, which is only a way of escaping pain by starving into dullness all the highest powers of your nature" (286; bk.5, ch.3) has been mistaken for George Eliot's view by critics who read the novel as a tragedy of misguided and pointless repression and regression.[7] But the arbitrariness of such a reading has been clearly demonstrated by John Hagan, who notes that the narrator terms Philip's desperate plea a "sophistry" and Maggie's resistance a "true prompting against a concealment that would introduce doubleness into her own mind, and might cause misery to those who had the primary natural claim on her" (54-55).

Once, in reply to Philip's timid reproof that she could never love him as much as Tom, Maggie answers simply, "Perhaps not; but then, you know, the first thing I remember in my life is standing with Tom by the side of the Floss, while he held my hand; everything before that is dark to me" (268; bk.5; ch.2). The reader who enters into George Eliot's view of the origin of human sympathy in the first affections of childhood will recognize the ineluctability of Maggie's decision to give Philip up, unjust as it seems. To require her to sacrifice her primary family ties to more recent sympathy is self-contradictory, since her affection for Philip itself, in this view, actually *depends* upon her primary ties with family which are the root of all subsequent affection.

The moral dilemma posed for Maggie by her love for Stephen reveals more fully how morality depends on the individual's awareness of the temporal continuity of his existence as well as its *solidarity* with all other human life.[8] For George Eliot, W.J. Harvey observes, "to lose one's roots is to lose that sense of oneself as part of the continuum of things, to blind oneself to that sense of looking before and after which is so necessary for maturity" (182). To succumb to the evil of egoism, as Maggie does momentarily in her "Great Temptation," is to live in a disconnected present. In allowing herself the forbidden joy of dancing with Stephen she rationalizes: "This one, this last night, she might expand unrestrainedly in the warmth of the present, without all those chill eating thoughts of past and future" (386; bk.6, ch.10). Likewise, when she sets out with Stephen on their fateful boat ride, we are told that "memory was excluded" (407; bk.6, ch.13). Again her yielding is described as a hiatus in the continuity of her life: "They spoke no word; for what could words have been but an inlet to thought? And thought did not belong to the enchanted haze in which they were enveloped--it belonged to the past and future that lay outside the haze" (407; bk.6, ch.13).

The novel reveals an elaborate parallel between these moral struggles of the heroine and the collective experience of the community. St. Ogg's, a town which "carries the trace of its long growth and history like a millenial tree" and which is "familiar with forgotten years" (104; bk.1, ch.12), has had in its collective infancy a potential "fountain light" of compassion and moral force. Wiesenfarth points out that the legend of Ogg is a myth of the *origin* of the community (103), while Buckler relates the story to Genesis (153). The spontaneous unquestioning pity with which Ogg, the patron saint of the old town,[9] responded to the heart's need of the wayfarer thus parallels closely the formative "first affections" of Maggie's childhood. It is true that the significance of Ogg's example in the novel is complicated by George Eliot's well-known ambivalence regarding social-historical evolution. But in this novel the narrator, while echoing the conventional nineteenth-century meliorism George Eliot upheld throughout her career, repeatedly praises the greater intensity of emotion attained by past ages.

Like her fellow agnostic John Stuart Mill,[10] George Eliot admired the potential of the Christian religion at its best to inspire self-transcending enthusiasm, but lamented the deterioration of Christianity in her own day into empty ritualism. In *The Mill on the Floss*, the narrator reflects that "The days were gone when men could be greatly wrought upon by their faith." And in his interviews with Maggie, Dr. Kenn echoes much the same animadversion:

And the Church ought to represent the feeling of the community, so that every parish should be a family knit together under a spiritual father. But the ideas of discipline and Christian fraternity are entirely relaxed--they can hardly be said to exist in the public mind. . .and if I were not supported by the firm faith that the Church must ultimately recover the full force of that constitution which alone is fitted to human needs, I should often lose heart at observing the want of fellowship and sense of mutual responsibility among my own flock. (432-33; bk.7, ch.2)

Somewhat more problematic but still essentially approbative is the appraisal of the past intimated in the narrator's contrast between the ruins of the Rhone and the Rhine:

And that was a day of romance! If those robber-barons were somewhat grim and drunken ogres, they had a certain grandeur of the wild beast in them--they were forest boars with tusks, tearing and rending, not the ordinary domestic grunter; they represented the demon forces for ever in collision with beauty, virtue, and the gentle uses of life; they made a fine contrast in the picture with the wandering minstrel, the soft-lipped princess, the pious recluse, and the timid Israelite. That was a time of colour, when the sunlight fell on glancing steel and floating banners; a time of adventure and fierce struggle--nay, of living, religious art and religious enthusiasm; for were not cathedrals built in those days, and did not great emperors leave their Western palaces to die before the infidel strongholds in the sacred East? (237-38; bk.4, ch.1)

The common denominator among St. Ogg, the robber-barons of the Rhine valley, the cathedral-builders and the Crusaders--the redeeming grace, in the narrator's eyes, of this age of lawless violence--is the sway of "passionate impulse." This characteristic is of course the distinguishing mark of Maggie Tulliver as a child; and this implied link between the heroine's childhood and the barbaric Middle Ages is textually reinforced, as both Stump (105) and Harvey (175) have noted, by the child's punishment of her "fetish" doll.[11] Without resolving all the inconsistencies in George Eliot's view of historical evolution, Harvey's comparison between childhood and pre-civilized society is illuminating. Childhood, Harvey insists, with its spontaneous sympathy and sense of unity with creation which are the fountain-head of moral life in the adult, is itself actually *pre-moral*. And he cautions that while continuity with childhood is essential for George Eliot,

continuity is not sameness; merely to extend the pre-moral life of childhood into the adult world is disastrous. For the child is also a simple ego, with little sense of cause or consequence. Like an animal, like a savage, his moods are intense but fugitive, lacking the necessary sense of time before and time after. (183)

The admiration the narrator expresses for the intensity of passion and compassion in the age of Ogg and the robber barons does not constitute a retrogressive proposal to return society to the conditions of the Middle Ages, any more than Rousseau's *Social Contract* proposes a return to the state of nature. The ideal of modern society the novel implies is rather a community in which the ancient springs of feeling still flow, but channeled by the "labor of choice" (135; bk.2, ch.1), by "that necessary sense of time before and time after," sharpened and extended by modern science and the accumulation of "hard-won treasurers of thought which generations of painful toil have laid up for the race of men. . ." (225; bk.4, ch.3).[12]

We are told at the conclusion of the legend of St. Ogg that

it was witnessed in the floods of aftertime, that at the coming on of the eventide, Ogg the son of Beorl was always seen with his boat upon the widespreading waters, and the Blessed Virgin sat in the prow so that the rowers in the gathering darkness took heart and pulled anew. (105; bk.1, ch.7)

Ogg's legend, I believe, presents a complex allegory depicting the moral influence of the past on the present in the life of both individual and community. On one level Ogg's act of compassion stands for the passionate impulse characteristic of civilization's infancy and serving as the "root of piety" for the "mature" civilization. The rowers in the gathering darkness represent successive generations who, under the influence of Ogg's act of charity, struggle to "rescue" their fellow men, or struggle in the *darkness* with their own moral difficulties and dilemmas.[13] And in a more general way Ogg's deed stands for any of the innumerable acts of goodness, historic and unhistoric, on which "the growing good of the world is partly dependent" (*Middlemarch* 613; bk.8, "Finale"), sometimes through direct moral inspiration,[14] but also in incalculable, mysterious ways. For George Eliot, with all her enthusiasm for Comte and positivism, never denies the existence of an irreducible core of mystery in human affairs. In a well-known letter she speaks of "the mystery that lies under the processes" (*Letters* 3: 227). We recall the narrator's insistence in *The Mill* on the "mystery of the human lot" (238; bk.4, ch.30), a dimension of reality virtually ignored by the current generation but appreciated by the Middle Ages. And elsewhere she professes through Maggie, "I think there are stores laid up in our human nature that our understanding can make no complete inventory of" (226; bk.5, ch.1).[15]

The river, prominent in Ogg's legend and ubiquitous in the novel itself, is a multi-faceted symbol which further links ontogeny and phylogeny by reinforcing the novel's central vision of solidarity and continuity in life. The Floss ties the community of St. Ogg's both spatially to all living humanity and temporally to the life of the past and future. It "links the pulse of the old English town with the beating of the world's mighty heart" (238; bk.4, ch.1) while it binds the present population to the "ghostly boatman" who haunts it still. At the same time the river serves as a metaphor for the formation and function of habit in the moral experience of individual and community,[16] a concept central to George Eliot's problematical theory of determinism.[17] The language of channels and pathways gouged out in the mind by habitual acts and feelings, derived from G.H. Lewes and his fellow physiological psychologists (Shuttleworth 72), is frequently encountered in George Eliot's work. In the Proem to *Romola* we read that "The great river-courses which have shaped the lives of men have hardly changed; and those other streams, the life-currents that ebb and flow in human hearts, pulsate to the same great needs, the same great loves and terrors" (43). In the same novel we are told of Tito Melema that "The little rills of selfishness had united and made a channel, so that they could never again meet the same resistance" (106; bk.1, ch.9). And in her essay on "Historic Guidance," the novelist writes,

We study the preparation made for us by previous ages, and discerning how laborious devoted lives or grand jets of noble resolution have made *currents* of good effect reaching to ourselves, grateful admiring love is more or less stimulated by our contemplation; this sentiment reinforces our desire to exert some corresponding influence over the destiny of our own successors. (371, my italics)

Yet consciousness, as Shuttleworth reminds us, was by George Eliot's time already seen as multiple, "the confluence of many streams of sensation" (Lewes 2: 68; qtd. in Shuttleworth 73). And this conflicting plurality in the influence of the past on the present of both individual and the race is powerfully depicted in *The Mill on the Floss* through complication of the river symbolism. We recall the "fierce collision" of "opposing elements" (261; bk.5, ch.1) that is foreshadowed at the moment of Maggie's reacquaintance with Philip Wakem. And in fact at the climax of her moral experience, two opposing "currents" are perceived at work within her, one a habit of compassionate self-denial originating in early childhood, the other an appetite for personal enjoyment also present in her childhood but latent until quickened into an inexorable force by repeated indulgence just before her fatal lapse with Stephen. At the outset of her aquaintance with Stephen, though she is tempted by the delicious prospects of admiration and luxury such a relationship seems to offer, there are still "things in her stronger than vanity--passion, and affection, and long deep memories of earlier claims on her love and pity and the *stream* of vanity was soon swept along and mingled imperceptibly with that wider *current* which was at its highest force today. . ."(382; bk.6, ch.9; my italics). The difference in magnitude between the two opposing forces depicted here--one a mere "stream," the other a "wider current"--augurs that the latter will eventually prevail. But first Maggie must be "Borne Along by the Tide" of egoism (bk.6, ch.13), the long deep habits of self-renouncing compassion momentarily overmastered by the "feeling of a few short weeks" (413; bk.6, ch.14). During her abortive elopement with Stephen it seems to Maggie "that the tide was doing it all--that she might glide along with the swift silent stream, and not struggle any more" (403; bk.6, ch.13). As she lies down to rest on the deck of the ship, "she was being lulled to sleep with that same soft stream still flowing over her" (412; bk.6, ch.13). And when her better self inevitably reasserts itself, "it came with the memories that no passion could long quench: the long past came back to her, and with it the fountains of self-renouncing pity and affection, of faithfulness and resolve" (450; bk.7, ch.5).

Analogous to the struggle between egoism and duty raging within Maggie is the tension between these two elements within the community. "The mind of St. Ogg's did not look extensively before or after," we are told. "It inherited a long past without thinking of it, and had no eyes for the spirits that walk the streets" (106; bk.1, ch.12). Maggie's transient state of mind at the moment of yielding to temptation is here revealed as the habitual mode of consciousness for most of the inhabitants of the ancient town. And near the end of the novel Dr. Kenn laments that "At present everything seems tending toward the relaxation of ties--toward the substitution of wayward choice for the adherence to obligation, which has its roots in the past" (433; bk.7, ch.2). Here as elsewhere in the text, the notion of ontogeny recapitulating phylogeny is inherent in the duality of "the past" that Dr. Kenn invokes: the people of St. Ogg's are oblivious both to their individual pasts with the duties that inhere in them and also to their communal history with its exemplary instance of compassion for suffering. Even if we regard the legend of St. Ogg entirely as a myth created by the community, its moral significance for the present is the same: "They are unfaithful to that generous impulse of their ancestors that gave rise to the legend of St. Ogg and recognized the validity of the heart's need" (Wiesenfarth 109).

Yet though its efficacy is mysterious and problematic, St. Ogg's deed of mercy does not fail to transmit its currents of benevolence down to the narrative present of the novel and beyond. For Ogg seems clearly to be reincarnated in several characters in the novel in their moments of charity and compassion. Bob Jakin, an unlikely avatar nonetheless linked to the Saint through his association with boats and water, repeatedly offers help to Tom and Maggie and responds to Maggie's heart's need without questioning it when she is in disgrace.[18] More unmistakeable is the link between Ogg and Dr. Kenn (curiously overlooked by Wiesenfarth). When Maggie first sees the clergyman his face seems "to tell of a human being who had reached a firm, safe stand, but was looking with helpful pity towards the waves" (381; bk.6, ch.9). And when he advises Maggie in her time of utmost need, he does so in precisely the spirit of the legendary boatman. We recall the word of the transfigured woman of the legend upon reaching the shore: "Ogg the son of Beorl, thou art blessed in that thou didst not question and wrangle with the heart's need, but was smitten with pity, and did straightway relieve the same" (105; bk.1, ch.7). Though *reason* dictates marriage between Maggie and Stephen as the expedient involving the least evil, we are told that Dr. Kenn "entered with all the comprehension of a man who had known spiritual conflict, and lived through years of devoted service to his fellow-men, into that state of Maggie's heart and mind which made the consent to the marriage a desecration to her: her conscience must not be tampered with. . ." (434; bk.7, ch.3).

During the "Final Rescue" with which the novel ends, the actual drama of St. Ogg and the Virgin is re-enacted with Maggie seeming to reincarnate alternatively the two figures of the legend. First, in setting out in a boat on the flood, she assumes the role of Ogg (Fisher 68). Then, with Tom at the oars, she is transformed into the Madonna always seated in the prow of Ogg's boat in the floods of aftertime (Bevan 74; Wiesenfarth 120). Though Maggie cannot save Tom's life, "the benevolent force of her past," as Bevan asserts, "is nontheless affirmed: Tom renounces pride and calls her 'Magsie'"(75). I would suggest that in fact both Maggie's pasts are confirmed by her final act of love, the "deep, underlying, unshakable memories of early union" with Tom (453; bk.7, ch.5) and, even deeper, the racial memory of St. Ogg's long-ago deed of mercy.

Maggie's actual knowledge of the St. Ogg legend is documented only once, near the end of the novel, through her dream on board the ship with Stephen:

She was in a boat on the wide water with Stephen, and in the gathering darkness something like a star appeared, that grew and grew till they saw it was the Virgin seated in St. Ogg's boat, and it came nearer and nearer, till they saw the Virgin was Lucy and the boatman was Philip--no, not Philip, but her brother, who rowed past without looking at her; and she rose to stretch out her arms and call to him, and their own boat turned over with the movement, and they began to sink, till with one spasm of dread she seemed to awake, and find she was a child again in the parlor at evening twilight, and Tom was not really angry. (412-13; bk.6, ch.14)

This dream, emerging from the individual and collective unconscious, provides the impulse for Maggie to renounce Stephen.[19] The shifting identity of the boatman in the dream reflects the twin sources of her renewed moral strength in her own early affections for Tom and Philip and in the legacy of Ogg. Her breach of faithfulness to her individual and racial pasts is symbolized by Tom's (the boatman's) refusal to look at her.

The benevolent influence on Maggie of a larger communal past takes a tangible form in her reading of Thomas a Kempis. Wiesenfarth explains that *The Imitation of Christ* "amplifies the meaning of St. Ogg by formulating the way an individual can understand his position in relation to other men" (114). It is significant that at least two human intermediaries are involved in the transmission of Kempis' message across the centuries to Maggie: the "quiet hand" (253; bk.4, ch.3) that directs her to certain passages in the text and Bob Jakin, who, himself impelled by memories of their early friendship (Buckler 152), gives her the book. The documentation of these intermediaries reinforces our sense of a historical continuum of human sympathy of which Maggie is the culmination and beneficiary.

But the moral value or significance of Maggie's renunciation of Stephen, like that of her rupture with Philip earlier, has been questioned repeatedly.[20] It is true that while the touchstone of George Eliot's moral system is the well-being of others, Maggie's ultimate refusal to marry Stephen comes too late to avert the suffering caused by her temporary lapse and indeed appears to effect no happiness nor alleviate any pain in the world around her. But those who deny the meaning and value of Maggie's choice have failed to grasp the breadth and complexity of the novelists's moral vision, the web-like interconnectedness she perceives pervading all human affairs. Everywhere in her work we are reminded of the incalculable, inevitable and infinite diffusiveness of good and evil in this organic universe: "So deeply inherent is it in this life of ours that men have to suffer for each other's sins, so inevitably diffusive is human suffering. . ." (*MF* 215; bk.3, ch.7); or as Adam Bede puts it, "You can never do what's wrong without breeding sin and trouble more than you can ever see" (*AB* 169; bk.1, ch.16).

I believe Myers is mistaken in categorically denying the utilitarian basis of George Eliot's morality (66-67). But certainly hers is an elusive and problematic form of utilitarianism, not to be confused with the sort of crude balancing of immediate consequences which Dr. Kenn rejects in his deliberations over Maggie's plight. Rather, it is utilitarianism with "a large vision of relations" (239; bk.4, ch.1), an absolute conviction, part scientific and part mystical, of the inevitability of evil's begetting evil, balanced by a corresponding faith that the currents of beneficence springing from Maggie's compassionate choice will one day re-emerge in the stream of human time.

NOTES

1. See for example Pinney, "Wordsworth's Influence on George Eliot" and Dunham.
2. W.J. Harvey asserts that the "recapitulation theory" was current in Europe before Haeckel's well-known formulation of it in 1866. And he contends that "this conviction is a part of the tap-root of George Eliot's 'ideology'" (153). In a more recent study Stephen Jay Gould attributes to Charles Bonnet (1720-93) "the first extensive parallel between ontogeny and the history of life" (18). For a discussion of the terms "ontogeny," "phylogeny," and "evolution," see Gillian Beer (15).
3. Ernest Bevan points out that while Maggie Tulliver resembles Dorothea Brooke and Gwendolen Harleth in her struggle to accomodate the needs of the imaginative self with worldly conditions, *The Mill on the Floss* differs from the later novels "by explicitly treating the relationship between childhood past and adult present" (69).
4. Compare Pip's departure from childhood in chapter 19 of the profoundly Wordsworthian *Great Expectations*, where as Jerome Buckley has noted (292) the language echoes that of the end of *Paradise Lost*.
5. For example Knoepflmacher (216-17) and Graver (198).
6. For example: "Her tender, tranquil affection for Philip, with its root deep down in her childhood. .seemed now to make a sort of sacred place, a sanctuary. . ."(359; bk.6, ch.7).
7. For example William R. Steinhoff, Jerome Thale and Elaine Showalter.
8. These terms, which the novelist used in her essay "On Historic Guidance" ("More Leaves" 371), have been compared by Suzanne Graver to Comte's "Social Dynamics" and "Social Statics" (154).
9. According to Joseph Wiesenfarth, the legend of St. Ogg "is a rewriting of the legend of St. Christopher, as told by Anna Jameson, George Eliot's 'private hagiographer'" (106). See Jameson, *Sacred and Legendary Art* 2:47-57.
10. See *On Liberty* 50-51.
11. Later in the novel, Stump observes, the Middle Ages are characterized by "a rigorous superstition, that lashes its gods or lashes its own back."
12. Basil Willey sees as the main impulse of George Eliot's work "a conservative-reforming one" (204), while Pinney notes that "the political and social reforms approved in the novels turn out to be not innovation but renovation" (39). A contrasting view is that of Suzanne Graver, who asserts that any suggestion of evolutionary progress in the novel is simply "denied by the resolution of the conflict, which depends on the writings of a medieval monk and primitive kinship needs (198-99); see also Shuttleworth (58).
13. The words "rescue" and "darkness" function as leitmotifs in the novel, symbolizing respectively moral salvation or triumph and the difficulty and obscurity of moral choice.
14. "The historian guides us rightly in urging us to dwell on the virtues of our ancestors with emulation" (*The Temptations of Theophrastus Such* 320).
15. The compatability of scientific curiosity with a certain transcendentalism or mysticism in a mind like Eliot's is cogently argued by Gillian Beer: The novelist's and the scientist's enterprise is fired by the same prescience, the same willingness to explore the significance even of that which can be registered neither by instruments nor the unaided senses, the same willingness to use and outgo evidence. . .The imagery of transcendence, of the invisible world, is one which George Eliot shares. The microscope and the telescope, by making realizable the plurality of worlds, scales and existences beyond the reach of our organization, were a powerful antidote to that form of positivism which

refused to acknowledge possibilities beyond the present and apparent world. . .Far from eschewing mystification, the extension of possibility through scientific instruments and scientific hypothesis-making actually gave at this time a fresh authority to the speculative and the fictive. Projects cannot rest in the present--they rely upon extension and futurity. (151-52).

16. Like Spencer, George Eliot believed that acquired moral characteristics could be transmitted genetically (Paris 59).

17. For the seminal discussion see Levine.

18. Stump (100), Wiesenfarth (119) and Buckler (152) all link Bob Jakin to St. Ogg. Buckler points out significantly that Bob befriends Maggie "for memory's sake" (152).

19. I am indebted here to Shuttleworth's fine analysis of the function of individual and collective subconscious in the novel (67-73).

20. For example by Steinhoff, Thale, Bennett and Lerner.

WORKS CITED

Beer, Gillian. *Darwin's Plots: Evolutionary Narrative in Darwin, George Eliot and Nineteenth-Century Fiction.* London: Routledge and Kegan Paul, 1983.

Bennett, Joan. *George Eliot: Her Mind and Her Art.* Cambridge: Cambridge University Press, 1962.

Bevan, Ernest. "Maggie Tulliver and the Bonds of Time." *Victorian Institute Journal* 12 (1984):63-76.

Bourl'honne, P. *George Eliot: Essai de biographie intellectuelle et morale 1819-1854.* 1933. Rpt. New York: AMS, 1973.

Buckler, William E. "Memory, Morality and the Tragic Vision in the Early Novels of George Eliot." *The English Novel in the Nineteenth Century: Essays on the Literary Mediation of Human Values.* Illinois Studies in Language and Literature 63. Urbana: University of Illinois Press, 1972. 145-63.

Buckley, Jerome. *Season of Youth: The Bildungsroman from Dickens to Golding.* Cambridge: Harvard University Press, 1974.

Dunham, Robert H. "Wordsworthian Themes and Attitudes in George Eliot's Novels." Dissertation, Stanford University, 1972.

Eliot, George. *Adam Bede.* Ed. Gordon S. Haight. San Francisco: Rinehart, 1948.

_____. *The George Eliot Letters.* Ed. Gordon S. Haight. 7 vols. New Haven: Yale University Press, 1954-55.

_____."Historic Guidance." In "More Leaves from George Eliot's Notebook." *Huntington Library Quarterly* 29 (1966):353-76.

_____. *The Impressions of Theophrastus Such.* Edinburgh and London, 1879.

_____. *The Mill on the Floss.* Ed. Gordon S. Haight. Boston: Houghton Mifflin, 1961.

_____. *Romola.* Ed. Andrew Sanders. New York: Penguin, 1980.

_____. *The Temptations of Theophrastus Such.* Edinburgh and London, 1879.

Fisher, Philip. *Making Up Society: The Novels of George Eliot.* Pittsburgh: University of Pittsburgh Press, 1981.

Graver, Suzanne. *George Eliot and Community.* Berkeley: University of California Press, 1984.

Hagan, John. "A Reinterpretation of *The Mill on the Floss*." *PMLA* 87 (1972):53-63.

Harvey, W.J. "Idea and Image in the Novels of George Eliot." Rpt. in *Critical Essays on George Eliot.* Ed. Barbara Hardy. New York: Barnes and Noble, 1970. 151-98.

Jameson, Mrs. Anna. *Sacred and Legendary Art.* 2 vols. Boston: Houghton, n.d.

Knoepflmacker, U.C. *George Eliot's Early Novels: The Limits of Realism.* Berkeley: University of California Press, 1968.

Levine, George. "Determinism and Responsibility in the Works of George Eliot." *PMLA* 77 (1962):268-79.

Lewes, G.H. *The Physiology of Common Life.* 2 vols. London, 1859-60.

Mill, John Stuart. *On Liberty.* Ed. Currin V. Shields. Indianapolis: Bobbs-Merril, 1977.

Myers, William. *The Teaching of George Eliot.* Leicester: Leicester University Press, 1984.

Paris, Bernard J. *Experiments in Life: George Eliot's Quest for Values.* Detroit: Wayne State University Press, 1965.

Pinney, Thomas. "More Leaves from George Eliot's Notebook." *Huntington Library Quarterly* 29 (1966):356-76.

_____."Wordsworth's Influence on George Eliot." Dissertation, Yale University, 1960.

Redinger, Ruby V. *George Eliot: The Emergent Self.* New York: Knopf, 1975.

Showalter, Elaine. *A Literature of Their Own: British Women Novelists from Brontë to Lessing.* Princeton: Princeton University Press, 1977.

Shuttleworth, Sally. *George Eliot and Nineteenth-Century Science: The Make-Believe of a Beginning.* Cambridge: Cambridge University Press, 1984.

Steinhoff, William R. "Intent and Fulfillment in the Ending of *The Mill on the Floss.*" *The Image and the Work.* Ed. B.H. Lehman. Berkeley: University of California Press, 1955. 23-51.

Stump, Reva. *Movement and Vision in George Eliot's Novels.* Seattle: University of Washington Press, 1959.

Thale, Jerome. *The Novels of George Eliot.* New York: Columbia University Press, 1959.

Wiesenfarth, Joseph. *George Eliot's Mythmaking.* Heidelberg: Carl Winter-Universitatverlag, 1971.

Willey, Basil. *Nineteenth-Century Studies.* London: Chatto and Windus, 1961.

CRITICAL RESPONSE TO
SILAS MARNER

ELIOT TO JOHN BLACKWOOD

The George Eliot Letters, 1978

24 FEBRUARY 1861

. . .I don't wonder at your finding *Silas Marner* rather somber. . .But I hope that you will not find it all a sad story, as a whole, since it sets--or is intended to set--in a strong light the remedial influences of pure, natural human relations. The Nemesis is a mild one. . . .

THE SATURDAY REVIEW

13 April 1861

UNSIGNED REVIEW

. . .There are two points especially with regard to the poor which George Eliot has mastered, and the mastery of which lends a lifelike reality to *Silas Marner*. These are the frankness of the poor and their religion. . . .
. . .The classes which the author can draw, and those alone, have been drawn. . . .There is, again, nothing painful in *Silas Marner*. The secret is one that it is not distressing either to have concealed or to find out, and the misery of those who are miserable is not of a very intense kind. We are left unembarrased to enjoy those pictures of humble life which have constituted the great merit of

George Eliot's works, and which appear in this new volume with as much freshness, novelty, and humour as ever. All that can be said against *Silas Marner*. . . is that it is shorter, and therefore slighter. . . .

THE TIMES

29 April 1861

E.S. DALLAS

To George Eliot belongs this praise--that not only is every one of her tales a masterpiece, but also they may be opened at almost any page, and the eye is certain to light upon something worth reading--some curious dialogue or vivid description, some pregnant thought or happy phrase. *Silas Marner* is, like the rest of her fictions, full of matter and delightful in manner. It is a picture of secluded village life in the midland counties in the early part of the present century, and we owe not a little gratitude to the author for the good which she has done, as well as for the amusement which she has imparted by means of such pictures. She has given dignity to the life of boors and peasants in some of our bucolic districts, and this not by any concealment of their ignorance, follies, and frailties, nor by false colouring, bombastic sentiment, and exceptional events, but by a plain statement of the everyday life of the people. The charm of George Eliot's novels lies in their truthfulness. Nothing is extenuated nor aught set down in malice. We see the people amid all their grovelling cares, with all their coarseness, ignorance, and prejudice--poor, paltry, stupid, wretched, well-nigh despicable. This mean existence George Eliot raises into dignity by endowing it with conscience and with kindliness. There is nothing glittering about it. Here we have no mock heroics. There is not the slightest attempt to represent the boor as a village Hampden, not the passing pedler as a poet wanting the accomplishment of verse. The personages of the tale are common, very common people, but they are good and kind, hardworking and dutiful. It is very wonderful to see how their lives are ennobled and beautified by their sense of duty, and by their sympathy with each other. It is the grandest of all lessons--the only true philosophy--the most consoling of creeds--that real greatness is within reach of the poorest and meanest of mankind. Wealth, glory, the pride of intellect, and the advantages of personal form--these are rare gifts, which seem to be scattered at random among the good and the bad; and in this ambitious age, when we see every one hastening to be rich and covetous of distinction, it is pleasant to be reminded that the honest man is the noblest work of God. George Eliot reminds us of it in her own genial way--transporting us into the midst of these stupid, common-place inhabitants of Raveloe--making them move before us and speak as if they lived, and making us feel a warm interest in all their petty concerns and humble endeavours. Such a novelist, while she amuses, teaches us. We open her volumes confident of most brilliant entertainment, and we close them wondering at the art of a writer who manages to reverse a time-honoured phrase and to render us, not sadder and better, but merrier and better.

While this is the general effect of all George Eliot's tales, it is most marked in what is still her greatest work--*Adam Bede*. The present tale, which is complete in one volume, has for its hero a sort of Seth Bede, and this statement will indicate to most persons the excellences and defects of the novel. A novel of which a Seth Bede is the hero must, of necessity, be less absorbing, and ought to be shorter, than one which could boast such a hero as Adam. Silas Marner is, like Seth, a simple-hearted and not very clear-headed Methodist, who, after going through a great deal of trouble, and having his life embittered by disappointment, slander, and ingratitude, comes at last to see an overruling justice in human affairs, and to put trust in his fellow men. In a world so full as this is of sin and suffering, it is difficult for the victims to believe in the benignant order of the universe. There could not be a more unfortunate victim than poor Silas Marner. He is cheated of his good name and branded as a thief through the instrumentality of his dearest friend; his betrothed, on whom he had set his heart, leaves him to marry this ingrate; afterwards he is suddenly robbed of all his hardwon savings, and he finds himself without means, and all alone in the world. The good and kind but weak-minded man curses his destiny, and cries aloud in his despair that there is no God, but only a devil on the earth. He is petrified; all the springs of his life are dried up; he withdraws from the society of his fellow men; all trust is gone, and he has neither physical nor intellectual energy enough to work his way back. How is this man to be recovered? It is to the moralist a most tempting question--to the novelist a most difficult one. It is easy according to the more common theories to suppose a man preached into contentment, or suddenly 'revived' by a spiritual convulsion. We are not aware, however, that Job ever got much good from the preaching of his friends, and it must be confessed that spiritual revivals and convulsions are not the ordinary means of reformation. Reformation of character and change of views are generally the result of long discipline, and we gather from the motto on the title-page of the present work

A child more than all other gifts,
That earth can offer to declining man,
Brings hope with it, and forward-looking thoughts[1]

that George Eliot meant to exhibit the unconscious influence of a child in gradually redeeming and reviving what may be almost described as a lost soul.

The author appears, however, to have stopped short of her design, and to have satisfied herself with stating the result instead of detailing the process. In two-thirds of the volume we have Silas Marner before us in his hopeless, helpless estrangement from his fellow men. The picture of his silent misery is filled in so carefully, the canvas is spread so large, and we are introduced to so many of his neighbours, that when, at the 240th page, we find the weaver of Raveloe adopting little Eppie as his own child we feel that the story is about to commence. Still more do we feel this when, a few pages further on, just as the first part of the tale is about to close, and while the motto on the title-page is ringing in our memories, we read that though now there are no white-winged angels to lead men from the city of destruction, still a hand is often put into theirs to lead them gently into a calm and pleasant land, that such a hand is to lead Silas Marner into the light, and that the hand is a little child's. . . .

. . .This is the burden of the book expressed in comical fashion. The weaver of Raveloe is very much in the position of the man of Uz. He is surrounded with comforters, most of whom are even less sympathizing than the comforters of Job, and he sinks into a deeper despair than that of the most patient of men, for, as we have said, he cursed and denied God in his affliction. The picture of his misery and the discipline of his repentance are but a homely, human version of the older and diviner drama. Instead of supernatural incidents and divine colloquies, we have ordinary accidents and village prattle. Instead of the Deity coming forth to justify his afflicted creature and to teach him better, a little child proves to the world the good qualities of his heart, and gives light and liberty to his understanding. It is a noble lesson, beautifully taught, though in saying thus much we run a risk of conveying the impression that George Eliot belongs to the class of religious or moralizing novelists who have rendered hateful the very idea of serious purpose in a novel. This is not the case, however. Hers is a very spiritual nature, and she cannot choose but regard life from a very lofty point of view. But her novels are true novels, not sermons done into dialogue. The moral purpose which is evident in her writing is mostly an unconscious purpose. It is that sort of moral meaning which belongs to every great work of art, and which no elevated mind can get rid of. She tells a simple story without the least idea of inculcating any copy-book lesson, but by merely elevating the reader to her mount of observation she cannot fail to suggest to the mind some profound reflections.

NOTE

1. Wordsworth's 'Michael', 146-8.

WESTMINSTER REVIEW

July 1861

UNSIGNED REVIEW

It is a great gain, because full of promise to her readers, that the last of George Eliot's works is undoubtedly the finest, the stream of thought runs clearer, the structure of the story is more compact, while the philosophical insight is deeper amd more penetrating than in any of her former productions. It has been said that *Silas Marner* is deficient in interest, but the only element of interest in which it can be called wanting, is that which is supplied by the vulgar excitement of exceptional circumstances or of abnormal characters. In *Silas Marner*, the dead level and dry bones of English country life fifty years since, are illumined and vivified by a power of sympathetic insight which is one of the rarest intellectual gifts. There is nothing so difficult to a cultivated intellect as to enter into the mental states of the ignorant and uninformed, it is an accomplishment of genius alone, the minutest analysis, and the most comprehensive inductions are but tools and helps in such a task. In the progress towards clear conceptions of any kind, the vestiges of the confused notions they replace are trodden out, the memory of our first feeble intellectual life is as irrecoverable and obscure as that of our physical birth. Insight into the past conditions of our own minds, is one of the rarest acquisitions of reflection; and the difficulty of attaining such insight when times and men foreign to ourselves are concerned is so great, that it is only within the last generation that even history has aspired to do more than chronicle the events of each succeeding year.

Heretofore novelists have either relied on an interesting and well-constructed tale, or on the gradual and skilful development of a well-considered plot, or on unexpected solutions of prepared difficulties; and when this has been the case the study of character has generally been weak and incomplete; or they have seized upon some particular type of character the growth of which they wish to display, and in this case the circumstances in which the hero or heroine is placed are generally forced and unnatural, being neglected as subordinate to the main purpose of the author. The most remarkable peculiarity and distinguishing excellence of *Silas Marner*, is the complete correlation between the characters and their circumstances; the actors in this story come before us like the flowers of their own fields, native to the soil and varying with each constituent of the earth from which they spring, with every difference that is implied in defective or excessive nutriment, but yet no more the creatures of blind chance, each asserting his own individuality after his kind, and none overstepping the possibilities of culture furnished by such a world-forgotten village as Raveloe. It is impossible to dissociate any of the characters from the village in which they were born and bred--they form an organic whole with Raveloe; they are not connected with it by any external, or even humorous bands, but by vital threads that will not bear disruption. The stranger Silas is at last assimilated by the little society, and only truly lives when the process has been completed. Nothing can be more profound than this picture of the manner in which all human beings are influenced by their environment, the consequence of this most wonderful fitness between the characters and the scene of their life, is that on laying down the book we do not dwell upon Silas Marner or Godfrey Cass or Dolly Winthrop, or any particular character, but are forced to embrace them all with their restricted country life; nothing short of all Ravloe satisfies the memory; there is no episode that can be detached from the story, no character that can be spared, much less conceived other than it shows itself; there is about them all a certain absoluteness like that which characterizes the works of nature.

In her former works the author has taken a more or less critical position over against society; in the present one, though criticism cannot sleep in such an intellect, she appreciates more fully the strange compensations which accompany incomplete states of development, and brings out, without express statement, that conclusion which has so often stood at the commencement of many a feeble sermon, that there is but little connexion after all between a high moral character and clear conceptions of morality.

The profound insight with which the seed of retribution is shown shrouded in every act, and the intimate fitness which this retribution assumes in her hands is beyond praise; truth calls not for praise, but demands acknowledgement. Novels claim to illustrate the instructiveness of life; but this instructiveness, however, is in direct proportion to the truth of the picture, and the light thrown on it by the author. Mostly it is the case that where the reflections are true and just, the situations are exceptional, or where the circumstances are those of every-day life, the remarks on them are weak, trivial, or obvious. Of *Silas Marner* it is impossible to say which is most admirable, the vivid painting of life itself, or the profound remarks on the progress of that life; nor is this all, the kindly humour which glows through every judgment is as conciliating as the verdict is convincing, and the more so as the author shows no foregone purpose in the construction of the fable, but leaves it to bear its own fruit. It not so much directly instructs as adds to the experience of its readers, and like life itself adds to it in proportion to their power of understanding the results it offers. . . .

THE WEAVER OF RAVELOE: METAPHOR AS NARRATIVE PERSUASION IN *SILAS MARNER*

Studies in the Novel, 1983

MERI-JANE ROCHELSON

The strong presence of the narrator in George Eliot's novels and the extensive use of metaphor within their texts are both significant characteristics of Eliot's art, and both have received a great deal of critical attention. For the most part, previous studies have focused on either the narrator alone[1], or on the imagistic content of metaphors without reference to the narrator.[2] A few writers on George Eliot's metaphors, however, have gone beyond the tracing of images in relation to theme, and have begun to look at some of their more rhetorical functions.[3] My study proceeds from the belief that metaphors in fiction contribute to meaning not only by illuminating the ideas in a novel, but also by helping to create the narrator who must make the reader understand, and believe in, those ideas.

This discussion of how the narrator of *Silas Marner* is created, in part, by the metaphors she[4] makes is based on Aristotle's notion of the "ethos" of a speaker. In the *Rhetoric*, Aristotle asserts that ethos, or "moral character. . .constitutes the most effective means of proof," and that a speaker "persuades by moral character when his speech is delivered in such a manner as to render him worthy of confidence."[5] While the persuasive power required by a writer of fiction is of a subtler kind than that expected of a political orator, still the need for persuasion exists. Before any narrative meaning can proceed from author to reader, the reader must be persuaded that he wants to keep on reading, that what he can obtain from the reading experience will be worth the having. By creating a narrator to whom the reader wants to listen--whose personal qualities, character, and values are such that the reader is willing to join him through the novel--the author brings about the most important relationship in the narrative. If the ethos of the narrator is right, then the bond will be created; the reader will go on reading and, under the guidance of the narrator, will come to understand the fictional world in the way the author wants him to. If the ethos is wrong, however, and the reader does not develop just the right amount of trust or distrust in his narrative guide, or if he misses cues for questioning or accepting or pondering because he is alienated, confused, or--as might happen in some modern fiction--inappropriately engaged, then the effect of the entire novel will be lost.

By examining the use of metaphor in George Eliot's novels, one can learn a great deal about the ethos of that narrator whose presence is so substantial in her works, and about the ways Eliot's narrative method itself helps convey the world-view that underlies her fiction. I have chosen to focus my discussion first on a close reading of a passage of overt narrative commentary in *Silas Marner*, to see how metaphor interacts with other forms of persuasion to create the essential bond when the narrator speaks directly to the reader. Later I will deal with the use of metaphor in the presentation of characters, to see how the narrator employs metaphor--in one case quite effectively, in another less so-- to shape the reader's response to persons in the novel. By taking three somewhat different perspectives toward the analysis of metaphor as narrative persuasion in *Silas Marner*, I hope to suggest the range of potential in this approach for adding to our understanding of George Eliot's art.

A passage early in Chapter 2 illustrates how the narrator of *Silas Marner* uses metaphor to bring the reader into the world of the novel, as she explains to the reader of Silas's growing alienation from God. Many critics have commented on the way Eliot frequently shifts the perspective of her narrative, like the changing or refocusing of a lens,[6] and she does so in the following passage early in *Silas Marner*. The narrator begins at a medium distance: "And what could be more unlike that Lantern Yard world than the world of Raveloe?--orchards looking lazy with neglected plenty; the large church in the wide churchyard, which men gazed at lounging at their own doors in service-time; the purple-faced farmers jogging along the lanes or turning in at the Rainbow; homesteads, where men supped heavily and slept in the light of the evening hearth, and where women seemed to be laying up a stock of linen for the life to come."[7] The narrator describes Raveloe as an objective traveler might, surveying its landscape and inhabitants from sufficiently near to infer its complacent abundance, but at a distance that still prevents intimate acquaintance. The picture is in many ways inviting, but the remote perspective suggests a coolness or aloofness which is, in fact, confirmed in the second sentence: "there were no lips in Raveloe from which a word could fall that would stir Silas Marner's benumbed faith to a sense of pain." The narrator's view moves closer in, to Silas, and we see that his soul remains untouched by the bounty and activity around him.

There has not been much metaphor in this section so far, so that when it does appear--in the reference to a word that might "Stir. . .benumbed faith"--its effect is the more dramatic. Analogies have appeared in the paragraph to this point: the orchards "look" lazy, and the women only "seem to be" storing linen for the afterlife. These comparisons help assure the reader of the narrator's perceptive eye, and the content of the second is appropriate to the discussion of faith and varieties of belief that make up the subject of the passage. But that they are straightforward analogies, drawing attention through their form to the fact that the narrator is creating them and that the reality they illuminate is quite ordinary reality, makes one feel, too, how strongly the narrator is in control. This feeling that one is being led along by a calm, perceptive, controlled narrator contributes as much to one's sense of the comfort of Raveloe as the actual images themselves. It is thus not only the shift in perspective but also the shift to metaphor, that accounts for the discomfort produced by the sentence about Silas. His faith does not "seem" numb, it *is* numb, and it must be awakened to pain when it begins to feel.

Many theories have been advanced as to what makes up the rhetorical difference between similes and metaphors. Aristotle found simile "less pleasant" than metaphor because, since it contains a word that points out the comparison, simile deprives the listener of making the connection for himself.[8] More recent theorists, such as Max Black, find the difference between metaphor and simile to lie in the complexity of meaning produced by each, the simile presenting a static, clearly defined comparison, while the metaphor calls into play systems of implications and connotations, changing the meanings of both "principal" and "subsidiary" terms.[9] But similes and analogies, as George Eliot's own works show, can be quite as rich and suggestive in meaning as metaphors. The difference in effect lies, then, not only in the difference in content between the two types of expressions or in how much effort the reader must expend to understand that content, but also in the difference in relation between narrator and reader that the simile and the metaphor create. In the passage under discussion, the narrator, previously guiding and explaining, now asserts a comparison to the reader as a truth, assuming the reader no longer needs to be led by the hand but can apprehend the point of the comparison at once. At the same moment, the reader is both challenged by the narrator and accepted by her as an equal. Since the preceding analogies have helped establish the narrator as intelligent and perceptive, one willingly accepts the offer of equality and partnership. The bond between reader and narrator is thus subtly strengthened, throughout the novel, by shifts such as this one.

The movement from one means of explanation to another conveys the earnestness of the narrator's desire to explain, and at the same time suggests that nothing can be explained through only a simple presentation of the data. The narrator then makes clear that the shift in perspective (from Raveloe to Silas, from survey to community to analysis of character) and the shift in rhetoric (from literal speech, to analogy, to metaphor) are still not enough to make the reader understand just what Silas Marner is experiencing. The sentence about Silas's benumbed faith is therefore followed by another shift in perspective: "In the early ages of the world, we know, it was believed that each territory was inhabited and ruled by its own divinities, so that a man could cross the bordering heights and be out of reach of his native gods, whose presence was confined to the streams and the groves and the hills among which he had lived from his birth. And poor Silas was vaguely conscious of something not unlike the feeling of primitive men, when they fled thus, in fear or in sulleness, from the face of an unpropitious deity."

The wider view provides a comparison between Silas's plight and the lives of "primitive men," and results from the same philosophical impulse as the employment of analogy and metaphor. What the narrator suggests is that fullness of understanding can only be approached if one compares the situation at hand to other situations like it. At base is the idea that all things can be related; as readers, we feel the narrator to be someone who sees in the world a unity between the petty details of life and the cosmic beliefs of ancient men, who cannot tell the story of one weaver without joining it to the lives of all people in all time.[10] We also sense the narrator's erudition in the fact that she knows about primitive men and their gods; our faith in her reliability as guide and interpreter increases as we appreciate her wisdom. We are impressed by her compassion in going to such lengths to make sure we understand what she is saying, and we are flattered that this wise, all-seeing narrator assumes "we know," as she does, all about ancient religion.

The brief explanation of local deities is presented as a simple, literal, matter of fact. Having already established her own reliability, the narrator thus places the reader in an attitude of respect toward something he might otherwise have treated with some scorn. He is then prepared to sympathize with Silas in his loss of faith. But in a subtle way this particular analogy also prepares the reader to reject, along with the primitive superstitions, certain forms of Christian belief which Eliot is to supplant in the novel with a religion of human compassion. The images of primitive gods take their place beside the lots-drawing of Lantern Yard in a system of references throughout the novel to superstitious faiths whose foundations may be false but whose believers are sincere.

The comparison between Silas and the early believers is stated explicitly, and as the paragraph ends the narrator reminds us of the more immediate comparison with which it began, the contrast between Raveloe and Lantern Yard: "It seemed to him that the Power he had vainly trusted in among the streets and at the prayer-meetings, was very far away from this land in which he had taken refuge, where men lived in careless abundance, knowing and needing nothing of that trust, which, for him, had been turned to bitterness." All the strands of explanation gradually come together here, in a powerful, simple metaphor. The sense of the whole paragraph is finally epitomized in the last sentence of the passage, an example of the "summary metaphor" that characterizes Eliot's narrator's rhetoric. By its very existence as metaphor, this statement adds something to the narration that could not have been rendered exactly any other way: "The little light he possessed spread its beams so narrowly, that frustrated belief was a curtain broad enough to create for him the blackness of night."

This sentence moves from light to darkness as the chapter so far has moved from the spiritual brightness of Silas's early life to the blankness of his later existence. In the "blackness of night" we have the clearest presentation yet of just how desolate his spiritual state is. With the metaphor, a "curtain" comes down on the bright and active scene of Raveloe life; it is blotted out for the reader just as, for Silas, the benevolent possibilities of that life are made invisible by his disillusionment. It is as if the narrator knows the reader cannot truly understand Silas's plight unless he has all the facts, and through every possible means. If we understand the narrowness of his "light," we will not be too impatient with Silas when frustration removes it completely. And in taking such a well-worn metaphor as the "light of faith" and transforming it into a physical light one may possess--a feeble, useless light, at that--the narrator reveals the pathos of Silas Marner's situation while at the same time suggesting the homely, personal quality of faith. We are led to speculate as to the solace a faith might provide, were its light only wide enough.

To this point I have been concerned with the ways George Eliot uses metaphor in overt narrative commentary, both as part of the process of explanation, and in allying the reader with the narrator in that process. But although a reader's sense of "who the narrator is" may come first through such direct intrusions of the narrator's voice, the values of a narrator in any work are in fact presented all through the narrative, even in sections of free indirect speech, which are intended most closely to reflect the thoughts of characters. In *Silas Marner*, as we have seen, the ability to create metaphors reveals the narrator's generous, farseeing moral nature, and this connection between metaphor-making and character appears, as well, when she narrates her characters' ruminations in free indirect discourse.[11] When Godfrey Cass shrinks from confessing to his father the fact of his secret marriage, the narrator traces his reasoning as follows:

Why, after all, should he *cut off the hope* of them [favorable chances] by his own act? He had seen the matter *in a wrong light* yesterday. He had been in a rage with Dunstan, and had thought of nothing but a *thorough break-up* of their mutual understanding; but what it would really be wisest for him to do, was to try and *soften* his father's anger against Dunsey, and keep things as nearly as possible in their old condition. If Dunsey did not come back for a few days,. . .*everything might blow over*. (8:119-20, emphasis mine)

Godfrey's desperate rationalization is expressed in a series of metaphors so overworked they are clichés. Developed individually most of these metaphors could be reinfused with their original power; we have already seen what Eliot is able to do with the "light of faith." But piled one upon the other as they are here, these hackneyed phrases indicate only the barreness of Godfrey's verbal and moral resources, as well as the emptiness of his excuses. By ending the chapter with the feeble phrase, "everything might blow over," the narrator emphasizes the futility of all Godfrey's ill-expressed hopes. If we try to imagine the kinds of metaphors the narrator might use to comment on a situation of such moral complexity, we see the difference in ethos that can be revealed through metaphor. It is significant that when Godfrey finally confesses his guilt, but is prevented from easily "making things right," he expresses his resignation by turning around a cliché: "it *is* to late to mend some things, say what they will"

(20:237). Growth of understanding, for Godfrey, takes the form of seeing the limitations in metaphors made lightly.

For the most part George Eliot's touch is sure. In the narrator of *Silas Marner* she has created a wise, compassionate, earnest guide whom the reader willingly joins and follows. As presented by this narrator, the characters in the novel attain a reality which encourages the reader's concern for their fates. There is one case, however, in which characterization falls short of success, to a large extent because of an inappropriate use of metaphor and symbol. This is what we find in the treatment of Eppie.

Part of the problem stems from the novel's insistence on Eppie as Silas's new treasure, the replacement for his lost gold. She is introduced as an agent in the fairy tale plot,[12] her symbolic function noted by both narrator and characters. In the descriptions of Eppie's childhood, the narrator's attempts to portray infantile reality through her mischievous behavior are overshadowed by Eppie's symbolic presence as the replacement for the gold and the agent of Silas's regeneration. And although the reader may well sympathize with the process Eppie brings about, this sympathetic involvement is won more by the narrator's comments and generalizations than by her actual depiction of Eppie as Silas's child. Since none of the other characters in the novel have such a purely symbolic presentation, the child Eppie stands out as an anomaly.

Part Two of the novel presents greater difficulties. Eppie, grown to young womanhood, has already helped reintegrate Silas into the human community. She still must serve to effect Godfrey Cass's chastening, but she carries out this function not much differently from the ways in which other, less symbolic, characters perform theirs. Thus, although the identification of Eppie with the gold remains strong (the section begins "sixteen years after Silas Marner had found his new treasure on the hearth"), the reader is also invited to view Eppie as a "rounder" character, with her own emotions, decisions, and individual destiny. The narrator's metaphors, however, interfere with one's acceptance of Eppie in this light.

Specific metaphors, as well as more indirect images, depict Eppie as something of a playful animal. She jokes about Aaron Winthrop, "laughing and frisking" (16:199), and is shown in affectionate communication with the animals around her home, including, "a meek donkey, not scornfully critical of human trivialities," and various dogs and kittens with other human attributes. Personification is used quite effectively in other places by the narrator as in the ironic allegorization of "inquiry" that starts Chapter 10, and the "importunate companion, Anxiety," who appears at its end. But in these cases the more abstract metaphors are appropriate where they appear, and consistent with the ethos of the narrator that has been established. The personifications of domestic animals do not seem to fit their context, because a conflict exists between the content and rhetoric of these metaphors and the implications inherent in other equally strong images.

Max Black has suggested that the best way to help a child understand what a metaphor is would be to give him examples of personification.[13] This does not mean that all personifications are childlike, but it does suggest that they can be particularly accessible to children. If we are to accept that the narrator, through her choice of metaphors, creates an ethos that embodies for the reader a mode of explanation, then the ethos presented in this section to some extent alienates the reader. Both the form and content of the metaphors present a mode of seeing associated with children, who as readers would certainly not have responded properly to the narrator as previously developed. The reader may justly ask why he is now appealed to in this childlike way, and who, in fact, is making the appeal.

What one seems to experience in this part of the narrative is an indirect presentation of Eppie's childlike ethos. The problem, of course, is that Eppie is not a child, but a young woman about to be married. The "playful animal" has another side; Eppie's sexuality is suggested repeatedly in the image of her garden,[14] in the unruliness of her hair, and even in her exuberant behavior. That married life is so strongly symbolized by Eppie's garden suggests that the narrator intends sexual awakening to be seen as part of Eppie's fulfillment. But the childish innocence that may also be meant to show the success of Eppie's upbringing does not fit. The metaphors conveying a childlike view of the world are at war with the notion of Eppie as a woman, and finally they overpower it.

It may be that Eppie's innocence is essential to the happy ending the fairy tale plot requires. But Eliot has trouble with happy endings; they tend to become, in her work, too happy, too conventional. Perhaps it is because she believes, with the narrator of *Silas Marner*, "that life never *can* be thoroughly joyous" (17:220). Straining for the conventions of peaceful contentment, in the portrait of Eppie the narrator fails to reconcile happiness with the complexity of human fates on which the rest of the novel insists.

The relative failure of Eppie's characterization is, however, only the exception that proves the rule. Looking at metaphor as part of a narrator's rhetoric provides an additional dimension to one's understanding of how meaning is conveyed to the reader of a novel. The extent to which a narrator uses metaphor, as well as when and how he uses it, affects the way a reader reponds to him--and thus to the narrative--at each point. In *Silas Marner*, the narrator's use of analogy and metaphor allies the reader with her in the process of explanation; at the same time it reveals her own sense of how difficult any explanation is. The moments at which she chooses to employ metaphor, and the kinds of metaphors she chooses, help so strongly to shape one's views of characters and events that at least once the narrator's metaphors produce a response in conflict with what the author seems to have desired.

In *Silas Marner* the use of analogy in narration also has a strong thematic appropriateness. Silas is the "weaver of Raveloe" in more than the literal sense; his misfortune unites his neighbors to him in sympathy just as

Eppie reawakens his own sense of ties to the community. The raveled threads of the village are woven into a fabric as Silas and his neighbors each come to see how, despite their first feelings of strangeness from each other, they are in fact mutually connected. By using analogy and metaphor as her predominant means of explanation, the narrator allows the reader similarly to see relationships among apparently disparate phenomena. The theme of universal interconnectedness, which in some way underlies all Eliot's novels, is thus presented through the method of narration, itself, based in the idea that things can best be understood when viewed "in the light of" each other.

NOTES

1. Also known, for much of the twentieth century, as the "intrusive narrator." In "George Eliot and the Omniscient Author Convention," *Nineteenth-Century Fiction*, 13 (1958), 81-108, and in his chapter on the omniscient narrator in *The Art of George Eliot* (London: Chatto and Windus, 1961), W.J. Harvey summarizes and refutes the arguments of its detractors.

2. Among these are--to list only a few--Reva Stump's full-length study of *Movement and Vision in George Eliot's Novels* (1959; reissued New York: Russell & Russell, 1973); articles on one image traced through one novel, such as Clyde de L. Ryals's "The Thorn Imagery in *Adam Bede*," *Victorian Newsletter*, No. 22 (Fall 1962), 12-13; on one image traced throughout the novels, as Barbara Hardy's "The Moment of Disenchantment in George Eliot's Novels," *Review of English Studies*, NS 5 (1954), 256-64; and on patterns of imagery within one novel, as William R. Steinhoff's "The Metaphorical Texture of *Daniel Deronda*," *Books Abroad*, 35 (1961), 220-24.

3. See, for example, John Holloway's chapter on Eliot in *The Victorian Sage: Studies in Argument* (London: Macmillan, 1953), and Janet K. Gezari, "The Metaphorical Imagination of George Eliot," *ELH*, 45 (1978), 93-106. Two early essays which concern the structuring function of imagery, but which also suggest the role metaphors play in uniting author and reader, are Mark Schorer's "Fiction and the 'Matrix of Analogy,'" *Kenyon Review*, 11 (1949), 539-60, and Barbara Hardy's "Imagery in George Eliot's Last Novels," *MLR*, 50 (1955), 6-14, later incorporated, with slight revision, into Chapter 11 of *The Novels of George Eliot: A Study in Form* (London: Athlone Press, 1959). Carol Howe Spady, in her essay, "The Dynamics of Reader Response in *Middlemarch*," *Rackham Literary Studies*, No. 9 (Spring 1978), 64-75, examines how metaphors "humanize" the reader of the novel. Spady's essay, which only recently came to my attention, is similar to mine in its analytical approach. Finally, an important but controversial contribution to the study of metaphor in Eliot's narrative method is J. Hillis Miller's "Optic and Semiotic in *Middlemarch*," in *The Worlds of Victorian Fiction*, ed. Jerome H. Buckley, Harvard English Studies, 6 (Cambridge: Harvard University Press, 1975), pp. 125-45. In brief, Miller finds the models of totalization in *Middlemarch* to be in combat with incompatible metaphors of vision. He concludes that the narrator is finally "entangled and trapped" in the "web of interpretive figures," the coherence of the novel shattered on a "battleground of conflicting metaphors" (p. 144). Although *Silas Marner* is a less complex novel than *Middlemarch*, my own analysis should suggest the more positive conclusions that may be drawn from Eliot's use of multiple metaphoric models.

4. K.M. Newton, in "The Role of the Narrator in George Eliot's Novels," *Journal of Narrative Technique*, 3 (1973), 97-107, argues that Eliot intended her narrator to be seen as male, and at least never explicitly said anything to the contrary. Newton prefers to use the masculine pronoun for the narrator, to underscore the fact that narrator and historical author are not the same (p. 98; J. Hillis Miller makes a similar point in "Optic and Semiotic," p. 130, n. 5). No critic, as far as I know, however, has ever used the feminine pronoun to refer to the narrator of a male author's work simply in order to preserve this distinction. The narrator of George Eliot's novels strongly invites

identification with an authorial voice, and to all readers after 1859, the author in question was known to be a woman. Except in discussions of *Scenes of Clerical Life* or "The Lifted Veil" (the "masculine" references in other novels are problematic), the narrators in George Eliot's fiction may justifiably be referred to as female. This does not imply that the narrator *is* George Eliot (or Marian Evans Lewes), but simply that the reader hears a female voice in the narrator's control and omniscience.

5. Aristotle, *The "Art" of Rhetoric*, trans. John Henry Freese, Loeb Classical Library (Cambridge: Harvard University Press; London: Heinemann, 1926; rpt. 1967), p.17 (I,ii,4). The issue of metaphor and the ethos of the narrator in fiction is discussed by Wayne C. Booth in "Metaphor as Rhetoric: The Problem of Evaluation," *Critical Inquiry*, 5 (1978), 49-72.

6. An especially perceptive analysis of the technique may be found in Elizabeth Ermarth's essay "Method and Moral in George Eliot's Narrative," *Victorian Newsletter*, No. 47 (Spring 1975), 4-7.

7. George Eliot, *Silas Marner: The Weaver of Raveloe*, ed. Q.D. Leavis (Harmondsworth: Penguin, 1967), Chapter II, pp.63-64. All subsequent references in text are to this edition.

8. Aristotle, p.397 (III,x,3).

9. Max Black, "Metaphor," (1954), in his *Models and Metaphors* (Ithaca, N.Y.: Cornell University Press, 1962), pp.25-47.

10. This belief in analogy as the basis for understanding finds support in George Eliot's essays as well as in her novels. In "The Future of German Philosophy," a review of Otto Friedrich Gruppe's *Gegenwart und Zukunft der Philosophie in Deutschland*, Eliot affirmed her agreement with Gruppe that abstract ideas must be attained "by an ascent from positive particulars." Abstractions arise from perceptions or judgments, she writes, and "every judgment exhibits itself as a comparison, or perception of likeness in the midst of difference: the metaphor is no mere ornament of speech, but belongs to its essence" (*Leader*, 6[1855], 723-24; rpt. in *Essays of George Eliot*, ed. Thomas Pinney [New York: Columbia University Press, 1963], pp.152,151).

11. Gezari notes this relationship between "metaphorical capacity and moral capacity" in Eliot's novels (p.103).

12. As Jerome Thale points out, "the Godfrey story. . .is realistic where the Silas story is pastoral and fairy-tale-like" (*The Novels of George Eliot* [New York: Columbia University Press, 1959], p.59). The treatment of characters within both stories is, however, largely realistic.

13. Black, p.26.

14. This sexual connotation holds, I believe, even if the garden is viewed as an image of Eden, as Joseph Wiesenfarth suggests in "Demythologizing *Silas Marner*," *ELH*, 37 (1970), 243-44.

CRITICAL RESPONSE TO
ROMOLA

THE ATHENAEUM

11 July 1863

UNSIGNED REVIEW

. . .But, read, as a consecutive whole, these scenes take their due place as the framework and background for the human characters, whose struggles and hopes and fears have a perennial interest, and which are in *Romola* as vivid as if they concerned English men and women of 1863. The amount of reading that the author must have achieved to get up the minute details of time, place, circumstance and costume, down even to the old proverbs, jokes and squibs of the passing moment,--to say nothing of the skill with which the aspect of the political questions of the period are grasped and presented to the reader, as they would have appeared to the eyes of those concerned in them, is marvelous;--a monument of patience and easy walking in heavy fetters, which commands the reader's wonder. But, then, the jokes are dried; the appearance of vitality given to politics and pageants long since dead and passed away is remarkable; but neither the politics nor the people are really alive,--they are only well dried, preserved and coloured, and the reader feels as though he were ungrateful, in not being better entertained by all that has cost so much time and labour. . . .Read, however, as a whole, this framework is less oppressive, whilst the human interest takes its due place and proportions. There are noble things to be found in *Romola*, which will make the reader's heart burn within him. It will be scarcely possible to rise from the perusal without being penetrated by "the joy of elevated thoughts," without feeling a desire to cease from a life of self-pleasing, and to embody in action that sense of obligation, of obedience to duty, which is, indeed, the crowning distinction that has been bestowed on man, the high gift in which all others culminate. This is high praise; and a work that can produce this effect, if only on a single reader, has not been written in vain. . . .

THE SPECTATOR

18 July 1863

R.H. HUTTON

. . .The great artistic purpose of the story is to trace out the conflict between liberal culture and the more passionate form of the Christian faith in that strange era, which has so many points of resemblance with the present, when the two in their most characteristic forms struggled for pre-eminence over Florentines who had been educated into the half-pedantic and half-idealistic scholarship of Lorenzo de Medici, who faintly shared the new scientific impulses of the age of Columbus and Copernicus, and whose hearts and consciences were stirred by the preaching, political as well as spiritual, of one of the very greatest as well as earliest of the reformers--the Dominican friar Savonarola. No period could be found when mingling faith and culture effervesced with more curious result. In some great and noble minds the new Learning. . .grew into a feeling that supplied all the stimulus of fever, if not the rest of faith, and of these the author has drawn a very fine picture of the blind Florentine scholar, Romola's father, Bardo, who, with a restless fire in his heart, 'hung over the books and lived with the shadows' all his life. Nothing is more striking and masterly in the story than the subtle skill with which the dominant influence of this scholarship over the imagination of the elder generation of that time,--the generation which saw the first revival of learning is delineated in the pictures of Bardo and Baldassare. In the former you get something like a glimpse of the stately passion for learning which, in a later age (though England was then naturally behind Italy), took so vital a hold of the intellect of Milton, and overlaid his powerful imagination with all its rich fretwork of elaborate classical allusion. In the latter character,-- Baldassarre, the same impression is conveyed in a still more subtle and striking form, because by painting the intermittent flashes of intellectual power in a scholar's failing memory, and its alterations with an almost animal passion of revenge, we gain not only a more distinct knowledge of the relative value in which scholarship was there and then held as compared with other human capacities, but a novel sense of sympathy which, in an age of diffused culture like this, it is not very easy to attain with the extravagance, as we should now think, of the price set upon it. There are few passages of subtler literary grandeur in English romance than that which paints the electrifying effect of a thrill of vindictive passion on Baldasarre's paralyzed memory, in recalling once more his full command of Greek learning, and the sense of power which thus returned to him. . . .

ELIOT TO RICHARD HUTTON

The George Eliot Letters, 1978

8 August 1863

I am sorry she [Romola] has attracted you so little; for the great problem of her life, which essentially coincides with a chief problem in Savonarola's, is one that readers need helping to understand. But with regard to that and to my whole book, my predominant feeling is,--not that I have achieved anything, but--that great, great facts have to find a voice through me, and have only been able to speak brokenly. That consciousness makes me cherish the more any proof that my work has been seen to have some true significance by minds prepared not simply by instruction, but by that religious and moral sympathy with the historical life of man which is the larger half of culture.

THE WESTMINSTER REVIEW

October 1863

UNSIGNED REVIEW

....The strong hold which George Eliot lays on the intellectual and ethical side of all that comes before her mind, and the predominant critical tendency of her mode of thought, make it more necessary with her than with other authors that she should have the direct support of personal experience for the external circumstances in which she places her characters. Her imagination has a strong bias towards moral conceptions rather than towards sensuous, much less passionate ones; with her passion and direct action lie strangled in thought, and deeds present themselves to her rather as problems than as facts. In those dramatic conceptions which give force, unity, and rapid action to a tale she is comparatively deficient. The keenness of her mind urges her on to results, and thought and feeling have so much the upper hand that the lower and more picturesque qualities of our nature have but little attraction for her. The moral progress of mankind is a far higher thing to her than the finest poetry, which is but an instrument in that progress. This bias leads her to treat the events by which she develops the characters of her stories with too great an arbitrariness, and to disregard their natural sequence in a manner which strongly contrasts with the inexorable consecutiveness of every step in the development of the characters themselves. In the minute analysis of moral growth she has no equal; no one has so fully seized the great truth that we can none of us escape the consequences of our conduct, that each action has not only a character of its own, but also an influence on the character of the actor from which there is no escape; "our deeds are like children that are born to us; they live and act apart from our own will. Nay, children may be strangled, but deeds never: they have an indestructible life, both in and out of our consciousness." The strength with which this truth is here expressed shows the deep feeling from which it arises. To this deep moral maxim George Eliot constantly recurs, not in *Romola* only, but in *Romola* it forms the central idea to which all else is made subservient; the external machinery of the tale is but the means by which it shall be set in an adequate light, considerations of probability are comparatively small matters, and the most fortuitous coincidences are accepted without a pang so that they do but aid in the display of that which is of more importance to the author than any superficial likelihood. If it were possible for her to consider the external circumstances in which she places her hero, apart from the influence those circumstances are intended to exercise on him, and as governed by laws of their own, she would be the first to recognize how remarkable an accumulation of improbable coincidences she heaps on Tito's head. But this is the greatness of George Eliot, that where others are feeble, she is strong, and it is only to be regretted that she is too regardless of that much less difficult accomplishment which is within the reach of any one with one tenth of her genius. On this account, we think it is to be regretted that *Romola* is an Italian story, and a story of the fifteenth century.

. . .Again we do not recognize the truth of detail in a description of public life so remote from us as we should the features of our own time, and the author has not the power to carry us away from the description she gives. The historical background, too, somewhat oppresses the human interest of the tale, and in its ultimate impression affects us like a mediaeval painted window, in which the action has to be disentangled from the blaze of colour and over-whelming accessories. To this source may be traced much of that want of appreciation with which the book has met. The general novel-reader is impatient at such details as those of the entry of Charles VIII, and of the Auto-da-fé of Vanities, and longs to hear more of that struggle between Romola and her husband which comes home to his business and bosom. There is another reason why *Romola* is not popular with the crowd. George Eliot's deep insight into the self-questioning human mind places her among those "neutrals who alone can see the finer shades of fact which soften the antithesis of virtue and vice, who are not distressed to discern some folly in martyrs and some judiciousness in those who burn them." The lofty superiority from which she draws the inspiration of that neutrality meets with no answering voice in the souls of the multitude. How few in these questions are not in some sense partisans, and where will they find a weapon to their hands in the pages of *Romola*? There is another result of this scientific insight, which, from the point of view of art, exercises a hostile influence over the power of the author's best scenes: they are so philosophically treated, and so full of the subtlest analysis of the varying motives which struggle for the mastery in the actors, that we are in constant danger of being more attracted by the treatment of the moral question than interested by its bearing on the fate of those whom it affects. We have heard many say that they cannot interest themselves in Tito and Romola, but we never heard any one who was capable of entering into the special purpose of this history who thought himself fully able to express his admiration either of the deep insight displayed in it or of the delicate beauty of the distinctions and qualifications by which it is preserved from any excess or exaggeration. . . .

. . .We cannot escape from the feeling that the chief interest of *Romola* reposes on ideas of moral duty and of right which are of very modern growth and that they would have been more appropriately displayed on a modern stage. The lovely and noble Romola would even now be more admired than loved, and surely we have not retrograded in devotion to all that is good and beautiful. It is not yet given to every one to love a Romola. Tito, too, seems to us to smack more of the intellectual strength and moral weakness of the nineteenth century than of the strong faith and equally strong passions of the age of Caesar Borgia and Machiavelli. Nothing can surpass the skill with which he is displayed, gradually entangled in the web of his own subtleties; but he would have cut short his trials with steel or poison in the age in which he is represented as enduring them. Instead of being content with frightening a wife he no longer loved when she threatened him with exposure and ruin, he would have relieved himself from that fear in a very different way within twenty-four hours. But he is a child of the nineteenth century, and shrinks from the more practical procedure of the fifteenth. He is Hetty, but a man, and not a fool. Indeed, the deepest and most powerful conception of the whole book is this of Tito--amiable, with great abilities and no vices, but living in other men's regards, and shunning every form of personal discomfort; weak, but not naturally wicked. How sad the view of life which at last leads such a man to commit some of the basest deeds, and yet who can say one feature of this wonderful portrait is at all exaggerated? Where was there ever a moral more forcibly set forth? Let no man sport with his existence.

. . .George Eliot is always charming in her treatment of children; they have not yet become the theatre of those conflicts which she hates, and she loves them without distrust or remorse. How admirably this episode is made to show that a man may be a villain and yet have soft affections, and a noble woman be jealous of something higher than mere personal fidelity to herself. . . .But there are no artifices in George Eliot's art. The true reason is, that she does not sufficiently sympathize with such depths of passion to give them adequate expression; they are so repugnant to her that she hardly compassionates the wronged old man, and certainly does not sufficiently display these features of his character which caused him to be successively forsaken by the woman he loved and by the boy he had adopted and tenderly cared for. How was it that he who so longed to be loved was denied all answer to his yearnings where he had set his heart? It can only be because his vindictive hate had so debased him, even in the mind that conceived his character, that no room was left for sympathy; and the savage animalism of his passions lowering him to the brutes that made George Eliot less human to one who had put off what alone interests her as distinctively human. This concentration of self in the reckless pursuit of a personal gratification is the strongest expression of that tendency in our race which is uniformly decried throughout *Romola*, whether it shows itself in the luxurious self-indulgence of Tito or in the noble Romola when she essays to throw off the trammels of a life that no longer answers to her ideal. The same idea is prolonged into the treatment of Savonarola, whose personal aims and longings for the glory that he thought his due are made to be his ruin, and to furnish the road to his defeat and death. That this is a true view of his character is in accordance with all we know of him, and connects him in a peculiar way with the ethical basis of the tale. His influence on its progress is but slight; the power which he exerted for a time over the imagination of Romola was not so much personal as the effect of the new views of duty which he brought before her; Christian morality could have found its way to an intellect like hers without the necessity of an intermediate human idol, and would not then have so failed her when she could no longer lean on his character for support. We do not mean that there is not much profound psychological insight displayed in the treatment of their mutual relations, but that all else in the story which is concerned with Savonarola leaves the reader but slightly moved and but feebly interested; it sinks down into that picture of ancient Florence which is so full of learned detail, and which stands in such grievous need of a central light which shall harmonize the whole. . . .

ROMOLA AND THE PRESERVATION OF HOUSEHOLD GODS

Cithara, May 1984

HENRY ALLEY

Romola's place in George Eliot's creative development has been difficult to determine, not only because of Eliot's own statements of doubt and agony,[1] but also because of what seems, in her previous works of full-length fiction, to be an almost linear progression of subjects, a projection that is suddenly interrupted by *Romola*, a novel of distracting erudition and remote characters, many of whom are themselves scholars. To step from merry England to late fifteenth century Florence is to endure a kind of cultural shock within the canon of an individual artist.

Romola is, however, continuous with the fiction before and after it, in that a common denominator, an emblem, almost, of an aged, kingly father and proud supporting daughter--that of Oedipus and Antigone at Colonus--informs and links two pairs of novels on either side of the conventionally established division in Eliot's career: *The Mill on the Floss* and *Silas Marner*; *Romola* and *Felix Holt*. How a young woman nurtures age, how she may derive and apply messages from the past, and how she may transcend a strong family *hubris* were more than themes to Eliot; they were a haunting, iconographic symbol--Maggie tending to the stricken Mr. Tulliver, hoping he might retract his curse; Eppie leading Silas through the unnamed town, in search of Lantern Yard; Romola reaching down a copy of Nonnus to the blind Bardo in the darkened library; and Esther, as a token of penitence, quietly brushing her father's hair. In Sophocles' *Oedipus at Colonus*, much of this father-daughter relationship is established in the short exchange, very close to the opening:

Oedipus Help me sit down; take care of the blind man.
Antigone After so long, you need not tell me, father.[2]

In the chapter, "The Blind Scholar and his Daughter," it is as if Romola and Bardo had just spoken these same lines, when the narrative commentary follows: "As Romola said this, a fine ear would have detected in her clear voice and distinct utterance, a faint suggestion of weariness struggling with habitual patience"[3]--even when the issue is the referencing of an obscure text rather than simple physical support. For Eliot to make the scene at one with Sophocles is to delineate the way tragedy exists from "generation to generation" and from novel to novel, and to prepare the way for Piero di Cosimo, an artist who, like the narrator herself, perceives the mythological, the heroic, within the everyday. In fact, when one looks at the novel's plot structure, the world of ancient Thebes seems to be suggested as much as that of Renaissance Florence: an old blind man, of noble lineage, uses his daughter as his "eyes" and as a sensitive intermediary to the outer world. He has cursed his son, but the daughter, in her dual love, never relents in her tenderness for both. When the father and brother are dead, the story pivots when the daughter, bearing out pride of the family name, defies the egotism and narrowness of the outer world in order to fulfill pledges to those who have died or are about to die. For Romola as for Antigone, the underworld, housing the family ghosts, often seems to require a stronger commitment than the daylight world of intriguing politicians and lovers.

This emblematic relationship between Romola and her father should not be confused, however, with Dorothea's slavish marriage to Casaubon. Romola's bond, although including that of an amanuensis, is also one of "sacramental obligation" (Ch.27,310), that has grown out of returned love and nurturance as well as a sense of inner and outer subordination. Although Bardo's bullying chauvinism and his even more imprisoning tenderness--which acknowledges, in a paternal but hurtful way, the capacities of Romola's "feminine mind" (Ch.5,100)--suggest something of the nightmare Dorothea enters in *Middlemarch*, Bardo's ends are critically different from Casaubon's[4]--as is, ultimately, his treatment of the principal woman in his life. Unlike the Key to All Mythologies, the father-scholar's plans can be seen as a potential benefit to the community at large--a library for the people of Florence--not just the assurance of an immortal name. Unlike Dorothea, Romola cannot, at the center of the novel, simply remove herself from the clutch of a dead hand. Her relationship to the past must be sustained and yet qualified. Romola is more firmly in the tradition of Maggie Tulliver, who inherits positive as well as negative legacies from her once known and living father, and she anticipates Esther Lyon, who will grow into a heroic appreciation of Rufus while he is still alive.

Ironically, Romola's protection of Bardo and his memory is her first source of liberation, her means of escaping the stifling feminine world of subjection, of "Reality, Books, and Waking Dreams," which incarcerated Maggie. Once her father is dead, her sense of familial piety throws her into direct conflict with the serpentine Tito, the husband who would have destroyed even what small freedom she knew as a daughter. Tito's wholesale destruction of Bardo's library is a pivotal point in the life of Romola's psyche, when she must choose between coerced and truly felt commitment:

> Romola sat silent and motionless; she could not blind herself to the direction in which Tito's words pointed; he wanted to persuade her that they might get the library deposited in some monastery, or take some other ready means to rid themselves of a task, and of a tie to Florence; and she was determined never to submit her mind to his judgment on this question of duty to her father; she was inwardly prepared to encounter any sort of pain of resistance. (Ch.32,352)

Thus when "the pride and fierceness of the old Bardi blood had been thoroughly awaked in her for the first time" (356), there is no doubt that Romola can stand up to Tito's "masculine predominance," because she can counter him on his own ground as well as wife to husband. In a parallel manner, Silas, in adopting his mother's characteristics, acquires a "fierceness" which puts Godfrey Cass in his place.

The moment of Romola "discrowning" herself is a response to both an inner need and a message from the grave. As she glides out of Florence, she sees her father's library being carried away and feels "less that she was seeing the imprisoning stones, where her hand could not reach his to tell him that he was not alone" (Ch.36, 386). This act of defiance, as well as tender recollection, constitutes Romola's first step into the world of activity, to apply, enrich, and also defy the circumscribed life of stoical scholarship. Savonarola, when he meets her on the road, is Thomas à Kempis giving a reborn Maggie a true opportunity to make use of self-renunciation. Romola has all of suffering, transitional Florence before her, for "the giant forces" are very much alive and shaking the world, whereas Maggie has nothing before her except a provincial and morally static St. Ogg's. Romola can become the visible Madonna of Maggie's dreams.

This idealization, which has troubled critics from virtually the novel's publication, does not seem so unlikely or disturbing when one considers the case of the multi-dimensional Lydgate, who, like Romola, must "come to us in our need with a more sublime beneficence than that of miracle workers"[5] because his own private life is desolate. Romola's obeying Savonarola's arresting voice does not spring so much from an improbable magnaminity as it does from a desire to redirect her energies and tenderness. In essence, Savonarola tells her that if she cannot return for the sake of her husband, she can at least return for Florence. In his influential article, "*Romola* as Fable," George Levine typifies many critics when he says that Romola "fails utterly on almost every occasion to live up to the supposed Bardo-like pride."[6] However, Romola, in retracing her steps, in living at an emotional distance from her husband, and in transforming her valued but insular education into charitable activity, is surely asserting pride and--in Eliot's world--a pride of the most enlightened sort:

All that ardour of her nature which could no longer spend itself in the woman's tenderness for father and husband, had transformed itself into an enthusiasm of sympathy with the general life. (Ch.44,463)

For this sort of life, Romola has had excellent training, not only from Savonarola but, indirectly, from her father as well. Both father and daughter can be seen as spiritual exiles, devoted to a proud pledge of conduct within a resisting context-- in Bardo's case, the scholarly world of Florence; in Romola's case, her own marriage.

It is important to point out that Romola, in her new role as the Visible Madonna, forms a full daughterly attachment to Bernardo del Nero as well as Savonarola. She becomes ardently and ideally devoted to both; however, her very compelling humanness keeps her from seeing, as the reader does, that eventually a violent contradiction will arise. For the time being, a passionate commitment to one's "close relations" (Ch.56,552)--which constitutes the fullest assertion of the Bardo legacy--urges her love of her godfather, just as it urges her through Florence, tending to the needy and the sick, who form, on their own, a second family, or second group of close relations. Romola never serves Savonarola in any truly political way; Florence only enlarges the possibilities for developing her sense of personal commitment. Thus she must, in her groping, very human way discover that when the laws of the city, even Savonarola's City of God, conflict with the higher laws, a choice must be made and one's "reverential memories" (Ch.59,576) affirmed, since they were the source of the more communal virtues in the first place. She must ultimately side with Bernardo and, by extension, her father.

At the start of her second, or Christian, phase, Romola is outfitted with a modernday assumption--namely that no grandeur can exist within the historic context one lives in--so that she herself becomes more accessible to the modern reader--"she had been brought up in learned seclusion from the interests of actual life, and had been accustomed to think of heroic deeds and great principles as something antithetic to the vulgar present" (Ch.27,311)--a quote which is reminiscent of the speculative Mrs. Farthingale of *Scenes of Clerical Life* and the bookworm readers who are exhorted in the pages of *Adam Bede* and *The Mill on the Floss*. *Romola* comprises a new direction for Eliot, however; for we are allowed, for the first time, to identify with a romantic attitude toward the past and then grow into an appreciation of the immediate life of the text, as the heroine herself becomes both heroic and committed to the life around her. Such a strategy is essential to this historical novel, where the danger of excessive remoteness and glamor is omnipresent.

The veneration which Romola grows toward is clearly illustrated in the later episodes with her godfather. In many ways, he is Bardo taken to the political arena, and because of this he best mirrors the new psychic dimension she has acquired. When, at last, she becomes disillusioned with the government of Savonarola, she is brought, in heroic fashion, to recollect all of Bernardo's virtues, at the point when he is most reviled:

Her mind rushed back with a new attraction towards the strong worldly sense, the dignified prudence, the untheoretic virtues of her godfather, who was to be treated as a sort of Agag because he held that a more restricted form of government was better than the Great Council, and because he would not pretend to forget old ties to the banished family. . . .Her affection and respect were clinging with new tenacity to her godfather, and with him to those memories of her father which were in the same opposition to the division of men into sheep and goats by the easy mark of some political or religious symbol. (Ch.52,527)

Romola has learned much from both men--integrity, reverence for the past, and, finally, resistance to categorical judgments. The "Pleading" chapter brings into strong juxtaposition what we have seen at every major climax of her previous novels, the vision of the Letter and the vision of the Spirit: Adam and Irwine on the eve of Hetty's trial, Tom and Maggie in the Red Deeps, Cass and Silas after the disclosure of Eppie's parentage, and now Savonarola and Romola on the eve of another hanging.[7] It is, of course, the ancient conflict of Creon and Antigone, but in her fiction, Eliot is much surer about who is right than she is in her famous essay. When Romola proves unable to persuade Savonarola into clemency and Bernardo is thus forced to mount the scaffold, Cennini foresees how the execution will raise "the old Bardi blood" in Romola, and raise it it does, bringing her to a strong awareness of her heritage:

> Romola was feeling the full force of that sympathy with the individual lot that is continually opposing itself to the formulae by which actions and parties are judged. (Ch.60,583)

If the individual lot cannot be sympathized with, then all communal demands become meaningless. This insight Savonarola has lost just at the moment it has become abundantly and bitterly clear to Romola. In the final seconds, she "rescues" Bernardo from anonymity, through her assurance that he has become a part of her "sacramental obligation."

> She seized the fettered hands that were hung down again, and kissed them as if they had been sacred things.
>   "My poor Romola," said Bernardo, in a low voice, "I have only to die but thou hast to live--and I shall not be there to help thee."
>   "Yes," said Romola, hurriedly, "you will help me--always--because I shall remember you."
> (Ch.60,584)

In Eliot, remembrance becomes the dividing point between significance and oblivion--not through fame or glory, but through the individual's ability to save another from the unvisited tomb, by making the person, in essence, a part of one's household gods.

The third stage of Romola's education consists of a refining and enlarging of these abilities. Severed, now, from all Florentine ties, she is ready to "drift away" to a place where her beneficience can become even more secularized and is ready, once she returns, to meet again the character who appears in the final lines of the Epilogue and has formed, all along, a second moral center, Piero di Cosimo. At just those moments when Romola begins reaching beyond the Christian confines of Savonarola's government, Eliot begins reminding the reader that as an artist, Piero has also been a preserver of household gods.[8]

In light of the complicated message which Eliot wanted to develop in the Epilogue, her choice of the historical Piero seems particularly apt. His paintings, when divided according to their mythological versus Christian subject matter, form, at least initially, a rather violent conflict, and there is a particularly narrative quality to his work that is missing from that of some of his contemporaries--one which Eliot may have identified with.[9] It is quite possible, also, that his *Story of Silenus* painting suggested the characters of Ariadne and Bacchus[10] or that "his" *Teseo e Arianna, Bacco e Arianna* (at that time erroneously assigned to him) inspired in Eliot the kind of moral and originally mythological contrast so characteristic of her.[11] In the early parts of the novel, Tito plays Bacchus to Romola's Ariadne, but in his perfidy, he is much more like Theseus. More importantly, the obscurity of Piero's fame and the sketchiness of Vasari's account of him gave Eliot a freedom which would have been lost in the recreation of a Botticelli. She could make his artistic vision more a reformulation of her own. In this sense, she is very much like Piero of the novel (or better, he is like her), who, when assigned Tito's project based on Ovid, protests when the information becomes too binding.

In being part of a larger context, Piero must be brought into the Epilogue as a living being, because he is the novel's consistently best example of the broad humanity, freed from conventional religion, which is embodied in the narrator herself. His attitude toward Tito is at one with hers, and his perceiving Sinon in his modernday face constitutes the sort of hybrid of immediate observation and classical acumen that Eliot strove to convey in her own work. More specifically, his sketch of Tito serves as an interruptive, moral commentary on the outward revel the groom-to-be wishes to create, and "the painted record" becomes at one with Eliot's own puncturing sentences, once the Bacchic beauty has been conceded. As Tito himself says, "That is a subject after your own heart Messer Piero--a revel interrupted by a ghost" (Ch.18,247). It is a subject very much after Eliot's heart, and once one considers how many interrupted revels exist in *Romola*, the very structure of the novel seems to grow out of Piero's vision. His Masque of Time, which disrupts "The Day of the Betrothal" chapter and closes Book I, is the pictographic analogue to the narrator's own positioning of characters through time and space, in order to bring about a reckoning with death and the self. Both Piero and the narrator are stage managers of Nemesis.

Piero's omniscience is further underscored by his enlightened use of classical history and literature, not only for their bright, decorative value but also, as has been suggested earlier, for their stunning and sometimes stark relevance to the present. What Eliot does as a narrator in her rather shrill discussion of Aeschylus' *Eumenides* (Ch.11,168-9), she does better through the character of her very attractive artist, who catalyzes the fear of Nemesis within the audience of the novel's *dramatis personae*. Like Mr. Cleves of "Amos Barton," Mr. Irwine of *Adam Bede*, and Mrs. Garth of *Middlemarch*, Piero is able to read, immediately, the classical configuration beneath the minutiae of the present, and also like them, he is one of those rare creations in fiction who arrives morally ready-made but is, at the same time, altogether convincing. His opinions of others are those of the author, and in speaking them always vehemently and sometimes tactlessly, he is spared, as is Herr Klesmer of *Daniel Deronda*, from becoming too perfect.

For Romola, he is the best means of preserving the past that has become sacred to her, both when it is alive in her imagination and when it has become eclipsed by her commitment to Savonarolan charity. In Book II, no longer bound as her father's handmaiden, she yet seeks his portrait "as Oedipus," drawing on Piero's original vision in Book I of the two of them as the mythic father and daughter at Colonus. The important suggestion is that Romola's perception is now approaching Piero's; she sees into people, into their strengths and faults, and forms, in her mind, a balanced and universal image. Alive, Bardo was only to serve as a model for the Theban king, a Florentine in ancient Greek costume; dead, and therefore perceived at a distance, he becomes Oedipus, with his *hubris*, blindness, and yet his power and love as well. Combining all of these elements, the portrait is the perfect visual corollary to Eliot's own portrait of words in "The Blind Scholar and his Daughter" and also to the tracing out of the shadowy archetypes of the father-daughter, Oedipus-Antigone groupings in the previous novels.

Once completed, Piero's painting crops up at certain strategic points throughout the remainder of the novel, as a special narrative signpost. As Barbara Hardy writes in a recent essay, "In *Romola* the objects which precipitate crisis or turn action also tend toward conspicuous symbolism."[12] In Chapter 31, the painting serves as an important catalyst to Romola's and Bernardo's discussion and recollection of Bardo's disappointed quest, and as a means of initiating a more life-like image in the minds of both. Later, after Romola has fought with Tito over the library and has disengaged herself from him for the first time, she is shown to start up "as if some sudden freedom had come, and going to her father's chair where his picture was propped, [fall] on her knees before it and burst into sobs" (Ch.32,359). When preparing to leave Tito, Romola places the portrait, along with her mother's, into a trunk that is to be sent to Bernardo for safe keeping, as a part of a trust of "sacred memory" (Ch.35,390). Finally, the portrait is referred to by Lillo in the Epilogue, when he is brought to ask some of the novel's major questions.

Romola's relationship to the image of her father, as preserved by Piero, is a changing and dramatic one. The image is classical and is thus reminiscent of the books they studied together. When, in Book III, Romola slips into the contradiction of supporting The Pyramid of Vanities and yet remaining her father's daughter, Piero, quite appropriately, is the one to appear and point it out:

"And I should like to know what the excellent Messer Bardo would have said to the burning of the divine poets of these Frati, who are no better an imitation of men than if they were onions with the bulbs uppermost. Look at that Petrarca sticking up beside a rouge-pot. Do the idiots pretend that the heavenly Laura was a painted harridan? And Boccaccio, now: do you mean to say, Madonna Romola...you have never read the stories of the immortal Messer Giovanni?" (Ch.49,501)

This is her father's arresting voice, and Romola is forced to admit that she has read Boccaccio's stories and that "there are some things in them I do not ever want to forget." We know from the early chapters that Boccaccio was sacred to her father, and although she thinks herself able to dismiss the writer for now, his work will be one of the first things she will think of, once her disillusionment with Savonarola is sealed (Ch.61,588). We also know that Boccaccio was central to Eliot's own reading, and that he was part of the list that she devoted herself to while researching the backgrounds of *Romola*.[13] For the historical Piero, Boccaccio's *Genealogy of the Gods* constituted the central source for several of his mythological paintings, and it is possible that Eliot speculated over this book's possibly being his source, had he ever really taken up Oedipus and Antigone at Colonus as a subject.[14] Whatever her specific historical knowledge, Eliot makes it clear that Bardo's library cannot be denied or burned, any more than the true spirit and sympathy of Savonarola's life and work--once the egotism, the rigidity, has been removed.

The other writer who is defended, Petrarch, provides a bridge to the novel's Epilogue, and here, in the last pages, he is saved from the flames of Christian fanaticism. In the Epilogue we are also back with Bardo again, who, in Chapter 5, quoted in visionary fashion the Petrarchan defense of reading: "Books delight our inmost selves, they speak to us, advise us, and are united to us by a kind of living and clear friendship" (Ch.5,97,n.). Romola, in teaching Lillo Petrarch's *Rime*, is preserving the best of her father's legacy, as enriched by what she has learned in the Christian phase of her life. Very tellingly, the *canzone* that Lillo is reading from speaks to a young man who may be the new hope for a restored Rome, a restored Italy. Perhaps Lillo will rise to that promise, through his godmother's careful assemblage of the best elements of the human psyche. This concept of Romola, uniter of disparate elements in the soul, is most appropriate for these final pages, for indeed here she is presented as an artist, a portrait maker belonging to the school of Naturalist Idealism,[15] like Piero and Eliot.

There are three portraits that she paints for Lillo, those of Bardo, Savonarola, and Tito, forming a triptych of her own, which recalls not so much Piero's Bacchic tabernacle as his Sketch of the Three Masks. The Stoic, The Magdalen, and the Satyr symbolize, as W.J. Sullivan has pointed out,[16] the lives of these three men, respectively; and the child in the sketch "whose cherub features rose above them with something of the supernatural promise in the gaze which painters had by that time learned to give to the Divine Infant" (Ch.3,79), represents not only the younger Romola, who has learned from each early in her life, but also, I would add, Lillo, on the eve of his being presented with their histories, as narrated by his godmother. Of Bardo, her final evaluation is, "he had the greatness that belongs to integrity; he chose poverty and obscurity rather than falsehood" (674-5)--which anticipates the Finale of *Middlemarch*, in which the whole egoistic problem of fame is supplanted by the legacy of goodness bequeathed by dead souls, whether known or anonymous. In this way, Romola returns to her vision of her father as Promethean,[17] a portrait which is itself very

Piero-like, in acknowledging the *agon*, the pride, and the heroism of the subject. It is no accident that when discussing Bardo, Lillo mentions the old portrait of him, since it is meant, once again, to stir veneration without distortion, criticism without hostility.

The same may be said of the second part of the triptych, Savonarola, who "had the greatness which belongs to a life spent in struggling against powerful wrong" (675), and therefore who represents that active spirit so fatally missing from the Bardo library. W.J. Sullivan, when he says that Romola's final state becomes that of the stoic, or that of Bernardo or Piero himself, does not take into account the Frate's role as a household god.[18] Restored again, in memory, to the sphere of private life, his previous concern for the growing sympathy of men and women becomes a luminous and vital example; it is retrieved. That his private self is rarely evoked in the novel constitutes a major artistic problem,[19] but in regard to the book's developing themes, it is entirely consistent that Romola keep his day sacred, that his physical and psychic portraits be brought in, just as were Bardo's.

Tito, the last man presented in Romola's triptych, is restored to his morally neutral nature at the story's opening. The fact that then he was no perfidious Bacchus but simply an *exemplum* of raw potential is emphasized. That he became like many of Eliot's chivalric discards--Arthur Donnithorne, Stephen Guest, and Harold Transome to come--men who possess an aberrant sense of their own gallantry--is also stressed. But the parts of him that may be preserved, his charm and magnetism, are also included in the portrait, even though he is no household god.

Petrarch's "gentle spirit" promises, then, to be a composite of the qualities which the novel has idealized and which Romola has come to teach by her own words and actions. The Epilogue is itself a kind of shrine, and a totally private one at that, which carries forward the Bardo legacy of scholarship and familial devotion and the Savonarolan tradition of service to the world at large. Piero must arrive with flowers even for the dead ascetic he dislikes, since his example and the gifts he bears serve as a second balance to the all too unworldly Frate, who wanted "to burn colour out of life" (Ch.49,500). Together, Piero and Romola form the best synthesis of the pagan and Christian elements which have been warring since the novel's Proem, and together they serve as the best corollary to Eliot the psychologist and the artist. Just as Eliot had to pick and choose among the various qualities of Vasari's Piero in order to construct her indirectly idealized painter, so her resultant creation, as an artist, must see into others in order to fashion characters of mythological resonance. So too must Romola, in reaching the novel's conclusion, pick and choose among the qualities of Bardo, Savonarola, and Tito in order to form her triptych of the completed human psyche, her greatest shrine to her household gods, since, in a Piero-like manner, it uses the best of each without distortion, and in the end, transcends them all.

NOTES

This article was made possible through the support of the Office of Research at the University of Oregon.

1. Gordon S. Haight, *George Eliot: A Biography* (New York: Oxford University Press, 1968), pp.351 and 361-62.
2. *Oedipus at Colonus*, Robert Fitzgerald, trans., in *Sophocles I*, eds. David Greene and Richmond Lattimore (New York: Washington Square Press, 1967), p.82. It is clear that George Eliot was thinking repeatedly of this play close to the time of *Romola*'s creation, not only from her references in *The Mill on the Floss* but also from an entry in her notebook (*A Writer's Notebook: 1854-1879 and Uncollected Writings*, ed. Joseph Wiesenfarth [Charlottesville: University Press of Virginia, 1981], p.19, entry 43.)
3. George Eliot, *Romola*, ed. Andrew Sanders (New York: Penguin Books, 1980), Ch.5,95. All further references are to this edition.
4. A number of critics have noted a parallel. Felicia Bonaparte (*The Triptych and the Cross: The Central Myths of George Eliot's Poetic Imagination* [New York: New York University Press, 1979], p.43) sees a similarity in that both scholars possess very incomplete knowledge, and Andrew Sanders (*The Victorian Historical Novel, 1840-1880* [New York: St. Martin's Press, 1979], p.191) links them through the implied and stated allusions to Milton's blindness. Susan M. Greenstein ("The Question of Vocation: From *Romola* to *Middlemarch*," *Nineteenth Century Fiction*, 35, No.4 [1981], 500) finds them united through a mutual desire to enslave: "her father's request imposes a task on her as onerous and pointless as the one Casaubon tries to force upon Dorothea, although Romola dearly wishes to discharge it in devotion to his memory."
5. George Eliot, *Middlemarch*, ed. W.J. Harvey (Baltimore: Penguin Books, 1965), Ch.66, 720.
6. In *Critical Essays on George Eliot*, ed. Barbara Hardy (London: Routledge and Kegan Paul, 1970), p.84.
7. In "*Romola* and the Myth of the Apocalypse" (in *George Eliot: Centenary Essays and an Unpublished Fragment*, ed. Anne Smith [Totowa: Barnes and Noble, 1980], pp.83-4), Janet Gezari points out that, historically, Savonarola did not have the opportunity to influence the Bernardo verdict. This fact highlights, even more, Eliot's determination to oppose the two worlds and to undermine, ultimately, her heroine's worship of the Frate. Andrew Sanders sees an interesting parallel between the "pleading" scene and the great debate between Angelo and Isabella in *Measure for Measure* (*The Victorian Historical Novel*, p.179).
8. The history of Piero's rise in critical stature is a rather dramatic one. Initially taken as a fictional embodiment of Vasari's cranky hermit, he is given one of his first serious treatments in Barbara Hardy's *The Novels of George Eliot: A Study in Form* ([New York: Oxford University Press, 1959], pp.170-6), where his visionary qualities are brought to the fore. Edward T. Hurley's "Piero di Cosimo: An Alternate Analogy for George Eliot's Realism" (*The Victorian Newsletter*, 31 [1967], 54-6) works to establish Piero's "insight into the actual" (54), an ability that best represents Eliot herself and her belief that art must transcend crude realism. William J. Sullivan's crucial articles, "Piero di Cosimo and the Higher Primitivism in *Romola*" (*Nineteenth Century Fiction*, 26, No. 4 [1972], 390-405) and his "The Sketch of the Three Masks in *Romola*" (*The Victorian Newsletter*, 41, [1972], 9-13), show the corollary between Piero's values and those guiding Romola's education. As a further development of Hardy, Gezari's "*Romola* and the Myth of the Apocalypse" stresses Piero's ability to see through the externals of characters, Tito especially.

9. See Mina Bacci, ed., *L'opera Completa di Piero di Cosimo* (Milan: Rizzoli Editore, 1976). Many of the mythological paintings may be grouped together as stories, and several of the religious ones narrate sacred legends through their background figures. In general, the secular works are flamboyant, sometimes violently so, and are probably responsible to the term "primitivism" being applied so often. R. Langton Douglas, in his study, *Piero di Cosimo* (Chicago: University of Chicago Press, 1946) argues, however, that this vision changed toward the end of the historical Piero's life, as shown by his masterpiece, *The Story of Prometheus* panels: "The men that he now represents are no longer in a state that was but little above that of the animals: they are 'as Gods knowing good and evil'; they have to bear the inevitable penalty that the gift of such knowledge brought with it" (p. 81).

10. Barbara Hardy writes that the sources of the triptych may have been found in "aspects of several of Piero's paintings which she would either have seen or read about in Vasari's detailed descriptions. Possible sources in the paintings themselves are the *Ariadne* itself, though here there is no resemblance except in the character of Ariadne, and also the *Mars and Venus and her Loves and Vulcan*, and *Perseus Frees Andromeda*, both of which might give the suggestion for the loves and the strange sea-monster" (p. 173). Although Hugh Witemeyer argues that "there is no evidence that George Eliot knew any of his work at first hand, beyond what she learned from the *ecphrases* of Vasari" (*George Eliot and the Visual Arts* [New Haven: Yale University Press, 1979], p. 200), it seems highly improbable that such a thorough researcher as Eliot would create an entire chapter without familiarizing herself with at least some of her historical model's *opus*. The *Oedipus and Antigone at Colonus* that her character proposes is suggested more by his *Prometheus* and the two earlier paintings in *Vulcan* series than it is by anything described in Vasari.

11. For a description of the apocryphal *Teseo e Arianna*, and *Bacco e Arianna*, see Mina Bacci, *Piero di Cosimo* (Milan: Bramante Editrice, 1966), p.122.

12. "Objects and Environments" in Barbara Hardy, *Particularities: Readings in George Eliot* (Athens: Ohio University Press), p.154.

13. Haight, p.350.

14. Boccaccio provided the source for the *Vulcan* and *The Story of Prometheus* paintings (Douglas, p. 81). For Boccaccio's version of the Oedipus legend, see *Genealogie Deorum Gentilium Libri* (Vincenzo Romano, ed. [Bari: G. Laterza and Sons, 1951], I, 113-4).

15. See G.A. Wittig Davis, "Ruskin's *Modern Painters* and George Eliot's Concept of Realism," *English Language Notes*, 18, No. 3, (1981), 200.

16. See *Victorian Newsletter*, No. 41, 9.

17. Ch. 5, 102-3. Bardo also refers to having "the *aes triplex* of a clear conscience," a reference to the *Odes of Horace* but also, as T.E. Page says (ed., *Carminum Libri IV* [London: Macmillan and Co., Ltd., 1962], p.143), to the *Prometheus Unbound* of Aeschylus.

18. *Victorian Newsletter*, No. 41, 13.

19. As in the case of Tom Tulliver, who creates similar difficulties for *The Mill on the Floss*, the Creon side of the argument is editorially defended but rarely evoked. Savonarola really does not arrive center-stage until Chapter 62; for the rest of the novel he exists as little more than a meandering postscript or admonishing voice. This failure in characterization is perhaps the only important one in the novel; however, it does qualify our responses to Dino, who is his convert, and to Romola, who agonizes over exhortations that come, as it were, from behind a curtain. When Eliot draws it, it is too late, and just as when Tom chastises and redirects Maggie, one finds it difficult to understand why such an empty voice should cause such an intelligent heroine such struggles.

CRITICAL RESPONSE TO
FELIX HOLT, THE RADICAL

THE TIMES

26 June 1866

E.S. DALLAS

      Hitherto Miss Austen has had the honour of the first place among our lady novelists, but a greater than she has now arisen--a lady who in grasp of thought, in loftiness of feeling, in subtlety of expression, in fineness of humour, in reach of passion, and in all those sympathies which go to form the true artist has never been excelled. In the art of weaving a narrative Miss Austen is still pre-eminent among women. Nothing can be more natural than the way in which she evolves an event, leading up to it with the clearest motives and the most likely accidents, never saying too much, never too little, nothing too soon, nothing too late; sparing of reflection, and letting her characters speak for themselves. George Eliot has not attained this ease of story-telling because she has to deal with subjects far more difficult than Miss Austen ever attempted, with wilder passions, with stronger situations, with higher thoughts. Miss Austen scarcely ever gets out of the humdrum of easy-going respectable life; she can therefore well afford to be calm and neat in arranging every thread of the narrative she has to weave. George Eliot undertakes to set forth the issues of a more tumultuous life, to work out deeper problems, and to play with torrents where Miss Austen played with rills. But if thus dealing with stronger forces she has been as a rule unable to give to her plots the finished ease of movement for which her predecessor is famous, she on the other hand succeeds in veiling any deficiency of story by the wondrous charm of her style. We don't know any Englishwoman who can be placed near her as a writer of prose. There is such a pith in her thinking, such a charm in her writing, such a fresh vigour in the combination of both, that--begin where we will in her volumes--we go on reading, now startled by some strange suggestive thought, now tickled by her humour, now touched by her pathos, and ever fascinated by the results of delicate observation and fine literary polish. Her style is very rich, and not only rich with the palpable meaning which in each individual sentence she has to express, but rich also in those swift, indescribable associations which well chosen words recall, allusions to past reading, the reflected sparkle of past thinking, the fragrance of past feeling.

But, great as the charm of her style is, it is not her most attractive quality. Style will go far to cloak the deficiencies of a story, but it will not account for the strong interest which 'George Eliot' always contrives to awaken. The secret of her power is to be found in the depth and the range of her sympathies. She gets to the heart of her characters, and makes us feel with them, care for them, like to know about them. Even if they are stupid people who lead dull lives, she has the happy art of making us take an interest in their story and wish to hear it out. When we come to care for people--men or women--it really does not much matter what their story is: it fixes our attention. And for the most part we care or don't care for people according as we understand them or not. Dugald Stewart somewhere makes a rather suggestive remark to the effect that many of us are supposed to be wanting in benevolence when we are only wanting in attention or in imagination. The cruelties which we inflict on each other and our indifference to each other's sufferings are the result not of a cruel disposition, but of blindness and thoughtlessness and incapacity of imagination. And so it comes to pass that in most cases, if we can only be made to see people as they are, we learn to care for them. 'Seeing,' says the proverb, 'is believing;' but seeing is also feeling. And this is George Eliot's great gift that she sees and makes her readers see the personages of her tale; and we cannot truly see them, with all the stern conflict of their lives and with all the skeletons which they keep in their closets, without sharing in their hopes and fears, mixing in their griefs, and tasting of their joys. Be the man ever so dull, we become part of him and have a personal interest in his story the moment we can see him and understand him as George Eliot enables us to do. Great is Miss Austen's art of weaving a plot, and great is George Eliot's charm of style; but grandest of all as a means of exciting interest is that sympathy which sets a living character before us, and enables us not merely to see it, but also to feel it. . . .

ELIOT TO SARA SOPHIA HENNELL

The George Eliot Letters, 1978

13 JULY 1864

. . .Surely that is a strange perversion into which men's minds have been led by long and various causes--to think that unless life can be made perfect, unless the prospects of humanity can be made to appear the very best, strong moral motives are gone! As if the very absence of that highest security were not a more urgent reason for at least diminishing the pressure of evil, for worshipping the goodness and the great endeavours that are at least a *partial* salvation, a *partial* redemption of the world?

FREDERIC HARRISON TO ELIOT

The George Eliot Letters, 1978

19 JULY 1866

. . .Positivism is a conception of society with all the old elements reknit and recast. In it society and men exist under the old relations reharmonized. Its dogma is vast, abstract, unpopular. The social and human form is eminently sympathetic, capable of idealization, and popular. Comte designed to close his life by the work of moulding the normal state into an ideal in a great comprehensive poem--a task which he would never have accomplished and did not begin. But some one will some day. In the meantime the idealization of certain normal relations is eminently the task of all art. . . .

. . .I suppose an ideal tale relating to [the] state of society which should have subjectively and objectively realized in its completeness a Positive system of life would be, even if an artistic marvel, valuable and intelligible exclusively (like Bekker's Charicles) to the actual student of Comte; as one might suppose a romance of society in Mars or Venus, with habits and customs of the Martial and Aphrodisian natives might be to an astronomer. I presume no true art is directly didactic or dogmatic. But I can conceive--and forgive me for wearying you with a dream--an ever present dream of mine that the grand features of Comte's world might be sketched in fiction in their normal relations though under the forms of our familiar life. There is nothing in Positive existence which is not on the depths of human nature and civilized society. There is no social force which it uses which is not now in germ or in disuse present around us--no human passion which it supposes absent or which it will not set itself to govern. Now I have imagined the temporal and the spiritual power outlined so in their main functions--the home, the school, the temple, the workroom, the teacher, the ruler, the capitalist, the labourer, the wife, the mother, the child, of the future might be drawn so as to do no violence to our familiar ideas yet consciously standing in their normal place. Types of these all exist about us. All I conceive is a state of society sufficiently favourable for them to develop themselves freely, and hold their natural relations, a surrounding adequate for them to perform normally where for instance the moral and practical forces are sufficiently elevated to control without arousing too strong resistance, and where the good forces are sufficiently strong to show their value by practical results. . . .

ELIOT TO FREDERIC HARRISON

The George Eliot Letters, 1978

15 AUGUST 1866

. . .That is a tremendously difficult problem which you have laid before me, and I think you see its difficulties, though they can hardly pass upon you as they do on me, who have gone through again and again the severe effort of trying to make certain ideas thoroughly incarnate, as if they had revealed themselves to me first in the flesh and not in the spirit. I think aesthetic teaching is the highest of all teaching because it deals with life in its highest complexity. But if it ceases to be purely aesthetic--if it lapses anywhere from the picture to the diagram--it becomes the most offensive of all teaching. Avowed Utopias are not offensive, because they are understood to have a scientific and expository character: they do not pretend to work on the emotions, or couldn't do it if they did pretend. I am sure, from your own statement, that you see this quite clearly. Well, then, consider the sort of agonizing labour to an English-fed imagination to make art a sufficiently real back-ground, for the desired picture, to get breathing, individual forms, and group them in the needful relations, so that the presentation will lay hold on the emotions as human experience--will, as you say, "flash" conviction on the world by means of aroused sympathy. . . .

THE NATION

16 August 1866

HENRY JAMES, JR.

. . .George Eliot's humanity colors all her other gifts--her humor, her morality, and her exquisite rhetoric. Of all her qualities her humor is apparently most generally relished. Its popularity may, perhaps, be partially accounted for by a natural reaction against the dogma, so long maintained, that a woman has no humor. Still, there is no doubt that what passes for such among the admirers of Mrs. Poyser and Mrs. Glegg really rests upon a much broader perception of human incongruities than belongs to many a masculine humorist. As for our author's morality, each of our readers has felt its influence for himself. We hardly know how to qualify it. It is not bold, nor passionate, nor aggressive, nor uncompromising--it is constant, genial, and discreet. It is apparently the fruit of a great deal of culture, experience, and resignation. It carries with it that charm and that authority which will always attend the assertions of a mind enriched by researches, when it declares that wisdom and affection are better than science. We speak of the author's intellectual culture of course only as we see it reflected in her style--a style the secret of whose force is in the union of the tenderest and most abundant sympathies with a body of knowledge so ample and so active as to be absolutely free from pedantry. . . .

GEORGE ELIOT'S VISION OF SOCIETY IN *FELIX HOLT, THE RADICAL*

Texas Studies in Literature and Language, Spring 1975

LENORE WISNEY HOROWITZ

Not until *Felix Holt the Radical* does George Eliot bring industrial England from the periphery of her novels to the center. This is a dramatic shift in emphasis and brings to the forefront for the first time the profound concern with the problems of Victorian England characteristic of her mature fiction. Set in the year of the first election under the Reform Bill of 1832, *Felix Holt* presents a wide range of social problems and political philosophies. There is not only conflict among the social classes but intense rivalry among leaders who seek their support. But while the novel poses the problem of political leadership initially, conventional methods of political change are ultimately rejected in favor of a more far-reaching vision of social change. Instead of endorsing political reform, the novel creates a broad myth of social transition suggesting the selective incorporation of what is valuable in the past into a social order which is really new. This myth of social transition defines meaningful change as the reorientation of society towards the future rather than the past. While George Eliot's respect for the past and its precedents is clear in the novel, *Felix Holt* presents an urgent plea for the present to break free from the control of the past in the definition and solution of society's problems.

Although it is a dramatic change, the use of industrial England as the setting of *Felix Holt* grows out of George Eliot's experiments in the earlier novels. *Adam Bede, The Mill on the Floss,* and *Silas Marner* are set in the stable agricultural England of the past, but industrial England appears on the outskirts of the landscape. The Hayslope of *Adam Bede* is part of old England, but the impact of manufacturing is felt in Snowfield and in Leeds where Dinah Morris preaches. In *The Mill on the Floss,* St. Oggs is a nontechnical, provincial society, but Tom Tulliver is sent by his uncle Deane's grain company on "northern business" because of the impact steam has had on the market. Manufacturing becomes more important in *Silas Marner* since Silas is a cottage weaver, but the action takes place in Raveloe rather than in Lantern Yard, the manufacturing town, and Raveloe as yet "lay aloof from industrial currents."

While the problems of industrial England are brought more and more into the settings of these early novels, they play only a minor role. The complex problems of the new England are excluded in the resolution of each novel. Characters with a foot in both Englands end up by leaving the mills for the farm. Dinah Morris gives up Leeds for Hayslope, while Tom Tulliver exchanges a promising future in the thriving grain trade for the old family mill. The pattern of Silas Marner's moral regeneration involves leaving Lantern Yard and its problems behind; his brief return to Lantern Yard severs rather than strengthens his ties to the manufacturing town. Like Dinah Morris, he is saved in a sense by returning to old England and its values.

Such a solution to human and social problems is not possible in *Felix Holt* because industrial England is at the center of the novel's landscape and social problems play a major role. The novel's "Introduction" presents a striking picture of England in conflict by describing the reaction of a coach passenger journeying through the English midlands.

In these midland districts the traveller passed rapidly from one phase of English life to another: after looking down on a village dingy with coal-dust, noisy with the shaking of looms, he might skirt a parish all of fields, high hedges, and deep-rutted lanes; after the coach had rattled over the pavement of a manufacturing town, the scene of riots and trades-union meetings, it would take him in another ten minutes into a rural region, where the neighbourhood of the town was only felt in the advantages of a near market for corn, cheese, and hay. . . .The busy scenes of the shuttle and the wheel, of the roaring furnace, of the shaft and the pulley, seemed to make but crowded nests in the midst of the large-spaced, slow-moving life of the homesteads and far-away cottages and oak-sheltered parks. (Introduction, pp.5-6)[1]

The passenger observes the sharp contrast between old rural England, "the district of protuberant optimists, sure that old England was the best of all possible countries," and the new England feeling the impact of profound social and economic problems.

The breath of the manufacturing town, which made a cloudy day and a red gloom by night on the horizon, diffused itself over all the surrounding country, filling the air with eager unrest. Here was a population not convinced that old England was as good as possible. . . .(Introduction, p.5)

It becomes clear to the coach passenger that "town and country had no pulse in common." Rather than the traveler's vacillating movement from one England to the other, a more permanent reconciliation, a synthesis based on a "common pulse," is sought in the novel.

The novel focuses the conflict between old rural England and new manufacturing England in Treby Magna. Like Hayslope and Raveloe, Treby Magna is an England of the past. However, while the societies of the earlier novels were stable with elements of change only beginning to show, modern political and economic forces have undermined traditional community relations in Treby Magna and have created social unrest. Coal mines and a tape factory have brought a new population and new problems, and when the passage of the Reform Bill makes the town a polling place, Treby Magna "began at last to know the higher pains of a dim political consciousness" (ch.3, p.50). How and by whom the people should be led emerges as an important question. A broad spectrum of political philosophies is presented. Sir Maximus Debarry, the Tory landowner, is one of those "protuberant optimists" who uphold the old ways as best, while Garstin, the Whig manager of the Sproxton mines, seeks moderate change. The miners themselves, however, have quite different opinions and call for annual Parliaments and universal manhood suffrage.

To illustrate the problems involved in leading the people to dramatic social change, the novel focuses on two Radical leaders, Felix Holt and Harold Transome. Both endeavor to change society, but both fail in their efforts to lead the people, or to "head the mob" (ch.2, p.34), as Reverend Lingon, Harold's Tory uncle, puts it. The reasons for these failures are important. Harold's efforts to change society are partially undermined by a fallacy in his political philosophy. He believes that society will change for the better through the agency of "active industrious selfishness." When the Sproxton miners turn their power of self-assertion into mob violence, the danger of such a philosophy becomes clear. In the election day riot, "the multitudinous small wickedness of small selfish ends, really undirected towards any larger result, had issued in widely-shared mischief that might yet be hideous" (ch.33, p.329). Harold's view of social change based on "active industrious selfishness," like the economic Darwinism prevalent in the period, does not formulate any "larger result" than the satisfaction of self-interest, and George Eliot foresaw dangerous consequences for such limited social vision.

Harold does not look far enough into the future, nor does he see clearly how present problems are rooted in the past. Calling himself a "new man," Harold seeks to sweep away the corruption of the past. The danger of political leadership which is based on insufficient understanding of the linkage between present and past is reflected in the Oedipal nature of the Harold Transome plot. Harold's discovery of his private past ultimately wrecks his public career. When election posters expose the manner in which his family has gained possession of the Transome estate, Harold learns that he cannot be a "new man" because the past is the "father" of the present. The past cannot be disowned, as he discovers when he sees himself and his father, Matthew Jermyn, reflected in the mirror. The moment when Harold discovers who he is coincides with his final recognition of the ties between the present and the past. Harold's failure as a political leader suggests that it would be as unwise for society to abrogate the past with sweeping changes as it is for Harold to attempt to be a "new man";[2] one's "father" always turns up.

Unlike Harold Transome, Felix Holt sees the linkage between present and past clearly. He knows who his father is and judges his parent's accomplishments objectively and even scientifically. It is knowledge rather than prejudice that leads him to repudiate his father's patent medicines. While he acknowledges his father's good intentions, Felix's training as an apothecary's apprentice convinces him that these panaceas complicate rather than cure present ills. Because he understands the relationship between the present and the past, Holt's view of social change is more comprehensive than Harold's. Felix sees social change as the gradual replacement of what is outmoded. The old ways of doing things, which he at one point likens to irrigation canals and pumps, must not be destroyed until they can be replaced. Otherwise society would be left with no means to cultivate its "common crop." Holt's failure as a political leader is linked not to his ignorance of the past but to his inability to predict with accuracy the future consequences of his actions. This is precisely the lesson of Felix's disastrous attempt to control the direction of the mob during the election day riot. No man can predict the future, but Holt's effort to do so is made particularly difficult by the very sympathy which makes him sensitive to human misery, which makes the "spirit of innovation" a "part of religion" to him (ch.16, p.187). While Harold "disliked all enthusiasm" (ch.16, p.187), Felix is liable "to be carried out of his own mastery by indignant anger" (ch.30, p.292). Felix's decision to lead the mob is an act of impulse "in the midst of a tangled business" (ch.33, p.325), and reflects the narrator's observation that "nature never makes men who are at once energetically sympathetic and minutely calculating" (ch.33, p.325).

The novel's answer to the question, who shall lead the people, seems to be that social change cannot be brought about safely by political means.[3] The lesson that Felix finds when he "sees behind failure" is that he can best improve society by helping those few within his immediate reach, a very limited social role. Attempts to have a wider effect are fraught with danger to both society and the individual himself. The machinery of power is best left in the hands of those who will not seek drastic changes, and it is significant that the Tory Debarry and the Whig Garstin win the novel's election.

The political plot, however, fails to deal with the more far-reaching question raised in the novel's "Introduction," whether a "pulse in common" could be found between old England and the new. It can be argued that the question of social reform in the novel is larger than the question of who shall lead the people, that the political failures of Holt and Transome are only part of the novel's resolution of the problem raised in the "Introduction." The other aspect of the novel's total vision of society centers around the Transome estate and Esther Lyon's role as heir. The important contrast here is not between Harold Transome and Felix Holt as political leaders but between Felix Holt and Esther Lyon as, respectively, the "outsider" and the "insider" vis-a-vis the novel's society. Each has a different relationship to society and faces different problems. Their opposite and complementary patterns of development explore the relationship between society and absolute moral values central to the novel's resolution.

Felix Holt is an outsider because he does not fit comfortably into the social structure of Treby Magna. "Felix chose to live in a way that would prevent any one from classing him according to his education and mental refinement" (ch.22, p.227). Felix does not accept society's values and seeks a higher morality than class prejudice or what he calls "the ordinary Christian motives of making an appearance and getting on in the world." Instead, Felix is committed to the ideal of human brotherhood and equality, to what he calls "the labour and common burthen of the world" (ch.27, p.266), a commitment that is at once his great strength and weakness. However, while he is morally superior to characters who unthinkingly accept conventional values, Felix is ineffective because he does not have a viable role in society. While Felix's sense of social responsibility is close to "vocation" in the religious sense, and religious imagery abounds in the novel to describe it, it is not easy for him to translate this feeling of brotherhood into effective social action. As two Glasgow acquaintances put his problem, Felix's capacity for "large veneration" leads him to "banging and smashing" because he cannot find anything in society "perfect enough to be venerated" (ch.5, p.59). He bangs and smashes at conventional values, but he is unable to define the positive part of his social function, that "demagogue of a new sort" (ch.27, p.270) he desires to be.

An important reason for this difficulty is his fear of becoming entangled in society. He refuses to wear conventional clothes because he believes that they will "throttle" him and confine him in "straps." He sees women as a seduction into economic and class compulsions which would force him to compromise his integrity: "Men can't help loving them, and so they make themselves slaves to the petty desires of petty creatures" (ch.10, p.129). His desire for independence from the corruption of social relationships extends to children as well. While "a bachelor's children are always young. . .with a chance of turning out good" (ch.22, p.232-33), specific children would be a disappointment as well as a burden. Felix does not recognize that his refusal to become involved in social relationships hinders his effectiveness and makes him as irrelevant to society as the Byronic corsairs and renegades whose "idle suffering" he despises. As far as members of Treby society are concerned, Felix is as much in the wilderness following the "lawless life of the desert" as a "young Ishmaelite" (ch.37, p.363).

Felix's stance is not only ineffective but arrogant as well. No man should try to keep his hands so clean that he must "eat turnips," as Felix puts it, to subdue his natural desires for intimate social ties. Like Reverend Rufus Lyon, whose history prefigures Holt's development, Felix must enter society even if it means compromising the purity of his ideals. Lyon's love for Annette Bycliffe, "a being who had no glimpse of his thoughts induced a more thorough renunciation than he had ever known" (ch.6, p.93) in his solitary life of theological devotion. Similarly, Felix has to learn that self-sacrifice for other persons is as important as self-sacrifice for ideals. After learning through his experience in the riot that an aloof purity is not possible in society, he accepts the fact that it is not even desirable. He changes his role as a detached critic of society for the role of husband, father, family provider, and teacher, recognizing that his efforts will "never be known beyond a few garrets and workshops" (ch.45, p.443).

While Felix Holt, the outsider, is gradually brought from a position outside society to a definite place and function inside society, Esther Lyon's development begins from the opposite extreme and has an expanding rather than a contracting pattern. Esther is an insider, accepting conventional values and standards of behavior without questioning them. She insists on wax candles instead of tallow, includes Byron's *Poems* in her workbasket, and wonders how she can counteract the assumption current in good society that Dissenters are necessarily vulgar. It becomes clear that her views are based on a lack of sympathy for others, on a "wilfulness" or self-centeredness "that conceives no needs differing from its own, and looks to no results beyond the bargains of to-day" (ch.6, p.81).

The narrator makes clear, however, that Esther is capable of developing greater vision through sympathy; "Esther's dread of being ridiculous spread over the surface of her life; but the depth below was sleeping" (ch.46, p.458). By telling her that she is "trivial, narrow, and selfish," Felix shatters Esther's confidence in her values. His criticisms had "shaken her mind to the very roots" (ch.22, p.235). Her self-absorbed world breaks apart, and she sees, as he does, the absolute claims that others have on her sympathy. Esther's growth is linked, like his conversion in Glasgow, with religious images. "The first religious experience of her life--the first self-questioning, the first voluntary subjection, the first longing to acquire the strength of greater motives and obey the more strenuous rule--had come to her through Felix Holt" (ch.27, p.273). In this "baptism," sins against man rather than against God are washed away. She is no longer "dead in trespasses--in trespasses on the love of others, in trespasses on their weakness, in trespasses on all those great claims which are the image of our own need" (ch.13, p.161). After this process of "painfully growing into the possession of higher powers" (ch.22, p.235), of developing what Holt calls the "best self" to a "vision of consequences," Esther chooses a role in society that can express this higher morality. By refusing to marry Harold and become another Mrs. Transome, Esther puts into practice her idea that "the best life" is not the most comfortable but one in which "one bears and does everything because of some great and strong feeling--so that this and that in one's circumstances don't signify" (ch.26, pp.260-61).

As the outsider and the insider approach each other, their different weaknesses are highlighted. While he sees man's fundamental responsibilities as a human being clearly, the outsider finds it difficult to relate these "great claims" to social relationships. In terms of their humanity, all men are equal; in society, however, men have different responsibilities and privileges. The insider, on the other hand, feels at home in social relationships but does not see beyond narrow conventional values. From different directions, Felix Holt and Esther Lyon move towards a norm of behavior in which absolute human responsibilities become workable within social relationships. Their interacting developments are described as a kind of "leavening" process. "So fast does a little leaven spread within us--so incalculable is the effect of one personality on another" (ch.22, p.235).

It is at the critical moment in this leavening process that Esther Lyon enters her major role in the novel as the heir to the Transome estate. Educated by Felix Holt to a clear perception of the frequent conflict between social and human values, as the Transome heir she must face squarely the problems of wealth, property, and privilege in society. While the law designates Esther as the legitimate heir and the Transomes as arbitrary possessors of the estate, Esther considers the legal tie the arbitrary one and believes that possession through years of habit and expectation is the human and legitimate claim. She feels that her responsibility to the Transomes as human beings conflicts with the laws of society which distribute property without regard for human feelings. Esther comes to realize that the possession of property and privilege is attended with "circumstance" that only the egoist, like Mrs. Transome, can "sweep away." She finds it impossible to institute legal proceedings against fellow human beings with whom one should share rather than take.

Disposition of the Transome estate, however, raises even more profound problems than the proper relationship among members of society. The estate is really a symbol for England itself, its complex past, confusing present, and uncertain future. The estate functions in the novel as a myth of social transition which finds the common pulse between the old England and the new. Esther's role as heir of the past is crucial, much like Margaret Schlegel's role in *Howard's End*.

The care with which George Eliot worked out the details of the Transome will is known from her letters,[4] and the details, though tedious, are important to the novel's structure. John Justus Transome entailed the estate "on his son Thomas and his heirs-male, with remainder to the Bycliffes in fee" (ch.29, p.290). Neither Thomas Transome nor any of his male descendants has the power to dispose of the estate as he might see fit because at the end of the male line the estate is to pass to the Bycliffe family. The fee tail perpetuates the testator's view of what is right generation after generation, with no possibility for change until the end of the Transome line. There are other complications. By selling the base fee to the Durfey family, Thomas Transome deprived his male heirs of their just share in the estate. The Durfey-Transomes purchased not the estate itself but only the Transome interest in it and may thus possess the estate only as long as the Transome line exists. Tommy Trounsem, the old impoverished bill-sticker, is the "last issue remaining above-ground from that dissolute Thomas who played his Esau part a century before" (ch.29, p.291). Mrs. Durfey-Transome and the lawyer Jermyn compound this original injustice by engaging in "law-tricks" to prolong the Transome interest and to prevent the Bycliffe heir from obtaining the estate. As a result of Jermyn's efforts, Maurice Christian Bycliffe, Esther's father, is falsely imprisoned under the name of Henry Scaddon and dies during this confinement.

The discovery of the Bycliffe heir is of great importance to the novel's myth of social transition because only the Bycliffe heir can break the control of the past and dispose of the estate according to the needs of the present situation. Esther's struggle to decide what should be done with the Transome estate thus raises the problem of the proper attitude of the present towards the past, a problem faced, as we have seen, by Felix Holt and Harold Transome as well. Unlike Harold, Felix rejects only part of the past, his father's patent medicines, because he has learned that they reflect "ignorance" of man's real needs. While rejecting these outmoded remedies, however, Felix aligns himself with a different past better suited to his present priorities: "I have my heritage--an order I belong to. I have the blood of a line of handicraftsmen in my veins" (ch.27, p.270). Like Felix, Esther acknowledges herself as the heir of the past but takes from the past only what is of value to the new purposes of the present.

Esther's decision as heir is crucial since the estate represents the line of succession from the past to the present. The alternatives to her choice show that, while the novel's myth of transition preserves the ties to the past, it involves a revolutionary change in the direction of society. Were Esther not revealed as the Bycliffe heir or had she decided to renounce her claim to the estate, the Durfey-Transomes would retain possession of the estate and could claim legal title after twenty years. This would merely legalize their position as false or spurious heirs of the past. Were Esther to marry Harold, the Durfey-Transomes would possess the estate under the original terms of the will through Esther's legal title. In this way, the succession of the estate through sale and injustice would be affirmed and continued. In both alternatives, the present is essentially a continuation of the past, and this principle is repudiated in the novel's myth of social transition.[5] Esther reclaims the "pawned inheritance," and, as the only heir with the discretion of disposal, she divides the estate according to her newly developed vision of priorities. She conveys the major portion of the property to Harold and his mother and arranges for annuities for her stepfather and Holt's mother. Wealth is not necessary to her new life of moral purpose with Felix, only a small income of "two pounds a week" to buy books for a lending library. The bulk of the inheritance from the past is used to provide for members of the past generation while the present looks forward to a very different kind of future.

By ending the fee tail, Esther breaks the control of the past and aligns the present with the future. Her marriage with Felix Holt becomes a symbol for possibilities in society not dictated entirely by tradition. It is a union between two characters who are symbolically fatherless and thus not strictly tied to the class or to the past in which they have been brought up. Their social identities are flexible rather than fixed. Although he is of lower-class birth, Felix's education and intelligence raise him above it. Esther was brought up in the lower class but is of the aristocracy and half-French by birth. Their marriage cuts across class boundaries to embrace all segments of society in a way that tradition would make impossible. This union is connected not with conventional values of class and position but with more important human responsibilities. Felix gradually emerges as belonging to what the novel defines as an aristocracy not of birth but of behavior. Esther remarks that Felix's behavior to his mother is "the highest gentlemanliness, only it seems in him to be something deeper" (ch.22, p.234). This gentlemanliness is a deference to the human dignity of others rather than merely respect for social rank. According to the narrator, Felix's "look of habitual meditative abstraction from objects of mere personal vanity or desire" is "the peculiar stamp of culture," the culture of the "human face divine" (ch.30, p.300). This marriage between an outsider and an insider whose different strengths are combined and whose different weaknesses are corrected suggests a society in which absolute human values would govern social behavior.[6]

This marriage reaches back to the past through inheritance and forward to the future through imagery of family connections that extend to all the social classes. Felix sees himself as belonging to the family of society: "It is held reasonable enough to toil for the fortunes of a family, though it may turn to imbecility in the third generation. I choose a family with more chances in it" (ch.27, p.270). The creative energy of this marriage is highlighted by contrast with the "fortunes" of the Transome family. Imbecility in the third generation is precisely their fate in the case of the half-mad Tommy Trounsem as well as the "imbecile" Durfey, Harold's older brother. By turning his efforts to the aid of all his brothers, Felix, a "man of this generation," works for a future that will not repeat the errors of the past. The offspring of this marriage between outsider and insider, between absolute human values and social relationships, is a hopeful future for society, a young Felix with "a great deal more science than his father, but not much more money" (Epilogue, p.487).

Taken together, the political plot and what I have called the novel's myth of social transition provide a complex answer to the question whether a "pulse in common" can be found between old England and the new. The failures of Felix Holt and Harold Transome as leaders of the people make clear that there are no reliable political solutions to society's problems. As Holt, sounding very much like Matthew Arnold,[7] says to the Duffield workmen: "Now, all the schemes about voting, and districts, and annual Parliaments, and the rest, are engines, and the water or steam--the force that is to work them--must come out of human nature--out of men's passions, feelings, desires. Whether the engines will do good work or bad depends on these feelings" (ch.30, p.302). Moreover, to set up a political "engine" to endure for generations would condemn society to mechanical repetition with little opportunity for fresh evaluations of its problems, much like the Transome fee tail.

The political plot leads simultaneously, however, to the discovery of Esther Lyon as the true heir of the past, the Transome estate. The sequence of events that results in the failures of Transome and Holt to lead the people also leads up to the uncovering of Esther's claim to the estate. At Harold Transome's nomination speech, Maurice Christian recognizes Esther and resolves to profit by revealing her claim to the estate. During the election campaign, posters and handbills advertise the history of the Transome family and cast doubt on their claim to the estate. During the election day riot, Tommy Trounsem, the last male Transome, dies and Esther's claim to the estate becomes valid. The narrator's observations make clear that the timing of these events is important. Even though several characters learn about Esther's legal claim, information alone is not sufficient because, as the narrator says, "Esther's claim had not yet accrued" and "hurry was useless" (ch.30, p.306). In terms of the novel's structure, the appropriate moment for Esther's claim to become valid is the point at which her interaction with Holt has produced in her a sufficiently broad perspective on society's problems. Rather than Felix Holt or Harold Transome, it is Esther Lyon who makes the significant move for social change by disposing of the Transome estate according to her vision of present needs.[8]

In *Felix Holt*, the final emphasis is on hope for society. Esther Lyon's role in the novel's myth of social transition provides a broad perspective on society and its problems within which the political failures of Holt and Transome can be understood. The problem with England as presented in the novel is that society is dominated by ideas and attitudes that are over a century old, the fee tail of the Transome estate. The present lives in the form of the past. New conditions have arisen, but the mechanical succession from the past to the present prevents any single generation from reevaluating its future goals and its inheritance from the past. Reevaluation is necessary, but the only heir with the power of possessing the past in "fee simple" has been lost and must be found.

It is important that the heir has been lost for another reason. Because he has been temporarily disinherited, the heir is given the opportunity to break free from inherited values. The interaction between the outsider and the insider explores a wide spectrum of values from which the heir may choose. A strong connection is established in the novel between interruption in the direct line of succession from the past and the discovery of important human values. The *Duffield Watchman*, for example, praises Harold Transome for his "self-liberation from the trammels of prejudice. . .united with a generous sensibility to the claims of man as man, which had burst asunder, and cast off, by a spontaneous exertion of energy, the cramping outworn shell of hereditary bias and class interest" (ch.8, p.114). While inappropriate for Harold, the terms of this praise fit Esther Lyon well. She has the capacity for feeling that "breaks through formulas too rigorously urged on men by daily practical needs" (ch.46, p.456) and can judge the past in terms of a "generous sensibility to the claims of man as man." According to the novel's vision of society, then, social development would parallel the pattern of individual development.[9] The "spiritual convulsion" in Esther's personal life is matched, on the level of social development, by the temporary loss and discovery of the true heir of the past.

The confusion and dislocation between old England and the new described in the novel's "Introduction" is resolved in a vision of society as involved in a broad transitional process from the past to the future. The solution to present confusion is to find the true heir of the past, the only heir who can "cast off, by a spontaneous exertion of energy, the cramping outworn shell of hereditary bias and class interest" and rediscover the human values with which a better society can be built.[10] As the true heir of the past, Esther Lyon restores the proper line of succession by reclaiming the "pawned inheritance" but disposes of it in such a way as to orient the present towards a better future for men, towards the "transition of an improved heritage" as Reverend Lyon puts it. Political solutions to social problems are rejected because society should be truly "re-formed" with the new energy of love and sympathy, and not simply build another mechanical engine to entail on future generations.

I have suggested that *Felix Holt*'s setting makes it a transitional novel in terms of George Eliot's development, but it is a transitional novel in terms of her use of plot and character as well. Felix Holt is not the first outsider in George Eliot's novels. Earlier characters were also at odds with society because of their extraordinary beliefs and behavior. Dinah Morris is criticized by Mrs. Poyser for having ascetic ideas and for preaching, an unconventional occupation for a woman. Maggie Tulliver frequently says and does things that embarrass her Dodson relatives, staunch exponents of conventional virtues. Silas Marner is called "queer Master Marner" because of his antisocial behavior. Nor is Felix Holt the last outsider. In *Middlemarch*, the outsider will be called a "later-born Theresa" trying to fuse "spiritual grandeur" with "domestic reality." Daniel Deronda is perhaps the most explicitly defined outsider, a character "stirred with a vague social passion but without fixed local habitation to render fellowship real."

Although there are important variations, the outsider's marginal relation to society is generally represented in his fatherless and sometimes homeless condition, his commitment to wider values than narrow social conventions, and his consequent difficulty in defining a social role. His development generally takes the shape of a gradual entry into society by means of assuming specific social responsibilities. Not until *Felix Holt*, however, is the outsider's gradual movement into society integrally involved with an insider's opposite and complementary development. Felix Holt's movement into a fixed social position is at once result and cause of Esther Lyon's movement towards recognizing absolute responsibilities outside conventional distinctions of rank and privilege.

The relationship between Felix Holt and Esther Lyon is a formal achievement of great importance because it focuses the question of the relationship between society and absolute values which George Eliot sought to explore and resolve in all her fiction. This formal pattern has its origin in the earlier novels and in the even earlier short story "Janet's Repentance." But while outsiders and insiders had been previously combined, their developments were not interdependent. The stimulus for Adam Bede's growth as an insider is Hetty's tragedy, and Dinah Morris, the outsider, is also affected primarily by the suffering Hetty causes. Moreover, she never really becomes a major character.

In *The Mill*, Maggie's growth is not connected with the growth of an insider of comparable stature. After Book Four, Tom Tulliver moves into the background and remains unmoved in his commitment to conventional values until the flood brings about his awakening. *Silas Marner* is the first novel in which a double plot structure presents the complementary developments of an outsider and an insider, but Silas and Godfrey Cass develop independently until Eppie brings them together near the novel's end. In *Romola*, Savonarola's character is altered by the events in the shifting political life in Florence rather than changed through his relationship with the insider, Romola. While the development of the novel's other outsider, Tito Melema, is more fully presented than Savonarola's, it involves his relationship with Baldassarre more than Romola. It is not until *Felix Holt* that the developments of outsider and insider become directly linked, a significant achievement in using the conventions of the novel to illuminate the conflict between absolute and conventional values and the possibilities for their reconciliation.[11] This combination of characters is at the core of both *Middlemarch* and *Daniel Deronda*, although there is in both these novels an almost astonishing increase in scope and complexity especially since the outsiders continue to be involved with political ideals rather than with religion as in the earlier works.

The marriage between Felix Holt and Esther Lyon which reconciles absolute and conventional values also looks back to the earlier novels and ahead to her major achievements. Marriages conclude all but two of George Eliot's novels and bring together either an outsider and an insider (Dinah Morris and Adam Bede, Eppie and Aaron Winthrop, Felix Holt and Esther Lyon) or two outsiders whose entry into the social bond of marriage is equivalent to an entry into society itself (Dorothea and Will Ladislaw, Deronda and Mirah). These marriages, except in her first novel, are connected with important and well-developed patterns of inheritance. The heirs are symbolically fatherless, able to judge the past critically. Temporarily disinherited and "orphaned,"[12] Eppie, Romola, Esther Lyon, Dorothea, Ladislaw, and Deronda select from the past only what is important to present priorities.

Society for George Eliot is more than simply a condition of life to which the individual must adjust, however painfully. Its problems and possibilities for its reform are explored with increasing insight and comprehensiveness as stable societies like Hayslope and Raveloe are replaced with traditional societies beginning to change, like Treby Magna and Middlemarch, under the impact of modern political and economic forces, and finally, in *Daniel Deronda*, by contemporary society itself. The widening scope and complexity of George Eliot's investigation of society is made possible by her gradual development of significant formal techniques such as the interdependent developments of outsider and insider, marriage, and inheritance. *Felix Holt* is the key novel in understanding the way in which George Eliot gradually learned to shape formal conventions into a structure flexible enough to explore the upheaval of mid-nineteenth-century England and to interpret it finally as a transition to something better for men.

NOTES

1. All quotations are from *Felix Holt, the Radical*, ed. George Levine (New York: W.W. Norton, 1970).

2. In her review of Wilhelm Heinrich von Riehl's *The Natural History of German Life* for the *Westminster Review* of July, 1856, George Eliot agrees with his recognition of the organic bonds between society's present and past. Language is used as a metaphor, as Carlyle uses clothes, for man's changing social institutions. "Language must be left to grow in precision, completeness, and unity, as minds grow in clearness, comprehensiveness, and sympathy. And there is an analogous relation between the moral tendencies of men and the social conditions they have inherited. The nature of European men has its roots intertwined with the past, and can only be developed by allowing those roots to remain undisturbed while the process of development is going on, until that perfect ripeness of the seed which carries with it a life independent of the root. This vital connexion with the past is much more vividly felt on the Continent than in England, where we have to recall it by an effort of memory and reflection; for though our English life is in its core intensely traditional, Protestantism and commerce have modernized the face of the land and the aspects of society in a far greater degree than in any continental country" (*The Essays of George Eliot*, ed. Thomas Pinney [New York: Columbia Univ. Press, 1967], p.288).

3. For a fuller discussion of George Eliot's conservative attitude towards political solutions for social problems, see Thomas Pinney, "The Authority of the Past in George Eliot's Novels," *Nineteenth-Century Fiction*, 21 (September, 1966), 131-47.

4. On 9 January 1866, George Eliot wrote to Frederic Harrison for advice on the Transome will. Significantly, her major concern was the extent of time that the will would influence. She wrote, "I should be glad of as large a slice of a century as you could give me, but I should be resigned if I could get forty years." In three lengthy letters written on January 11, 27, and 29, Harrison suggested what amount to the broad outlines of the Transome will. See *The George Eliot Letters*, ed. Gordon Haight (Oxford: Oxford Univ. Press, 1954-56), IV, 216-32 and 237-40.

5. George Eliot rejected Frederic Harrison's suggestion that Esther turn out to be a Transome as well as a Bycliffe. As a Transome-Bycliffe, Esther would have been more closely allied with the past. See *Letters*, IV, 230-31.

6. Social distinctions do not disappear. George Eliot did not forsee any benefits from the abolition of the class structure, and was sympathetic to von Riehl's belief that "in modern society the divisions of rank indicate *division of labour*, according to that distribution of functions in the social organism which the historical constitution of society has determined" (*Essays*, p.296). In the "Address to Working Men, by Felix Holt," published in the *Blackwood's Magazine* of January, 1868, Felix Holt advises the working classes that, while their claims are just, these claims must find expression in changes that would not give a "fatal shock" to the "living body" of society as a whole. Particular changes "can be good only in proportion. . .as they put knowledge in the place of ignorance, and fellow-feeling in the place of selfishness. In the course of that substitution class distinctions must inevitably change their character; and represent the varying Duties of men, not their varying Interests" (*Essays*, p.422). In this way, social distinctions will gradually be unified with absolute moral values so that what von Riehl called "the principle of differentiation and the principle of unity" become "identical" (*Essays*, p.296).

7. Matthew Arnold uses the metaphor of machinery in *Culture and Anarchy*. "Faith in machinery is, I said, our besetting danger: often in machinery most absurdly disproportioned to the end which machinery, if it is to do any good at all, is to serve; but always in machinery as if it had a value in

and for itself" (*Culture and Anarchy*, ed. R.H. Super [Ann Arbor: Univ. of Michigan Press, 1965], p.96). Arnold identifies "machinery" with a wide range of things--railroads, coal, wealth, industrialism in general, religious organizations, and radical political movements like Jacobinism. Culture, which is concerned with man's spiritual development, must evaluate and direct society's economic and political machinery. "The idea which culture sets before us of perfection,--an increased spiritual activity, having for its characters increased sweetness, increased light, increased life, increased sympathy,--is an idea which the new democracy needs far more than the idea of blessedness of the franchise, or the wonderfulness of its own industrial performances" (p.109).

8. It is tempting to go so far as to suggest that it is Esther who is "nominated" on the day of Transome's nomination speech and who is "elected" on election day when her claim to the estate becomes valid.

9. David R. Carroll is one of the few critics to recognize that the fate of society itself is a central issue in *Felix Holt*. In his article, "*Felix Holt*: Society as Protagonist," in *Nineteenth-Century Fiction*, 17 (December, 1962), 237-52, he suggests that society's growth parallels Esther's development but does not link her role as heir to the Transome estate with George Eliot's vision of society.

10. In the "Address to Working Men, by Felix Holt," the opposition between a wisdom seen as "outside" society and the social structure is explained by Felix Holt. "Wisdom stands outside of man and urges itself upon him. . .before it finds a home within him, directs his actions. . . .But while still outside of us, wisdom often looks terrible, and wears strange forms, wrapped in the changing conditions of a struggling world. It wears now the form of wants and just demands in a great multitude of British men: wants and demands urged into existence by the forces of a maturing world. And it is in virtue of this--in virtue of this presence of wisdom on our side as a mighty fact, physical, and moral, which must enter into and shape the thoughts and actions of mankind--that we working men have obtained the suffrage. . . .But now, for our own part, we have to seriously consider this outside wisdom which lies in the supreme unalterable nature of things, and watch to give it a home within us and obey it. If the claims of the unendowed multitude of working men hold within them principles which must shape the future, it is not less true that the endowed classes, in their inheritance from the past, hold the precious material without which no worthy, noble future can be moulded. . . .Here again we have to submit ourselves to the great law of inheritance" (*Essays*, p.429). In this passage Felix Holt expresses rhetorically what the novel presents formally through the marriage of the insider-heir and the outsider.

11. The interrelated developments of the outsider and insider can be seen as George Eliot's effort to explore and try to resolve what she calls the conflict between Antigone and Creon in her article for the *Leader*, "The *Antigone* and its Moral" (29 March 1856). "Whenever the strength of a man's intellect, or moral sense, or affection brings him into opposition with the rules which society has sanctioned, *there* is renewed the conflict between Antigone and Creon" (*Essays*, p.265). Her belief that this conflict is an "antagonism between valid claims" is reflected in the complex "leavening process" in which the different weaknesses of the outsider and the insider are corrected and their different strengths combined.

12. Ian Adam has discussed the significance of "lost children" in terms of the problems in individual character development in "Character and Destiny in George Eliot's Fiction," *Nineteenth-Century Fiction*, 20 (September, 1965), 127-43.

CRITICAL RESPONSE TO
MIDDLEMARCH

ELIOT TO HARRIET BEECHER STOWE

The George Eliot Letters, 1978

8 MAY 1869

. . .that thought lies very close to what you say as to your wonder or conjecture concerning my religious point of view. I believe that religion too has to be modified--"developed," according to the dominant phrase--and that a religion more perfect than any yet prevalent, must express less care for personal consolation, and a more deeply-awing sense of responsibility to man, springing from sympathy with that which of all things is most certainly known to us, the difficulty of the human lot. I do not find my temple in Pantheism, which, whatever might be its value speculatively, could not yield a practical religion, since it is an attempt to look at the universe from the outside of our relations to it (that universe) as human beings. As healthy, sane human beings we must love and hate--love what is good for mankind, hate what is evil for mankind. For years of my youth I dwelt in dreams of a pantheistic sort, falsely supposing that I was enlarging my sympathy. But I have travelled far away from that time.

JOHN BLACKWOOD TO ELIOT

The George Eliot Letters, 1978

20 JULY 1871

I have read the second portion of *Middlemarch* with the greatest admiration. It is a most wonderful study of human life and nature. You are like a great giant walking about among us and fixing every one you meet upon your canvas. In all this life like gallery that you put before us every trait in every character finds an echo or recollection in the reader's mind that tells him how true it is to Nature.

It was a disappointment at first not to find any of my old friends of the former part, all except Lydgate apparently entirely strangers, but as you beautifully express it we never know who are to influence our lives while "Destiny stands by sarcastic with our dramatis personae folded in her hand."

SATURDAY REVIEW

7 December 1872

UNSIGNED REVIEW

. . .where a moralist and satirist quarrels with society he is very sure to be able to adduce an abundance of facts on his side. The quarrel with humanity in *Middlemarch* is its selfishness, and the quarrel with society is its hollow respectability. Human nature and society are hard things to defend; but care for self up to a point is not identical with selfishness; and respectability which pays its way and conducts itself with external propriety is not hollow in any peculiar sense. And we must say that if our young ladies, repelled by the faint and 'neutral' virtues of Celia on the one hand, and the powerfully drawn worldly Rosamond on the other, take to be Dorotheas, with a vow to dress differently from other women, and to regulate their own conduct on the system of a general disapproval of the state of things into which they are born, the world will be a less comfortable world without being a better one.

Dorothea is so noble and striking a character--her charm growing upon us as the story advances--she is so penetrated by a sense of duty, so ardent in her longing to make the world better and happier, that we would not introduce her as an example unfit for general imitation had the ordinary domestic type of woman with whom she is contrasted been drawn by a more friendly hand. Dorothea is born with the temper and the aspirations of a St. Theresa; to her the destinies of mankind, seen by the light of Christianity, made the solicitudes of feminine fashion appear an occupation for Bedlam. She will not ride, because all people cannot afford a horse. She takes no interest in art, because it is the delight of the few beyond the reach of material want. Her strength of opinions, and her propensity to act on them, thus put her from the first at odds with society, which, we are told, expected women to have weak opinions, 'while still finding its greatest safeguard in the security that opinions were not acted on.' As a foil to these high sentiments, we have her sister Celia, of whom Dorothea says that she never did anything naughty since she was born, and who really never goes contrary to our sense of what is amiable and dutiful in woman; though, not being in the good graces of the author, we are not allowed to find her attractive. Less clever than Dorothea, she has more worldly wisdom, which means perhaps more instinctive perceptions; and not feeling it her duty to subvert the world, she can take her place in it naturally. But surely it is not every girl's duty to refuse the advantages and pleasures of the condition in which she finds herself because all do not share them. She is not selfish because she is serenely happy in a happy home; and if she does her best to help and alleviate the suffering within her reach, she may comfort herself in the belief that the eye of Providence never sleeps.

It is certain that nothing in human nature in the way of a virtue or a grace will stand a strict analysis unshaken. The analytical mind is logically driven into disparagement. Thus Pascal, refining upon the pervading vanity of man, holds it impossible to escape from it. 'Those who write against glory wish for the glory of having read it; and I who write this have perhaps the same longing, and those who read me will have it also.' There is no escape but in the ideal. Perhaps such a state of mind almost leads to hardness where the sympathies are not active--which they are not with our author on first opening her story. Early during its progress we have at times said to ourselves, the subjects and sentiments are tragic, but not the persons; the writer does not identify herself with them. But such a writer too keenly enters into her creations not to become attached to them, and therefore sympathetic; and tenderness for human frailty, and belief in human feeling, with whatever alloy of self, give a pathos to the close which the beginning did not promise.

. . .As one book of this series followed another, each seemed to say, This is your benevolence, this your learning, this your family life, this your religion! The sleek trust in Providence which easy or grasping selfishness makes its boast is the particular subject of warning and contempt. The carefully elaborated character of Bulstrode, no hypocrite of the common type, but one who sincerely hopes to flatter Divine Justice into condoning the wrong done, and permitting ill-gotten gains to prosper on condition of a certain amount of service done, is a leading instance; but most of the selfishness of *Middlemarch* shelters itself under an assumed appeal from conscience to religion. Whether it be poor Celia justifying her girl's love of pretty things under the test that the necklace she longs for won't interfere with her prayers; or Mr. Brooke excusing a political move with one of his favourite summaries--'Religion, properly speaking, is the dread of a Hereafter'; or Mrs. Waule arguing that for her brother Peter to turn his property into Blue-Coat land was flying in the face of the Almighty that had prospered him, the appeal is uniformly a cover to the real thought or motive, and, as such, a fit subject for the satirist's pen. But every man's religion may be vulgarized if the alloy is too curiously sought for. We like things in groups; our preferences and convictions are tied together by association; but it is not always fair to couple the highest of these with the lowest, as though the same amount and quality of thought and conviction went to each. When we are told that Mrs. Bulstrode and Mrs. Pymdale had the same preferences in silks, patterns of underclothing, china ware, and clergymen, it does not prove the religion represented by the clergyman to be superficial and trivial, though it sounds so in such a conjunction. If *Middlemarch* is melancholy, it is due perhaps to its religion being all duty, without a sufficient admixture of hope. We miss the out-look of blue sky which is as essential to the cheerful portraiture of humanity by the moralist as a glimpse into the open is to the portraiture of art.

In so far as *Middlemarch* is an allegory Mr. Casaubon represents learning as opposed to science. Bunyan's Mr. Bat's-eyes is not more a personification of qualities than is Dorothea's first choice, with his lean person, blinking eyes, white moles, and formal phrases; with talents chiefly of the burrowing kind, carrying his taper among the tombs of the past in diligent exploration; his book, the 'Key to all the Mythologies,' itself a tomb. Altogether he is a striking figure, though now and then the author scarcely shows herself as entirely at home in his surroundings--for example, in his college jealousies and sorenesses--as we generally find her. As for Dorothea's sudden choice of him for a husband, it is not without precedent in real life, reminding us at once of Madame de Staël when a prodigy of fifteen gravely proposing to her parents that she should marry Gibbon; as fat a specimen of distinguished middle life as Mr. Casaubon was a lean one. The more a woman has aims of her own, and a sense of power to carry them out, the less is she guided by the common motives and aspirations of her sex. Personally we can acquiesce in her first choice more readily than in her second. There are two views of Ladislaw, who, we scarcely know on what reasonable grounds, is a great favourite with the author. He charms Dorothea by qualities exactly the reverse of her husband's; by his passionate prodigality of statement; by his ready understanding of her thoughts, which Mr. Casaubon always snubbed as long-exploded opinions, if not heresies; by the sunny brightness of his expression and hair, that seemed to shake out light when he moved his head quickly, 'showing poor Mr. Casaubon by contrast altogether rayless'; by his looking an incarnation of the spring which we must suppose he typifies; by his easy unconventional manners and attitudes, and indifference to the solid good things of life. All these are doubtless attractions. Nature has done much for him, but duty--by which all the other characters of the story are tested--altogether fails in him. He does what he likes, whether right or wrong, to the end of the story; he makes no sacrifices; even his devotion to Dorothea does not preserve him from an unworthy flirtation with his friend Lydgate's wife. He is happy by luck, not desert. Just as devotees of the Virgin are said to be saved at the last moment by a medal worn or a rosary said in her honour, so the chance of his choosing the right woman to worship (though not at the right time) saves him from the consequences of idleness and mere self-pleasing; while poor Lydgate--ten times the better man--suffers not only in happiness, but in his noblest ambitions, and sinks to the lower level of a good practice and a good income because he marries and is faithful to the vain selfish creature whom Ladislaw merely flirts with. We daresay, however, it is inevitable that a grand woman who never in her life called things by the same name as other people should not match in her own degree. There is quite enough of the vagabond in Ladislaw, in spite of his remote kinship with Mr. Casaubon, to make Mrs. Cadwallader's judgment stick by one, that Dorothea might as well marry an Italian with white mice; for the author spares us nothing, and allows his enemies to sum up his genealogy--'the son of a Polish fiddler, and grandson of a thieving Jew pawnbroker.' It is the man, not his antecedents, that the ideal woman cares for. But, after all, what is the example she sets? How does it differ from the ball-room choice of any ordinary girl who takes the pleasant fellow who pleases her fancy? not that it is reasonable to require or to expect her to make the same sort of mistake twice over. This Mrs. Cadwallader--a bright bit of worldly common sense always welcome in the county circle we get pleasantly familiar with--is, however, equally caustic upon both objects of Dorothea's choice. . . .

We have left ourselves no space for more than recognizing the immense amount of character described. The book is like a portrait gallery. . . .Though here we must point out some prejudices, as we would fain suppose them, which make the author hard upon natural distinctions of eye and complexion. All her weak and mean and knavish people are blond, as she calls fair-skinned: and blue eyes are uniformly disingenuous. The acutest observer is not free from prepossession. But what a ceaselessly busy observation; what nicety of penetration; what a tenacity of memory are indicated by these different social pictures! All the gradations of rank and class, nicely measured and appreciated, even while the distinctions of rank are represented as provoking the low ambition of common souls, and therefore things to be overstepped by natures of higher insight and more universal good will. In such questions the book is a deliberate challenge to society as at present constituted. Where we pause to doubt or to dispute we may detect an especial care and point in the wording, showing the author to be aware of the reader's arrested attention. . . .

BLACKWOOD'S MAGAZINE

December 1872

W. LUCAS COLLINS

. . .It is very noteworthy how many of the best novels of the present day touch with more or less distinctiveness upon questions of religious belief. We set aside, of course, those many stories--some excellent of their kind, others the veriest rubbish--which are confessedly stories with a purpose, written to advocate some favourite view, in which the illustration of certain theological tenets is of the very essence of the book. In these, if we only know the name of the writer-- sometimes a fairly accurate guess may be arrived at by merely glancing at that of the publisher--the reader is enable at once to forecast the kind of fare which is provided for him, and will proceed to read or not to read according as his bias may incline him. But even in those which assume no such didactic office, and whose writers would fairly repudiate any such design as proselytism, the great problems of religion, instead of being tacitly ignored or disguised in vague generalities, are assumed as having a momentous influence upon human life. They are not brought prominently into the foreground, perhaps, but they are evidently present to the mind of the writer as elements of grave importance. If our generation be indeed so irreverent and irreligious as it is said to be, the traces of this character are not to be found in our highest works of fiction. If there is scepticism in them, it is scepticism in the better sense of the word. The doubts are those of the honest doubter; the questioning is not of a sneering or captious kind, but has the earnest tone of the inquirer who seeks an answer. Even if prevalent forms of belief are sometimes held up somewhat rudely to the light, and shown to be here and there but threadbare spiritual raiment, it is without prejudice to the living body of truth which they are intended to clothe.

This is peculiarly the case with the works of the writer whose last production lies before us. Theological colour these volumes have none. Professions of a creed may seem to be even purposely avoided. But no one can say that their tones is other than reverent on religious questions. The unrealities of religion, whether they take the shape of formal act or fluent profession, are touched with a satire whose lash is not the less cutting because it is laid on with the most delicate wrist-play. People 'whose celestial intimacies seem not to improve their domestic manners,' who contrive 'to conciliate piety and worldliness, the nothingness of this life and the desirability of cut glass, the consciousness at once of filthy rags and the best damask,' find no mercy here. . . .And nowhere, read where we will, shall we find less religious narrowness, or a fuller confession of the spiritual needs of human nature. Indeed, the cry of the soul after something more satisfying than the mere husks of worldly well-doing and success seems uttered in these volumes with an intensity which is almost painful. True, we have no distinct ideal set up and recommended as really attainable; rather--and this gives to the work that remarkable tinge of melancholy which has been remarked, in spite of all their grace and humour, in most of its predecessors from the same hand--we are allowed to gather that for the most part ideals are attainable, and that the highest aspirations only serve to give a grandeur to the failure in which they inevitably end. . . .Take the characters in these volumes: all who set before them an object in life higher than their fellows, fail in its attainment. Casaubon is a failure, Dorothea is a failure, Lydgate is a failure more than all. It might seem, at first thought, as though the moral were as cynical as this--if you would escape disappointment, you must not seek to rise above the level of your fellow-creatures. It is Celia, with her kitten-like content and hatred of 'notions,'--Sir James Chettam, who 'doesn't go much into ideas,'--Will Ladislaw, with his amiable vagabond dilettantism, who looks upon all forms of prescribed work as 'harness,' and holds genius to be 'necessarily intolerant of fetters,'--Fred Vincy, with his goodhumoured gentlemanlike selfishness,--who come out, on the whole, with the largest share of commonplace happiness. But we are much mistaken if such be the moral which the author--if any moral be intended or permissable--would have us draw. The lines may be read another way. To have an ideal at which we aim, and that ideal of the highest kind, is worthy the life and the true life, though not of necessity that which attains its object or wins content. It is better to fail than succeed, if the aim has been noble in the one case, and mean in the other. . . .

FORTNIGHTLY REVIEW

19 January 1873

SIDNEY COLVIN

. . .In the sense in which anything is called ripe because of fulness and strength, I think the last of George Eliot's novels is also the ripest. *Middlemarch* is extraordinarily full and strong, even among the company to which it belongs. And though I am not sure that it is the property of George Eliot's writing to satisfy, its property certainly is to rouse and attach, in proportion to its fulness and strength. There is nothing in the literature of the day so rousing--to the mind of the day there is scarcely anything so rousing in all literature--as her writing is. What she writes is so full of her time. It is observation, imagination, pathos, wit and humour, all of a high class in themselves; but what is more, all saturated with modern ideas, and poured into a language of which every word bites home with peculiar sharpness to the contemporary consciousness. That is what makes it less safe than it might seem at first sight to speak for posterity in such a case. We are afraid of exaggerating the meaning of such work will have for those who come after us, for the very reason that we feel its meaning so pregnant for ourselves. If, indeed, the ideas of to-day are certain to be the ideas of to-morrow and the day after, if scientific thought and the positive synthesis are indubitably to rule the world, then any one, it should seem, might speak boldly enough to George Eliot's place. For the general definition of her work, I should say, is precisely this--that, among writers of the imagination, she has taken the lead in expressing and discussing the lives and ways of common folks--*votum, timor, ira, voluptas*[1]--in terms of scientific thought and the positive synthesis. She has walked between two epochs, upon the confines of two worlds, and has described the old in terms of the new. To the old world belong the elements of her experience, to the new world the elements of her reflection on experience. The elements of her experience are the 'English Provincial Life' before the Reform Bill--the desires and alarms, indignations and satisfactions, of the human breast in county towns and villages, farms and parsonages, manor-houses, counting-houses, surgeries, streets and lanes, shops and fields, of midlands unshaken in their prejudices and unvisited by the steam-engine. To the new world belong the elements of her reflection; the many-sided culture which looks back upon prejudice with analytical amusement; the philosophy which declares the human family deluded in its higher dreams, dependent upon itself, and bound thereby to a closer if a sadder brotherhood; the habit in regarding and meditating physical laws, and the facts of sense and life, which leads up to that philosophy and belongs to it; the mingled depth of bitterness and tenderness in the human temper of which the philosophy becomes the spring.

Thus there is the most pointed contrast between the matter of these English tales and the manner of their telling. The matter is antiquated in our recollections, the manner seems to anticipate the future of our thoughts. Plenty of other writers have taken humdrum and narrow aspects of English life with which they were familiar, and by delicacy of perception and justness of rendering have put them together into pleasant works of literary art, without running the matter into a manner out of direct correspondence with it. But this procedure of George Eliot's is a newer thing in literature, and infinitely harder to judge of, than the gray and tranquil harmonies of that other mode of art. For no writer uses so many instruments in riveting the interest of the cultivated reader about the characters, and springs of character, which she is exhibiting. First, I say, she has the perpetual application of her own intelligence to the broad problems and conclusions of modern thought. That, for instance, when Fred Vincy, having brought losses upon the Garth family, feels his own dishonour more than their suffering, brings the reflection how '*we are most of us brought up in the notion that the highest motive for not doing a wrong is something irrespective of the beings who would suffer the wrong.'* That again, a few page later, brings the humorous allusions to Caleb Garth's classification of human employments, into business, politics, preaching, learning, and amusement, as one which *'like the categories of more celebrated men, would not be acceptable in these more advanced times.'* And that makes it impossible to describe the roguery of a horse-dealer without suggesting that he *'regarded horse-dealing as the finest of the arts, and might have argued plausibly what it had nothing to do with morality.'*

Next, this writer possesses, in her own sympathetic insight into the workings of human nature, a psychological instrument which will be perpetually displaying its power, its subtlety and trenchancy, in passages like this which lays bare the working of poor Mrs. Bulstrode's faithful mind upon the revelation of her husband's guilt: 'Along with her brother's looks and words, there darted into her mind the idea of some guilt in her husband. Then, under the working of terror, came the image of her husband exposed to disgrace; *'and then, after an instant of scorching shame in which she only felt the eyes of the world, with one leap of her heart she was at his side in mournful but unreproaching fellowship with shame and isolation.'* Of the same trenchancy and potency, equally subtle and equally sure of themselves, are a hundred other processes of analysis, whether applied to serious crises--like that prolonged one during which Bulstrode wavers before the passive murder which shall rid him of his one obstacle as an efficient servant of God--or to such trivial crises as occur in the experiences of a Mrs. Dollop or a Mrs. Taft, or others who, being their betters, still belong to the class of 'well-meaning women knowing very little of their own motives.' And this powerful knowledge of human nature is still only one of many instruments for exposing a character and turning it about. . . .

Then, the writer's studies in science and physiology will constantly come in to suggest for the spiritual processes of her personages an explanation here or an illustration there. For a stroke of overwhelming power in this kind, take what it said in one place of Bulstrode--that 'he shrank from a direct lie with an intensity disproportionate to the number of his more indirect misdeeds. *'But many of these misdeeds were like the subtle muscular movements which are not taken account of in the consciousness; though they bring about the end that we fix in our minds and desire. And it is only what we are vividly conscious of that we can vividly imagine to be seen by Omniscience.'*

And it is yet another instrument which the writer handles when she seizes on critical points of physical look and gesture in her personages, in a way which is scientific and her own. True, there are many descriptions, and especially of the beauty and gestures of Dorothea--and these are written with a peculiarly loving and as it were watchful exquisiteness--which may be put down as belonging to the ordinary resources of art. But look at Caleb Garth; he is a complete physiognomical study in the sense of Mr. Darwin, with the 'deepened depression in the outer angle of his bushy eyebrows, which gave his face a peculiar mildness;' with his trick of 'broadening himself by putting his thumbs into his arm-holes,' and the rest. Such are Rosamond's ways of turning her neck aside and patting her hair when she is going to be obstinate. So, we are not allowed to forget 'a certain massiveness in Lydgate's manner and tone, corresponding with his physique;' nor indeed, any point of figure and physiognomy which strike the author's imagination as symptomatic. Symptomatic is the best word. There is a medical strain in the tissue of the story. There is a profound sense of the importance of physiological conditions in human life. But further still, I think, there is something like a medical habit in the writer, of examining her own creations for their symptoms, which runs through her descriptive and narrative art and gives it some of its peculiar manner.

So that, apart from the presence of rousing thought in general maxims and allusions, we know now what we mean when we speak of the fulness and strength derived, in the dramatic and narrative part of the work, from the use of so many instruments as we have seen. Then comes the question, do these qualities satisfy us as thoroughly as they rouse and interest? Sometimes I think they do, and sometimes not. Nothing evidently can be more satisfying, more illuminating, than that sentence which explained, by a primitive fact in the experimental relations of mind and body, a peculiar kind of bluntness in the conscience of the religious Bulstrode. And generally, wherever the novelist applies her philosophy or science to serious purposes, even if it may be applied too often, its effect seems to me good. But in lighter applications I doubt if the same kind of thing is not sometimes mistaken. The wit and humour of this writer every one of us knows and has revelled in; I do not think these want to gain body from an elaborate or semi-scientific language. In the expression of fun or common observation, is not such language apt to read a little technical and heavy, like a kind of intellectual slang? I do not think the delightful fun about Mrs. Garth and Mary and the children gains by it. I doubt if it is in place when it is applied to the mental processes of Mrs. Dollop or Mr. Bambridge. And when, for example, we are asked to consider what would have happened if Fred Vincy's 'prophetic soul had been urged to particularize,' that is what I mean by something like a kind of intellectual slang.

But all this only concerns some methods or processes of the writer, picked from random points in the development of her new story and its characters. What of these in themselves? Well, there comes back the old sense, of a difference to the degree to which we are aroused, attached, and taught, and the degree to which we are satisfied. The book is full of high feeling, wisdom, and acuteness. It contains some of the most moving dramatic scenes in our literature. A scene like that of Dorothea in her night of agony, a scene like that in which the greatness of her nature ennobles for a moment the smallness of Rosamond's, is consummate alike in conception and in style. The characters are admirable in their vigour and individuality, as well as in the vividness and fulness of illustration with which we have seen that they are exhibited. Dorothea with her generous ardour and ideal cravings; Mr. Brooke with his good-natured viewy incoherency and self-complacence; Celia with her narrow worldly sense seasoned by affectionateness; Chettam with his honourable prejudices; Ladislaw with his dispersed ambitions, and the dispositions and susceptibilities of his origin; Casaubon with his learning which is lumber, his formalism and inaccessibility of character, his distrust of himself and other people; Lydgate with his solid ambitions which fail, and his hollow which succeed; Rosamond 'with that hard slight thing called girlishness,' and all the faults which can underlie skin-deep graces; Bulstrode with the piety designed in vain to propitiate the chastisement of destiny; the witty unscrupulous rattle of Mrs. Cadwallader; the Garth household, the Farebrother household, the Vincys, the country bankers and country tradesmen, the rival practitioners, the horse-dealer, the drunkard who is the ghost of Bulstrode's ancient sin--all these are living and abiding additions to every one's circle of the familiar acquaintances that importune not. But as one turns them over in one's mind or talk, them and their fortunes in the book, with laughter or sympathy or pity or indignation or love, there will arise all sorts of questionings, debatings, such as do not arise after a reading which has left the mind satisfied. One calls in question this or that point in the conduct of the story; the attitude which the writer personally assumes towards her own creations; the general lesson which seems to underlie her scheme; above all, the impression which its issue leaves upon oneself.

The questions one asks are such as, within limits like these, it would be idle to attempt to solve, or even to state, except in the most fragmentary way. Are not, for instance, some points in the story a little coarsely invented and handled? At the very outset, is not the hideous nature of Dorothea's blind sacrifice too ruthlessly driven home to us, when it ought to have been allowed to reveal itself by gentler degrees? Is it not too repulsive to talk of the moles on Casaubon's face, and to make us loathe the union from the beginning? Is not the formalism and dryness of Casaubon's nature a little overdone in his first conversation and his letter of courtship? Or again, is not the whole intrigue of Ladislaw's birth and Bulstrode's guilt, the Jew pawnbroker and Raffles, somewhat common and poor? The story is made to hinge twice, at two important junctures, upon the incidents of watching by a death-bed. Is that scant invention, or is it a just device for bringing out, under nearly parallel circumstances, the opposite characters of Mary Garth and of Bulstrode--her untroubled and decisive integrity under difficulties, his wavering conscience, which, when to be passive is already to be a murderer, permits itself at last in something just beyond passiveness? Or, to shift the ground of question, does not the author seem a little unwarrantably hard upon some of her personages and kind to others? Fred and Rosamond Vincy, for instance--one would have said there was not so much to choose. The author, however, is on the whole kind to the brother, showing up his faults but not harshly, and making him in the end an example of how an amiable spendthrift may be redeemed by a good man's help and a good girl's love. While to the sister, within whose mind 'there was not room enough for luxuries to look small in,' she shows a really merciless animosity, and gibbets her as an example of how an unworthy wife may degrade the career of a man of high purposes and capacities. Celia, too, who is not really so very much higher a character, the author makes quite a pet of in comparison, and puts her in situations where all her small virtues tell; and so on. Minute differences of character for better or worse may justly be shown, of course, as producing vast differences of effect under the impulsion of circumstances. Still, I do not think it is altogether fancy to find wanting here the impartiality of the greatest creators towards their mind's offspring.

Then, for the general lesson of the book, it is not easy to feel quite sure what it is, or how much importance the author gives it. In her prelude and conclusion both, she seems to insist upon the design of illustrating the necessary disappointment of a woman's nobler aspirations in a society not made to second noble aspirations in a woman. And that is one of the most burning lessons which any writer could set themselves to illustrate. But then, Dorothea does not suffer in her ideal aspirations from yielding to the pressure of social opinion. She suffers in them from finding that what she has done, in marrying an old scholar in the face of social opinion, was done under a delusion as to the old scholar's character. 'Exactly,' is apparently the author's drift; 'but it is society which so nurtures women that their ideals cannot but be ideals of delusion.' Taking this as the author's main point (and I think prelude and conclusion leave it still ambiguous), there are certainly passages enough in the body of the narrative which point the same remonstrance against what society does for women. '*The shallowness of a water-nixie's soul may have a charm till she becomes didactic:*' that describes the worthlessness of what men vulgarly prize in women. '*In the British climate there is no incompatibility between scientific insight and furnished lodgings. The incompatibility is chiefly between scientific ambition and a wife who objects to that kind of residence.*' That points to the rarity of a woman, as women are brought up, who prefers the things of the mind to a luxury. '*"Of course she is devoted to her husband," said Rosamond, implying a notion of necessary sequence which the scientific man regarded as the prettiest possible for a woman.*' That points with poignant irony to the science, as to the realities of society and the heart, of men whose science is solid in other things.

It is perhaps in pursuance of the same idea that Dorothea's destiny, after Casaubon has died, and she is free from the consequences of a first illusory ideal, is not made very brilliant after all. She cannot be an Antigone or a Theresa. She marries the man of her choice, and bears him children; but we have been made to feel all along that he is hardly worthy of her. There is no sense of triumph in it; there is rather a sense of sadness in a subdued and restricted, if not now a thwarted destiny. In this issue there is a deep depression; there is that blending of the author's bitterness with her profound tenderness of which I have already spoken. And upon this depends, or with it hangs together, that feeling of uncertainty and unsatisfiedness as to the whole fable and its impression which remains with the reader when all is done. He could spare the joybells--the vulgar upshot of happiness for ever after--Sophia surrendered to the arms of her enraptured Jones--if he felt quite sure of the moral or intellectual point of view which had dictated so chastened and subdued a conclusion. As it is, he does not feel clear enough about the point of view, the lesson, the main moral and intellectual outcome, to put up with that which he feels to be uncomfortable in the combinations of the story, and flat in the fates of friends and acquaintances who have been brought so marvellously near to him.

That these and such like questionings should remain in the mind, after the reading of a great work of fiction, would in ordinary phrase be said to indicate that, however, great the other qualities of the work, it was deficient in qualities of art. The fact is, that this writer brings into her fiction so many new elements, and gives it pregnancy and significance in so many unaccustomed directions, that it is presumptuousness to pronounce in that way as to the question of art. Certainly, it is possible to write with as little illusion, or with forms of disillusion much more cynical, as to society and its dealings and issues, and yet to leave a more harmonious and definite artistic impression than is here left. French writers perpetually do so. But then George Eliot, with her science and her disillusion, has the sense of bad and good as the great French literary artists have not got it, and is taken up, as they are not, with the properly moral elements of human life and struggling. They exceed in all that pertains to the passions of the individual; she cares more than they do for the general beyond the individual. That it is by which she rouses--I say rouses, attaches, and elevates--so much more than they do, even if her combinations satisfy much less. Is it, then, that a harmonious and satisfying literary art is impossible under these conditions? Is it that a literature, which confronts all the problems of life and the world, and recognises all the springs of action, and all that clogs the springs, and all that comes from their smooth or impeded working, and all the importance of one life for the mass,--is it that such a literature must be like life itself, to leave us sad and hungry?

NOTE

1. 'their wishes, fears, anger, pleasures' (Juvenal, *Satire* I, 85).

THE MORAL IMAGINATION OF
GEORGE ELIOT

Papers on Language and Literature, Fall 1972

BERT G. HORNBACK

On 23 September, 1865, George Eliot began "Amos Barton," her first work of fiction. Just ten days earlier she had finished an essay for the *Westminster Review* with a warning to "any female reader who is in danger of adding to the number of 'silly novels by lady novelists.'"[1] It would be hard to imagine George Eliot herself ever needing to be warned against silliness; from the very beginning of her career her serious and intellectual bent was remarked by readers and critics. Yet this is not to say that her work is dry or academic or argumentative. It is didactic; but working through and from the logic of the imagination rather than the logic of reason. George Eliot never submits herself--and never asks her readers to submit themselves--to sentimental emotionalism; her style, her people, her situations, the whole of her fictions are denominated by her strength of mind. Still, such is that strength that what one comes away with is closer to "feeling" than it is to "idea"; and what I propose to explore in this essay is the nature of this "feeling," as it informs *Middlemarch*.

In a note composed sometime in the years immediately following the *Middlemarch* George Eliot wrote under the heading "Feeling is a sort of knowledge" that "What seems eminently wanted is a closer comparison between the knowledge which we call rational & the experience which we call emotional."[2] From this combination she thought men would derive a higher sympathy for their fellows--something much like Keats's "knowledge," which Douglas Bush defines as a "sympathetic understanding of the human condition."[3] Such an awareness is for George Eliot the highest and most noble of human pieties, the only true and relevant morality. And this is what she wanted to teach. The Puritan streak in her allowed her no room for the beautiful unless it was also good, and no room for the good unless it was also useful. F.W.H. Myers has written of what is now a famous conversation with her in 1873 in which "she, stirred somewhat beyond her wont, and taking as her text the three words which have been used so often, as the inspiring trumpet-calls of men,--the words *God, Immortality, Duty*--pronounced, with a terrible earnestness, how inconceivable was the *first*, how unbelievable the *second*, and yet how peremptory and absolute the *third*."[4]

George Eliot's writings are filled with statements of this thesis. When she discarded the ardent Evangelicalism of her girlhood in her early twenties, she did not lay aside with it the ideal of relevant morality. In October of 1841 she wrote:

Much is said about the love of the beautiful, and the idea of perfection as a characteristic of the refined mind, and as being the spring of all high attainment in the triple sisterhood, painting, poetry, and music. But there is a more important application of the terms, a moral one, which I trust we shall ever have before our mind's eye--the love of the beauty of holiness, and a continual yearning after a conformity to it, an habitual contemplation of Moral Perfection, and a dissatisfaction with all that falls short of that standard.[5]

That this art which has its source in the idea of moral perfection is also a duty is expressed in 1868:

The inspiring principle which alone gives me courage to write is, that of so presenting our human life as to help my readers in getting a clearer conception and a more active admiration of those vital elements which bind men together and give a higher worthiness to their existence. . . .I see clearly that we ought, each of us, not to sit down and wail, but to be heroic and constructive, if possible, like the strong souls who lived before, as in other cases [eras?] of religious decay.[6]

This sounds much like the mental and moral point of view of Dorothea Brooke, of course, in *Middlemarch*. The young woman who introduces the almost mystical idea of beautiful failure into English fiction--and this is keyed in the expansive ironies of the "Prelude"--wants to "judge soundly on the social duties of the Christian" (p.42), is anxious about "making my life good for anything" and learning "new ways of helping people" (p.52). Her constant question is the would-be activist's. She asks of Lydgate, concerning Casaubon's health, "Tell me what I can do" (p.200). Later, she asks herself "what should I do--" to help Lydgate and Rosamond (p.544). And again, wanting to be useful at Lowick she asks "What could I do?" (p.251). So much does she want to do something that she complains once pettishly that there is nothing wrong at Lowick: "Everybody was well and had flannel; nobody's pig had died" (p.555).

Dorothea's desire to do something finds its best satisfaction in her assistance to Lydgate which, though it does not save him his position, at least saves him from himself. The circumstances of Raffle's death suggest some sort of moral, perhaps even criminal conspiracy between Bulstrode and Lydgate. Dorothea, however, does not accept circumstantial evidence. She is naively prejudiced for Lydgate from the beginning, sure that "to find out the truth" and to "clear him" are the same undertaking (p.505). What is important here is not Dorothea's innocence or her prejudice, but the idea of the undertaking itself. "What do we live for," she asks, "if it is not to make life less difficult for each other?" (p.506). To Lydgate she says: "I would take pains to clear you. I have very little to do. There is nothing better that I can do in the world" (p.526). And to Rosamond: "How can we live and think that anyone has trouble--piercing trouble--and we could help them, and never try?" (p.548).

This insistence on social morality and charity is the main thematic emphasis of Dorothea's story; and it is this, rather than George Eliot's realism, or her carefully precise psychological insight, which creates the feeling of beauty and of life in the novel. To help others is one thing; to sacrifice oneself for the sake of others is something else. The communication of this something is George Eliot's greatest success in *Middlemarch*. Dorothea's simple attempt to help Lydgate leads her into a situation which challenges her to sacrifice herself--her pride, her dreams--for his honor. The climax comes at the end of her night of torment, as she surrenders her own desires and feelings in order to help Lydgate and to save his marriage. She asks herself: "What should I do--how should I act now, this very day, if I could clutch my own pain, and compel it to silence, and think of those three?" (p.544).

George Eliot is quite explicit in her revelation to us and to Dorothea of what it means to have asked such an heroic question as this. Immediately it is dawn, and Dorothea looks out onto a world in microcosm: "On the road there was a man with a bundle on his back and a woman carrying her baby; in the field she could see figures moving--perhaps the shepherd with his dog. Far off in the bending sky was the pearly light" (p.544). The relevance of this symbolic scene penetrates Dorothea's sympathetic soul, and she understands:

she felt the largeness of the world and the manifold wakings of men to labour and endurance. She was part of that involuntary, palpitating life, and could neither look out on it from her luxurious shelter as a mere spectator, nor hide her eyes in selfish complaining.

What she would resolve to do that day did not yet seem quite clear, but something that she could achieve stirred her with an approaching murmur which would soon gather distinctness (p.544).

What she does is make "her second attempt to see and save Rosamond" (p.545).

Dorothea's anxiety about doing good is at once typical of and more noble than the general mood and order of action in the novel; and both of these aspects of her character must be explored in order to learn how George Eliot's moral imagination forms and informs *Middlemarch*. The world of the novel is full of reforms and reformers. Lydgate would reform the practice of medicine; Mr. Brooke--under pressure, and with Ladislaw's help--would address himself to the question of political and land reform; Sir James is engaged in economic reform on his own property; the tenant farmer Dagley threatens Mr. Brooke with "the Rinform"; and in the background of the whole novel the House of Commons debates the first great Reform Bill of 1831-32. Dorothea's plans for building cottages are her link with this world of practical reform and, at the same time, the symptom or sign of her grander spiritual ambition. In this sense, the larger world of the novel is set as a background, sometimes supportive, sometimes contrapuntal, for Dorothea's story.

In her journal for 1 January 1869 George Eliot lists "a Novel called Middlemarch" as among her plans for the year.[7] Then in 1870 she began "experimenting in a story" on "a subject which has been recorded among my possible themes ever since I began to write fiction."[8] "A Novel called Middlemarch" was probably the story of Lydgate, the Vincys, the Bulstrodes, the Farebrothers, and the Garths; the other, later story was to be called "Miss

Brooke." By the spring of 1871, however, she had determined that "the work is called *Middlemarch*. Part I will be *Miss Brooke*."[9]

When George Eliot began to put Dorothea's story together with "Middlemarch" her problem was how to unite them. How could she make her heroine fit into "A Study of Provincial Life"? Dorothea scarcely belongs to the Middlemarch community in what she is or does--she would be terribly out of place, for example, at a dinner party at the Vincy's. Further, she is treated differently by her creator. Real authorial sympathy is invested in the various Middlemarch characters, certainly; but it is the condescending sympathy of a superior critical observer who is not actively involved with them. Dorothea's experience is felt much more viscerally and personally by George Eliot. This is not to say that Dorothea's experience is her creator's or that her character is autobiographically modeled. Rather, the point is that she is given more of soul, of spirit, of significant human individuality than the other characters are allowed, and this plenitude is what George Eliot responds to in writing about her. The Middlemarch people are all the subjects of a "Study"; and for all their rich vitality, they belong in a real and serious way to a research project almost as much as they do to imaginative literature. Dorothea, however, is observed, not studied. She is a creature more of "that experience which we call emotional" than of "the knowledge which we call rational" in the way she is presented. And her story is a richer, more intense experience for the reader than is the story of provincial Middlemarch.

At the center of the Middlemarch story stands Lydgate. Around him are circled Mr. Vincy, Rosamond, Fred, the Garths, Mr. Brooke, Ladislaw, Raffles, and Bulstrode. Each of them is related in some important way to Lydgate, except for Mr. Brooke and Fred, whose relationships with him are indirect, through Casaubon and Mr. Farebrother. Beyond their relationships with Lydgate, the characters of the outer circle also maintain significant relationships with their immediate neighbors: for example, Ladislaw with Brooke and Raffles, Raffles with Ladislaw and Bulstrode, and Bulstrode with Raffles and Vincy. Still, the most important relationships are with Lydgate, generally; and as each set of characters interacts with him, triangles of action are formed in the circle, segments of a web which has at its center the young doctor. It is almost as though the rest of the characters, except for Dorothea, feed from this center, dependent upon Lydgate for their action and involvement.

Lydgate is a social character as well as a character caught in society. Through most of the novel Dorothea, in contrast, has little to do with other people. When the story is concerned with Dorothea, it is usually concerned almost singly with her and ignores the other characters. All the attention is on her in her scenes with Celia, with Casaubon, with Ladislaw, and with Lydgate; they are merely her supports or foils. And her most fully realized moments are moments she spends alone. But when the scene focuses on Lydgate, it focuses on the heart of society, and suddenly all the rest of the characters appear and involve themselves with and around him in the poignantly abrasive play of life.

If this large novel is to hold together, of course, Dorothea too must become involved in the Middlemarch world. To do so, she must give up her romantic idealism and look at and work usefully among the petty but real people who live there. For all that George Eliot appreciates Dorothea's desires to do great things, she knows and remarks both their impossibility and Dorothea's fault. This is made clear in the often-discussed image of Dorothea's myopia, which is both literal and metaphorical. Dorothea tells Sir James that she is "rather short-sighted" (p.19); and Celia complains to her, "You always see what nobody else sees. . .yet you never see what is quite plain" (p.23). What Dorothea sees is usually the ideal vision, or the vision oriented to the ideal, that she wants to see. And busy thus blindly with her own dreams, she neither sees what is there to be seen nor does anything. At the very end of the novel she admits to Celia, "I have never carried out any plan yet" (p.566).

Dorothea's myopia finally means that, lost in her own world, she is piously selfish and naively egoistic. She wants to marry Hooker, Locke, Milton, Pascal, or Casaubon. She rejects Sir James's suit, and determines to give up planning cottages in order to be "uncivil" with him, crying--about the cottages, not Sir James--"It is very painful" (p.23). Celia, whom George Eliot has already established as the one who sees clearly, consoles her sister: "Poor Dodo. . . .It is very hard: it is your favorite *fad* to draw plans." But Dorothea will not accept this criticism: "How can one ever do anything nobly Christian, living among people with such petty thoughts?" she asks. And the narrator answers the rhetorical question: "Dorothea was too much jarred to recover her temper and behave so as to show that she admitted any error in herself. She was disposed rather to accuse the intolerable narrowness and the purblind conscience of the society around her" (p.23).

As the novel progresses, Dorothea begins to see more clearly both the world and her own place in it. She is disillusioned in her dream of Casaubon and in their marriage and begins to assert that strength of character which has been lost--hidden--in the lighter tissues of her own fantasies. Her determination to clear Lydgate of suspicion in the death of Raffles leads her to the meeting with Rosamond in chapter 77. She goes to offer her sympathy to Rosamond, and to pledge her faith in Lydgate's honor. But in seeing Rosamond and Ladislaw together she is shorn of sympathy, discovering what she thinks is Ladislaw's romantic dishonesty. When Dorothea returns from Lydgate's house, Celia notices that something has happened: "Dodo, how very bright your eyes are!. . .And you don't see anything you look at." Dorothea is seeing what she thinks is her own betrayal, by Will; and Lydgate's unhappiness coupled with her own is, to her, "all the troubles of all the people on the face of the earth" (p.535). This crisis comes as Dorothea says to herself, of Will, "Oh, I did love him" (p.542). The act that follows is her selfless act, done for the sake of others at great cost to herself.

And from this act of charity, of social morality, of heroism in truth and in Dorothea's own terms, comes her reward, and the fulfillment of George Eliot's novel.

But as many readers and critics have long said, her reward is only Will Ladislaw: a weak, unworthy, unsatisfactory, and unreal or unrealized creature with a rippling nose and coruscating hair. The key to this criticism seems to be in the term unrealized--and the result of examining what Will is realized as, may be to enable us to see him more positively. By looking carefully at how he is identified and defined in the novel and in relation to the real world upon which the novel is based we can discover why and how he can be Dorothea's reward, and why she has to sacrifice herself a second time--by giving up her future, it seems--to marry him.

One of the most remarkable aspects of *Middlemarch* has been, for many critics, its realism: the way in which the real world is woven together with the fictional. The history of England from 1828 to 1831 is an impressive part of the texture of the novel--so much so that English history and *Middlemarch* seem to be complementary. The medical education and opinions of Lydgate are real, current, and historically reliable. Dorothea's planning, Mr. Brooke's politics, Casaubon's scholarship are all drawn in reference to a real history, as has often been pointed out. But such historical realism is not in itself important to the novel or to the reader's experience of it. This historical, factual dimension becomes a part of the "feeling" that *Middlemarch* produces indirectly upon the reader, as this dimension supports the characters and gives them something like metaphysical validity and authority in their world. Their realization as characters is finally more imaginative than historical, or simply realistic.

Like most of the other characters in *Middlemarch*, Ladislaw is attached to history. Indeed, Will's attachment to historical fact is more direct and personal than that of any other character in the novel. Through this attachment, he is associated with a certain set of aesthetic, imaginative, and philosophic values which, as they are shared with Dorothea, become a kind of morality for George Eliot and provide the novel's resolution. Through these values, as through the other realistic and historical details of the novel, she creates its "feeling," the imaginative experience of the whole.

At the time in history of which she writes, George Eliot says, "Romanticism. . .was fermenting still as a distinguishable vigorous enthusiasm in certain long-haired German artists in Rome" (p.130). Ladislaw's sketching leads him to an association with one of those artists, Adolf Naumann. Joseph Jacobs has thought Naumann's character to be suggested by that of Johann Friedrich Overbeck (1789-1869), the father of the German Nazarene school, who worked in Rome after 1810.[10] Certainly Naumann is representative of that school. He describes Dorothea not so much in the vocabulary of the German Nazarene group as in related English Pre-Raphaelite terms, seeing her as "antique form animated by Christian sentiment--a sort of Christian Antigone--sensuous force controlled by spiritual passion" (p.132). That is to say, George Eliot is remarking on the past forty years earlier (*Middlemarch* was published in 1871-72, and its action transpires during 1828-31) in the vocabulary familiar to, as well as from the point of view of, a contemporary of the Pre-Raphaelites. Thus, for example, a few pages later she has Will characterize Naumann as "one of the chief renovators of Christian art, one of those who [has] not only revived but expanded that grand conception of supreme events as mysteries" (p.147)--which is to characterize him as a follower of the Nazarenes. It is not surprising that Will should be defined and situated in these terms, since from about 1850 the Nazarene school had its disciples in England in the Pre-Raphaelites, led in art and in literature by Dante Gabriel Rossetti. Will's interest in painting is influenced by Naumann's work, and he espouses something of the idea of Pre-Raphaelite poetry in saying to Naumann that "Language gives a fuller image [than painting], which [image] is all the better for being vague. After all, the true seeing is within' (p.133).[11]

Ladislaw's role in *Middlemarch* is in part established by means of this association with Pre-Raphaelitism, as it gives him a set of basic values from which to develop his personal identity. The historical association gives authority--but not necessarily approval--to his character and his way of life. It does not prohibit George Eliot's criticizing him for being a dilettante, though even in that criticism she seems to recognize the measure of his spiritual potential. When he gives up "poetic metres" and "mediaevalism"--which is to say the Pre-Raphaelite affectation--in exchange for the chance of "sympathising warmly with liberty and progress in general" (p.318), George Eliot comments that "Our sense of duty must often wait for some work which shall take the place of dilettanteism and make us feel that the quality of our action is not a matter of indifference" (pp.318-19).

Of course Will has never been a petty creature, just a dilettante. His moral point of view is basically similar to Dorothea's--and to Lydgate's. His religion, he says, is "To love what is good and beautiful when I see it" (p.271). True, by comparison with Dorothea's ambition, to *do* good for other people, Will's sounds--as his creator would have it--somewhat effetely aesthetic, "dilettantish." And adumbrating the decadents of the 1890's, he insists to Dorothea, "I don't feel bound, as you do, to submit to what I don't like" (p.271). Still, his point of view is important for the novel, and important for Dorothea to understand. Their confrontation in chapter 22 is a significant one. Will tells Dorothea:

"I fear you are a heretic about art generally. How is that? I should have expected you to be very sensitive to the beautiful everywhere."

"I suppose I am dull about many things," said Dorothea, simply. "I should like to make life beautiful--I mean everybody's life. And then all this immense expense of art, that seems somehow to lie outside life and make it no better for the world, pains one. . . ."

"I call that the fanaticism of sympathy," said Will, impetuously. ". . .The best piety is to enjoy--when you can. You are doing the most then to save the earth as an agreeable planet. And enjoyment radiates. It is of no use to try and take care of all the world; that is being taken care of when you feel delight--in art or in anything else" (pp.152-53).

Two similar but uncongenial idealisms meet here: the moral ideal, to which Dorothea is devoted, and the aesthetic ideal, by which Will wants to live. In the end they are reconciled by the necessary compromise which makes Will commit himself to work as "an ardent public man" and Dorothea settle for something like the "radiance" of goodness in which Will believes, so that "the effect of her being on those around her was incalculably diffusive" (p.578).

This ending is not a triumphant one for Dorothea. She still feels "that there was always something better which she might have done" (pp.575-76), and George Eliot concludes that her marriage to Will was not an "ideally beautiful act, but a sacrifice" (p.577). And although Dorothea believes (pp.374-75)--and George Eliot asserts (p.576)--that Will is no longer a dilettante, he is nevertheless not Hooker, Locke, Milton, or Pascal. He is, however, real and male, a husband for Dorothea and a father for her child. And he is prepared to work in the real world at doing practical things, "working well in those times when reforms were begun with a young hopefulness of immediate good which has been much checked in our days" (p.576). As for Dorothea, though she is happy in her life with Will, many people, according to George Eliot, "thought it a pity that so substantive and rare a creature should have been absorbed into the life of another, and be known only in a certain circle as a wife and mother. But no one stated exactly what else that was in her power she ought to have done" (p.576). Despite the resemblances and comparisons, Dorothea is not, after all, St. Theresa, Antigone, the Virgin Mary, or a queen.

Dorothea is only real, not mythical. And in being real, in becoming a woman of responsibility in the real world, she joins the community of Middlemarch. In so doing she proves the vitality and the significance of that community. As the reader looks back now on the "Study of Provincial Life" that he has read, the various characters exhibit a new depth, a new rich dimension of humanity which was not so evident before. There is a "feeling" that "radiates" from Dorothea, affecting one's sense of the whole novel. This happens by means of example and analogue: for not only do the comparative elements in plots and characterization support Dorothea, they are themselves elevated and enhanced by what they share with her.

The simplest analogue is the story of Fred Vincy and Mary Garth. Fred's generous irresponsibility is on the side of pleasure, and Mary's goodness is bound to duty. The reform of Fred puts him to work also--and then they are married, to live happily ever after in a romanticized descant of bliss sung above the central melody of the novel. A more serious parallel, and one opposite to the subplot of Fred and Mary, is Lydgate's story. His ambition is as uncomromisingly idealistic, originally, as Dorothea's. He looks to his profession as "the most perfect interchange between science and art. . .the most direct alliance between intellectual conquest and the social good" (p.99), and his enthusiastically conceived prospect is "to do good small work for Middlemarch, and great work for the world" (p.102). Lydgate fails in his grand ambitions, just as Dorothea does; but unlike her, he fails completely, ruinously, fatally. Dorothea's compromise is an honorable one made with reality, whereas Lydgate's is the sacrifice of his dignity, his honor, and his honesty. He compromises his life in order to please Rosamond's weakness and vanity, and instead of doing a realistically limited but respectable good for either Middlemarch or the world, Lydgate ends his days a prostitute to the wealthy and a specialist in the treatment of gout.

The echoes of Dorothea's character and career are obvious here. Perhaps there is also some useful connection to be drawn between the Bulstrode story and Dorothea's. In physical appearance Casaubon's double, Bulstrode is an unsavory advocate of strict Evangelical living whose piety is both a terrible private penance for himself and a self-righteousness used for the moral oppression of others. His power pervades the society of Middlemarch, and is woven carefully and fully into the fabric of the novel. Yet despite his obvious corruption, the author encourages some sort of sympathy for him--moreso than for Casaubon. George Eliot allows Bulstrode to be saved by his wife's compassionate loyalty and sympathy. In the space of five chapters she sets up three parallel tests of generosity, for Dorothea, Mrs. Bulstrode, and Rosamond. Like Dorothea, Mrs. Bulstrode responds to the test selflessly, with "new compassion and old tenderness" and a silent "promise of faithfulness" (p.518). Played against this response is Rosamond's assertion in the face of Lydgate's distress: "Whatever misery I have to put with, it will be easier away from here" (p.523).

In George Eliot's world happiness is a matter of the soul, and the success which the world usually recognizes is irrelevant. Early in her career she wrote, "If art does not enlarge men's sympathies, it does nothing morally."[12] The lesson of *Middlemarch* may be in the expansion of the capacity for sympathetic understanding, through the appreciation of Dorothea's story. The famous image of the pier-glass, in chapter 27, is descriptive of this phenomenon as well as of the organization of the novel:

Your pier-glass or extended surface of polished steel made to be rubbed by a housemaid, will be minutely and multitudinously scratched in all directions; but place now against it a lighted candle as a centre of illumination, and lo! the scratches will seem to arrange themselves in a fine series of concentric circles round that little sun. It is demonstrable that the scratches are going everywhere impartially, and it is only your candle which produces the flattering illusion of a concentric arrangement, its light falling with an exclusive optical selection. These things are a parable (p.182).

In *Middlemarch*, the complicated web of character relations can be described by reference to this image. At the same time, but thought of in a different way, this "parable" of "optical selection" can be useful in explaining how the complex focus of the novel works. All the characters are there, and their actions and interactions are as scratches on the surface of the Middlemarch mirror. In order to organize their activity the narrator must find some pattern therein which will help make it all intelligible. The focus George Eliot chooses--where she places her candle--is one means of achieving this meaning; and the "exclusive optical selection" which results is what ordinarily is called narrative point of view.

Lydgate is the focal character for Middlemarch activity, as I have said. By looking at him George Eliot brings the rest of her characters into the "web" of the action, and describes thus the representative world of her novel. Dorothea is outside the focus, originally, and must be seen by another light. But by means of the analogy between her story and character and Lydgate's, she is associated with that other focus, and a tie is established between the two. Finally, as Dorothea commits herself to action in the world of society, the two focuses fuse, and the several stories of Middlemarch which have already been ordered and organized to fit a single structure are seen in a new depth, with a new dimension, in the light of Dorothea's radiance. This sophisticated thematic and structural organization of the novel may be what George Eliot had in mind in saying that her "ideal" in writing *Middlemarch* was "to make matter and form an inseparable truthfulness."[13]

But what this truthfulness is, exactly, is another matter. One of the long-standing arguments among readers of George Eliot's novels is about her interpretation of the nature of human experience.[14] In *The Mill on the Floss* she writes: "the tragedy of our lives is not created entirely from within. 'Character,' says Novalis, in one of his more questionable aphorisms--'character is destiny.' But not the whole of our destiny."[15] A similar argument is presented in *Middlemarch* by the epigraph to chapter 4:

1st Gent. Our deeds are fetters that we forge ourselves.
2nd Gent. Ay, truly; but I think it is the world that brings the iron.

The idea appears again in such statements as the narrator's "Destiny stands by sarcastic with our *dramatis personae* folded in her hands" (p.122). Will's "I take Tamburlaine in his chariot for the tremendous course of the world's physical history lashing on the harnessed dynasties" (p.148) and the narrator's, again, in the last paragraph of the novel, "For there is no creature whose inward being is so strong that it is not greatly determined by what lies outside it" (p.577), are similar statements. But the epigraph to chapter 70 seems to agree with the proposition that "character is destiny":

Our deeds still travel with us from afar,
And what we have been makes us what we are.

George Eliot seems to be of two minds about the making of man's fate. She is not a simple determinist, yet she is unsure that human choice is ever really free. There is no contradiction inherent in such a view, of course. The problem arises in the difficult adjustment of emphasis which one must make in order to find a balance, a philosophical and practical equilibrium. Perhaps the most sophisticated and satisfactory formulation of this position is Walter Pater's, in the conclusion to his essay on Winckelmann, written in 1867:

What modern art has to do in the service of culture is so to rearrange the details of modern life, so to reflect it, that it may satisfy the spirit. And what does the spirit need in the face of modern life? The sense of freedom. That naive, rough sense of freedom, which supposes man's will to be limited, if at all, only by a will stronger than his, he can never have again. . . .For us, necessity is not, as of old, a sort of mythological personage without us, with whom we can do warfare. It is rather a magic web woven through and through us, like that magnetic system of which modern science speaks, penetrating us with a network, subtler than our subtlest nerves, yet bearing in it the central forces of the world. Can art represent men and women in these bewildering toils so as to give the spirit at least an equivalent for the sense of freedom?. . .Natural laws we shall never modify, embarrass us as they may; but there is still something in the nobler or less noble attitude with which we watch their fatal combinations. In those romances of Goethe and Victor Hugo, in some excellent work done *after* them, this entanglement, this network of law, becomes the tragic situation, in which certain groups of noble men and women work out for themselves a supreme *denouement.*[16]

Not only is the idea here very close to George Eliot's in its balance of necessity, responsibility, and sympathy; the images, even, are hers. The concern to "satisfy the spirit" of which Pater speaks is what Henry James called George Eliot's "extensive human sympathy."[17] The artist whose work is "so to rearrange the details of modern life, so to reflect it" as to achieve that end is she who writes of the "parable" of "optical selection" in chapter 27 of *Middlemarch*. And Pater's "magic web woven through and through us," that "entanglement" or "network of law," is what George Eliot saw before her as her work: "I at least have so much to do in unravelling certain human lots, and seeing how they were woven and interwoven, that all the light I can command must be concentrated on this particular web, and not dispersed over that tempting range of relevancies called the universe." But there is enough light, finally, for *Middlemarch* to seem a universe; and for George Eliot as well as for Pater this web of ordinary life becomes "the tragic situation, in which certain groups of noble men and women work out for themselves a supreme *denouement*." For George Eliot, this *denouement* can be worked out only in terms of the moral imagination, whose end is always "to enlarge men's sympathies" with each other, and whose means to that end is "radiance." It is the "spirit" of man that needs to be saved by art; and art works through "feeling," that "sort of knowledge" which so pervades *Middlemarch* as to be its most significant truth, the truth which may lead at last to wisdom.

NOTES

1. "Silly Novels by Lady Novelists," *Westminster Review* 66 (October 1856):461.
2. Quoted in Thomas Pinney, "More Leaves from George Eliot's Notebook," *Huntington Library Quarterly* 22 (1966):364.
3. John Keats, *Selected Poems and Letters*, ed. Douglas Bush (Cambridge, Mass., 1959), p.338.

4. F.W.H. Myers, *Essays--Modern* (London, 1883), pp.268-69.

5. Gordon S. Haight, ed., *The Letters of George Eliot*, 1 (New Haven, 1954-55):118.

6. See above p.594 [Editor].

7. See above p.598 [Editor].

8. Haight, *Letters*, 5:, 124, 127.

9. See above p.598 [Editor].

10. Joseph Jacobs, *Essays and Reviews* (London, 1891), p.72.

11. George Eliot went to see some of Rossetti's paintings in January of 1870, and then received a copy of his *Poems* (1870) from him early in May (Haight, *Letters*, 5:78, 98); see also James D. Merrit, *The Pre-Raphaelite Poem* (New York, 1966), pp.9-11.

12. See above p.590 [Editor].

13. Haight, *Letters*, 5:374.

14. The reviewers of *The Mill on the Floss* for *The Spectator* (7 April 1860) and *The Atlas* (14 April 1860) found some hint of the force of destiny governing the action of the novel. Reviewing *Middlemarch* for *The Spectator* (1 June 1872), Richard Holt Hutton called George Eliot "melancholy," "bitter," and "sceptical." For further contemporary remarks on George Eliot's philosophical position, see Edith Simcox, "*Middlemarch*," *The Academy* (1 January 1873), pp.1-4, and Sidney Colvin, "*Middlemarch*," *The Fortnightly Review* (19 January 1873), pp.142-47. Bernard Shaw has found that the characters of *Middlemarch* "have no more volition than billiard balls: they are moved only by circumstance and heredity": "Postscript. . .to the Preface," *Back to Methuselah, Complete Plays and Prefaces*, 2 (New York, 1963), pp.cv-cvi. Arnold Kettle writes that "George Eliot's view of society is in the last analysis a mechanistic and determinist one" and finds this the reason for the failure of her "Study of Provincial Life": *An Introduction to the English Novel*, 1 (London, 1951):185. George Levine has written an excellent essay on "Determinism and Responsibility in the Works of George Eliot" (*PMLA*, 77 [1962]: pp.268-79), concluding that she shared with John Stuart Mill the position that "the world is rigidly determined, even in cases of human choice, but that man remains responsible for his actions."

15. Part 6, ch 6. For the source of the quotation from Novalis, see W.E. Yuill, "'Character is Fate': a Note on Thomas Hardy, George Eliot, and Novalis," *Modern Language Review* 57 (1962): 401-2.

16. Walter Pater, *The Renaissance*, 2nd ed. (London, 1877), pp.224-25.

17. "*Felix Holt, the Radical*," *Nation* (16 August 1866), p.127.

IRONY IN THE MIND'S LIFE; MATURITY: GEORGE ELIOT'S *MIDDLEMARCH*

Virginia Quarterly Review, Autumn 1973

ROBERT COLES

George Eliot has built the whole novel *Middlemarch* around the theme of life's "indefiniteness," a word she stresses in the book's prelude. It is a prelude often analyzed, and one especially of interest today, when women are asserting their individuality and humanity against customs and laws (and generalizations) as embarrassingly irrational and insulting as they are instructive. (One century's, even one generation's, conventional wisdom is the next century's or generation's appalling stupidity.) Usually critics emphasize the connection between St. Theresa of Avila and Dorothea Brooke. Both are women very much curbed by the spirit of their time, yet gifted with energy and intelligence which, given other circumstances, might have been differently--in greater measure--put to use. The author intends no slight of what St. Theresa did accomplish--rather a lot--even as she has throughout the length of her novel extended the fullest of sympathy and respect to Dorothea. It is more a matter of recognition: some souls are passionate beyond the norm, and on that account fated for frustration. The destiny of such men and women may never suit their psychological and spiritual endowment. George Eliot was also haunted by those who never even come to be seen as "limited" by a particular historical era: "Here and there is born a St. Theresa, founders of nothing, whose loving heart-beats and sobs after an unattained goodness tremble off and are dispersed among hindrances, instead of centering in some long-recognizable deed."

She can be even more ironic, and in awe of life's unpredictability. Not only have there been those thwarted and disappointed who might have lived "an epic life"; some "born a Theresa" have ended up living "a life of mistakes." And the reason? She will side neither with "nature" nor "nurture"; perhaps some internal flaw, some "tragic failure" undercuts such would-be individuals of distinction, or perhaps it is the "meanness of opportunity" all too many, indeed the vast majority, of this world's growing children must accept, like it or not, as their inheritance. Still, she is not quite satisfied with that rather broad and flexible way of looking at human growth and development. Are women, for instance, afflicted with an "inconvenient indefiniteness," God-given most likely? She asks the question, and naturally has no answer. She herself is rather comfortable with "indefiniteness"; it is a psychological fact of life: "the limits of variation" to human behavior are rather broad--perhaps an unpromising way to start a novel which is called "a study of provincial life."

Throughout *Middlemarch* George Eliot seems unable to forget that word "indefiniteness." The novel's plot, its characters, its psychological and philosophical themes--they all resist clear-cut definition. In the eight books that make up the author's "study," stories give way to other stories; and unattractive individuals to our surprise demand our sympathy while those we have felt close to suddenly are found wanting. No central argument prevails, even as no one person dominates the narrative. It is a world of refined gradations we have to comprehend, a world where political reformers, bent on doing what obviously needs to be done, are shown to be, at the same time, foolish, frivolous, or uninformed. It is a world where hypocrites are not segregated and scoffed at; we meet one of them, get to know him well--and before we are through knowing him we have learned of his thoughtfulness, his sincerity, his genuine capacity for moral introspection. It is a world where well-meaning idealists falter and reveal severe mistakes in judgment. It is a world where neither abstract "social forces" nor "historical conditions" nor individual initiatives dominate; they all are mixed so subtly into a particular narrative, into a *story*, that they resist the critic's desire to extract them and weigh their separate "influence." It is the world of England's Midlands around 1831 and 1832, just before the Reform Bill was enacted; and there is no doubt that the values of every one of the individuals portrayed reflect that geographical and temporal fact.

On the other hand, various individuals (and not just the ones we meet at greatest length) are capable of being very much themselves. With a determined assist from the author, they say things that transcend any era's confines, and they not infrequently act in ways that jolt the reader; he has not been prepared by the author for what he learns has been said or done. It is almost as if George Eliot is determined that this long and ambitious story not be any one thing--but rather combine elements of fiction that other novelists are perfectly willing to sort out and use separately for particular novels.

George Eliot is not one to come up with unqualified "causes" to explain the direction of lives. She has written this novel to show not only how history limits would-be Theresas, but Lydgates as well. She is interested in how psychological flaws lend themselves to history's hand; and in particular, she is after an understanding--she knows it will always be limited--of her own kind: those who think a lot, as Dorothea's sister Celia (not a likely spokeswoman for the author) says, miss a whole lot. So, Dorothea and the young doctor Lydgate merge thematically. The latter has not just naïveté, plain and simple, but a version of it: he is unsophisticated enough to be so preoccupied with his own ideas that he overlooks Rosamond's. His condescension and attendant openness to psychological exploitation are not on the surface; I do not think they can be characterized as "unconscious" either. There is, quite simply, a limit to what any mind can hold. Lydgate's, as the author tells us, is intensely preoccupied with the strategy for a virtual war upon certain customs, upon human fallibility and credulity; under such circumstances he had no time to bear down on other issues

--and as well, no capacity to do so. We are not only *motivated* to do things, or ignore doing things; we make choices, and having done so, we have, as George Eliot puts it, a "preoccupation." As a result, things happen to us--and we are, psychologically, elsewhere: thinking, planning, dreaming, conspiring. An obsessed doctor has only so much time to analyze his would-be wife. The issue is not intentionality, open or disguised, but the range of experience that a finite human being can deal with. (God told Adam and Eve there *was* such a range, and it seems they had to find that out for themselves.)

As for Dorothea, she is no less fully occupied mentally. We felt close to Lydgate, and we are terribly moved by her predicament. In *Middlemarch*'s struggle between the "children of light" and the "children of darkness," she is clearly on "our" side, the side of those who read novels like *Middlemarch* and try conscientiously to apply its message to a later century's problems. Still, we have been forewarned with respect to her, also, and when George Eliot wants to exert caution on us she doesn't mince words: "Her mind was theoretic, and yearned by its nature after some lofty conception of the world which might frankly include the parish of Tipton and her own rule of conduct there; she was enamoured of intensity and greatness, and rash in embracing whatever seemed to her to have those aspects; likely to seek martyrdom, to make retractions, and then to incur martyrdom after all in a quarter where she had not sought it."

Dorothea's is the mind of one who knew by heart many passages of Pascal's *Pensées*. It is the mind of one who recognized and scorned the banalities and superficialities of provincial life. It is also the mind of one who--moving from irony to blunt critical comment--"retained very childlike ideas about marriage." And at this point "childlike" is linked with an interesting illustrative sequence: "She felt sure that she would have accepted the judicious Hooker, if she had been born in time to save him from that wretched mistake he made in matrimony; or John Milton when his blindness had come on; or any of the other great men whose odd habits it would have been glorious piety to endure; but an amiable handsome baronet, who said 'Exactly' to her remarks even when she expressed uncertainty--how could he affect her as a lover?"

Is it childlike to want to "save"--in this case, people from what seems to be their foreordained fate? When George Eliot wrote *Middlemarch* she had herself given up an earlier evangelical religion (her father's) and now preferred to talk of "human lots" and our "destiny," which in her mind has its own unfathomable momentum. It could be that for her "childlike" means ignorant or untutored or naive: to think that one has lived so little, or lived so long yet still so little, as to think that one can undo what has been fated. On the other hand, there is the issue of presumptuousness; and children can be that, too. Linked with presumptuousness, rather often, is self-righteousness.

A clue to the author's interpretation of Dorothea's "childlike ideas" comes much later on, when she has her thoroughly honorable and untainted Caleb Garth wash his hands of Bulstrode when his dubious past begins to be revealed. Confronted with a troubled soul, Garth rather too quickly passes judgment, missing thereby a great deal of moral complexity which the author takes pains to supply us--and connect to everyone, Garth included. Here Garth is being "childlike." Bulstrode rushes to save, willy nilly, and himself needs saving. Garth rushes to escape the presence of corruption, blithely unaware of his own complicity as a fellow human being and neighbor. Garth's "childlike" behavior is not without obtuseness and malice--and both stem from a version of the author's oft-mentioned "preoccupation," that of the self with itself. Charity is lost, because it requires a gesture outward. Common sense is lost, because it requires the same thing--a look at what is reasonably possible, as opposed to dreamed of or insisted upon. Those who designed the "French social theories" might not find such a conception of "childlike" congenial.

In fact the author might well have substituted "childish" for "childlike." The words have different connotations. The latter suggests the admirable qualities children often have, their directness, their charming and affectionate side, their lack of so many of the disguises it takes years of living to develop. The former refers to the petulance children can show, as well their undeveloped mentality, their ignorance, and even more, their inability to understand much of what is happening around them. Further, children love to pretend, build castles in the sky as well as on a nearby beach.

I write this as I work with Pueblo Indian and Chicano children in New Mexico. As I was going over *Middlemarch* yet again, trying to gain some sense of George Eliot's intentions, so to speak toward her various characters, I thought of a girl of eight I visited in one of the Pueblos north of Albuquerque. Once I asked her what she pictured her life like in the future. She was in a lively and frolicsome mood; maybe a teasing mood, though she would have denied that allegation. She thought for a minute, then told me she wouldn't mind "rescuing people." Well, of course, I wanted to know whether she had any people in mind. Yes, there is an uncle of hers, who has a bad leg, and can't walk well. And there is her grandmother, who feels tired all the time and gets chest pains when she exerts herself. There are also those various dead people she has heard about; some of them had very difficult lives, and she wonders whether "by some magic" they won't come back again, so that they can have an easier, better life. If so, she would certainly be right there, anxious to help them, busy "rescuing" them. In a final summary, she looked me right in the eye, a touch defiantly, and said: "Rescuing people is the best good you can do, if you get a chance." There followed a more historical discussion, initiated by her: the Pueblo Indians, she reminded me, have been helpful to other Indians--have rescued them by teaching them how to raise crops and live a less nomadic, more settled kind of life. I suppose I could have tried to push us back to a more psychological line of talk; though it could be that she, like George Eliot, knew a lot better than I how to "integrate" her particular imagination--her reveries, her aspirations, the "night-pictures" she speaks of seeing, while asleep--with her people's historical experience and their ongoing social and cultural life.

But ought I turn that child into an all-knowing authority, someone we must uncritically look up to? She can be silly and impractical. She can vex her parents no end with her peevish, obstinate ways. She can also ignore her younger sister's crying, immediate needs--as she goes about her own moment-to-moment play. Her mother has often had to warn me about something, and I will let her tell what it is: "She's wise, like you say. But she's not always wise. There will be times when I get so angry at her I have to fold my arms and grit my teeth, or else I'll hit her, and I don't want to do that. She'll be talking so nice, and meanwhile her sister is in trouble, and she hasn't helped. Or she'll be playing, and I'm in trouble, and she won't lift a finger--and it's she who's done the spilling or the breaking. Children have to learn to grow up, I guess. I tell my children that things don't just appear on trees, and meals just don't happen, and a house doesn't just become clean. You have to train yourself to pay attention to all the little things. You can't just be sitting and dreaming about rescuing people, like she told you, and all that. I rescue her every morning--from those hunger pangs she has when she wakes up. And let me tell you, I don't dream when I do my everyday work--cook and clean up and get the whole house organized so all of them are ready to go to work or school."

II

This is the one deviation in the direction of my own present "everyday work" that I will permit myself here. I do so because I believe the tensions George Eliot tries to bring alive in a Dorothea or a Dr. Lydgate are shared by those who never become as singular as they each did (by virtue of being made the center of an author's attention, in contrast to all those other Middlemarchers who are in the "background"), never mind as saintly and thereby historical a figure as a Theresa of Avila. And it is ironic that one like Pascal (were George Eliot writing today, Kierkegaard might replace him) becomes so influential to Dorothea. For all his force of mind, Pascal knew that religious faith had to be grounded, ultimately, in each person's ordinary, dreary perhaps, often boring, certainly undramatic daily life. There is a conflict in Dorothea and Lydgate, also in Ladislaw, between their secular faiths (which prompt their ambitions) and their everyday lives. That is, they feel the antagonistic tension between the prophetic and pastoral modes of living. Dorothea and Lydgate are heavily inclined toward the former; Ladislaw would like to be, but lacks the fierce will those other two possess.

Dorothea's "theoretic" mind, Lydgate's dreams of a new form of medical practice, have an enormous effect on their lives, not to mention the lives of others. Yet, at times that quality of her mind, those dreams of his, seem to be dispossessed, in a vacuum almost. We occasionally wonder what they do when they are not trying to implement their ideals. The author is tempted with the romantic hero--full of special and all too glamorous aspirations, and headed always for spectacular affirmation or an apocalyptic decline. Only at times, though; George Eliot wants to fix those two and everyone else in the world and show how Middlemarch sets limits on any mind's ingenuity or expansiveness, shapes even the most original of dreams. Of course she was tempted as a Victorian story-teller simply to let Dorothea loose, spring free Lydgate and his aspirations--and offer us their dramatic, not seriously impeded fulfillment. The two of them are memorable, and in so far as they become so, page by page, they obtain at least a share of the distinction each fervently sought--urged on by a mixture of egoism and moral uprightness that no one in his or her right mind can ever sort out into percentages.

The novel obtains momentum, however, because the novelist chooses to indicate the antagonism I mentioned between the pastoral and the prophetic. Even as a Pueblo mother can contrast her child's dream-like (childlike?) state with the demands that a given society makes on a girl of eight, never mind her older sister and brothers or her mother and father, so George Eliot begins *Middlemarch* by contrasting Celia's accomodating spirit to Dorothea's rebellious, at times almost agitated state of mind. We are disposed to scorn Celia; she questions no one or nothing, is willing to be dominated, taken for granted, denied her rights as an individual human being. On the other hand, the preface with its mention of Theresa is followed by a great deal of favorable comment on Dorothea and her aspirations. If Middlemarch or any other part of England is going to change, people will have to be brought to think more like her, less like Celia.

But nowhere does George Eliot make us feel that if Middlemarch *is* going to change, Dorothea and Lydgate will be the kind of people who do it. Nor is it that the two of them were a shade ahead of their time. Lydgate was; but he needn't have stumbled as he did. Dorothea might indeed have lived a different life, as the preface tell us, had she been born in some other place, at some other time. However, one cannot simply make that kind of extrapolation; in fact, the whole point of *Middlemarch* is to make clear what it means to be born in a particular place, to live at a certain time. There are traits that transcend place and time (one moves from Theresa to Dorothea to that Pueblo girl) but the setting for those traits is crucial and (as the length and complexity of this novel demonstrate) ought never be taken for granted. As for who or what *does* cause social change, the author seems to feel that the answer is to be found not in character portrayal so much as the vast yet detailed social portrayal, mediated through her characters, that is *Middlemarch*.

III

Middlemarch starts out with the words "Miss Brooke." The Midlands provincial world is almost assumed; for a while we get little formal description of it. Rather, the general atmosphere as well as various particulars of a sociological nature come through in the minor characters, whose various distinctions of speech and attitude have a cumulative effect as instruments of representation and analysis. And even more insidiously, as it were, Dorothea and Lydgate, Ladislaw, Bulstrode, and Rosamond, are made to reflect that same atmosphere.

By the end of *Middlemarch* we have been shown the power of a given social system; but Eliot's power as a novelist never wanes. She has created a character as well as evoked a rural scene at a given moment in history, and she remains faithful to her imaginative life as well as the world of Middlemarch. If she fails with respect to Dorothea, it is in denying her the intensity of scrutiny given Bulstrode. We are expected to accept Dorothea's personality as given; she is idealistic, she has the reformer's zeal, she believes in certain principles of justice and equality, stripped (one is to gather) of any Divine Sanction. She is never carried back in time, though, as Bulstrode is. The complexities of her life are those that grownups have to face, but because she is carried forward in time (inevitable in a novel like George Eliot's) the problem of repetition comes up. Why does she choose the men she does? What about her prompts such peculiar and recurrent self-abasement, a contrast indeed with the haughtiness she also keeps revealing?

Are those questions that belong to another age--ours? Even though the author is quite aware that we have to contend with an unconscious (she speaks of "invisible thoroughfares which are the first lurking-places of anguish, mania, and crime"), we may demand too much of her when we notice a little petulantly that she has not sufficiently analyzed those "first lurking-places" of Dorothea's. Yet, in the case of Bulstrode she shows herself willing and able to do more than take note of such "places." She goes into an extended analysis of what made this man what he has become; and for the most part her emphasis is retrospective and psychological rather than descriptive and sociological. From Bulstrode's tormented life, years in the making, we learn to think about people in one way. From Dorothea's persistent if flawed effort to make something of herself in relationship to a given society (and through the agency, it might be put, of two husbands), we pick up a quite different perspective. No portrayal in *Middlemarch* is exclusively psychological or sociological, but Bulstrode's motives get astonishingly intense scrutiny, and Dorothea's life to a considerable extent prompts us to think about provincial life in the first part of the 1830's. (I differ with Henry James, when he describes Bulstrode as "too diffusely treated.")

George Eliot operates out of a tradition of fervent moral Puritanism, with the Christian underpinnings considerably weakened but by no means abandoned. It is a tradition still alive; D.H. Lawrence and Faulkner belong to it. It is a tradition that takes seriously man's peculiar position on this earth, and concerns itself with judgment. There is nothing neutral or detached about D.H. Lawrence. He may despise elements of Chrisitianity and the middle-class commercial world that embraces the institutional church for its own purposes, but he has not lost interest in Heaven and Hell, in the saved and the damned. Nor is he afraid or undesirous of condemning or uplifting, if not rendering worthy of worship. Faulkner may be a little less explicit, but the message still gets across: there is good and evil, personified as well as distributed randomly; and the novelist must center his attention constantly on the struggle between the two. I suppose their attitude, very much George Eliot's, is one of moral earnestness. Sometimes in this century that earnestness takes on a decidedly psychological cast; and sometimes a cast of mind can become an obsession. But self-scrutiny was not invented in Vienna around the turn of this century, nor the psychological observer's ability to keep himself or herself substantially removed from a particular "subject," though still of opinion about the person's worth.

IV

In Bulstrode George Eliot had a chance to put her own religious experiences to work. She was, anyway, a moralist first, a romancer later. The man is thoroughly pompous and self-serving, also manipulative and power-hungry. When he first enters into a crisis, and begins to appear even more wicked and unsavory, we merely take note of the fact and feel further educated about the facts of life. Middlemarch, like other areas of this world, has its fair share of hypocrites and deceivers; bad has gone to worse under the careful tutelage of this student of "provincial life," and we, most likely eager to rejoice in the demise of at least one fraudulent man of influence, can only feel satisfied.

Suddenly a remarkable shift occurs in the novel, and soon enough we are deprived of a good deal of our pleasure. Satire is foregone. Mockery is lacking. Sympathy appears unexpectedly; but even more telling, Bulstrode is connected to all of us, not with a pointed finger, but in an almost offhand manner. We are ensnared when we had expected to stand removed and gloat. Bulstrode is in that sense quite definitely treated "diffusely." But when Henry James says "he never grips the reader's attention," his criticism might well be accepted only with a proviso: with good reason, because no reader accepts such a shrewdly and powerfully launched, such a penetrating, critique of his own "nature" as a human being, alive in a Middlemarch of his own, without an effort to let go and run.

In certain respects Bulstrode is the most powerfully drawn character in *Middlemarch*--the strongest person, the one we struggle with most, perhaps the one from whom we learn the most. Even in the prelude we are told that Dorothea will never quite live up to her possibilities. Dr. Lydgate wins our admiration; later on he disappoints us, or we cover up our impatience toward him with pity. Ladislaw is indeed weakly portrayed; if only he *were* a first-class dilettante-- anything to give some direction to his personality. Casaubon is not so easily dismissed, thanks to the author's stubborn sympathy for everyone she creates. But an old, tired man obsessed with obscure philosophical points is hardly the one to capture our imagination. He, too, becomes pitiable--and maybe at times defended by us as an object of exploitation: it is no joy to become an instrument of an another's moral passion. In contrast, Bulstrode seems to appear out of nowhere and ultimately vanish with no trace left--yet he is unforgettable, even haunting.

He is a banker at first acquaintance, a newcomer to Middlemarch, one who is selfish, and again, power-hungry, but also progressive. The old established wealth, such as that possessed by Dorothea's brother-in-law Sir James Chettam, is unobtrusive and arguably more dangerous. Sir James wants no changes. Why should a perfectly ordered and comfortable Middlemarch be undone by new ideas, new programs? He is the staunch conservative, not romanticized, however. He has his clear interests, and will fight to defend them. He is haughty, smug, self-satisfied--and headed for a decline in power as a result of the political reforms on the brink of being enacted. Celia loves him and he is good to her, provided she keep within the limits he has set. His antagonism to Dorothea is maintained throughout the novel--he had first wanted to marry her-- and only somewhat attentuated, in a live-and-let-live arrangement at the very end; for such stubborn pique we are disposed against him. He uses social custom to enforce his whims and prejudices. But his manners and background shield him from criticisms Bulstrode easily comes upon.

Sir James manipulates, pulls levers of influence, dominates, inflicts vengeance--but all the while displays impeccable manners. As a result he is seen as a proper gentleman. Refinement cloaks a mind's nature, a person's deeds. Bulstrode has no such sanctuary. He is blunt and forceful, looked up to because he is a man of means, but not for any other reason. No one in Middlemarch at that time wanted to lose its aristocrats; and one way of keeping them is to be blind to their schemes and warts, their solid capacity to be as malevolent as anyone else. Bulstrode was always there, a man to be feared and suspected. He may have done many things to warrant just such an attitude from his fellow Middlemarchers, but even before the critical drama of his life unfolds, we find him no mere greedy banker. His bluntness and candor contrast with the deceit that social prominence can cover up. His reformer's instincts are also apparent. He is a rational man, and impatient with outmoded traditions, or superstitions. He is with Lydgate in his desire to reform the medical profession. True, his progressive inclinations are with justice seen as excuses for his greed or ambition. If the old customs are ended, the old authorities weakened, his kind of aggressive wealth has a much easier time extending itself.

But reform was needed badly, and George Eliot makes it all too clear that the kind of enlightened, regenerative conservatism Edmund Burke placed his faith in was simply not forthcoming in Middlemarch. Sir James Chettam is no political monster, anxious to turn the clock back and keep everyone firmly under tow. He is quite simply self-contented without exception. He will lift no finger to make anyone else even remotely as well-off as he is. Consequently, others have to have the nerve, the drive, the skill and cunning, to move in, if not take over. Then it is, of course, that the Chettams of this world look surprised: why the uproar? And besides, look at those complaining or trying to exert their influence--their gall, their coarseness! Meanwhile, not a few people, whatever their actual needs, side with the Chettams. Perhaps they are people who have given up hope for any change in their own condition--or perhaps they find satisfaction in favoring what is established and has an aura of respectability and gentility, as against the brash, the new, the somewhat ungraceful. Perhaps, not unlike Hobbes or Edmund Burke, they prefer the authority that *is*, and dread the uncertainty if not the chaos which often enough accompanies social change.

There are rhythms to injustice which become familiar; new noises, however promising, only grate upon the ears. Nor is resignation of a highly philosophical kind to be dismissed as beyond the ken of a peasant. Caleb Garth, who abruptly turns on Bulstrode, is more than a peasant, anyway, though he has the somewhat exaggerated honor and righteousness city people in search of heroes sometimes grant peasants. They are felt to be so good, those men of the earth--so decent, so hard working, so uncorrupted, so near to being Rousseau's natural man. They are credited with seeing so much--more than the Bulstrodes, more than the Chettams, more than the Casaubons, even the Lydgates--and also with being beyond temptation: they hold everything together. However, the truth may simply be they stand with the prevailing system often enough, and block social and political changes that might well help them live better. They do so not out of virtue, nor out of malice, either. They do not wish to cut their noses to spite their faces. Resignation may indeed be the word. They feel in their bones what the new programs and leaders will bring: yet more mischief.

Against such a background of forces and counter forces, established authority and rising power, crying needs and grave doubts about anyone's reasons for meeting those needs, Bulstrode suddenly moves from a peripheral figure, one of those minor Middlemarchers who have mainly sociological interest for us, into the exact center of the novel's stage. With him comes Raffles, whose name and manner are right out of Dickens. With him, too, comes an acceleration of drama that almost takes the reader aback. After nearly five hundred pages of almost stately progression (which reflects England's remarkable nineteenth-century capacity for gradual but significant political transformation) we suddenly meet up with blackmail, night-terrors, political anguish, a virtual murder, followed by the swift exposure and ruin of a prominent citizen.

All this is done, however, with a minimum of melodrama. Even more important, the author shirks other temptations. She has already told us how pious a man Bulstrode is, how devoted to evangelical religion. She might easily have exposed not only him but his beliefs--his constant outward show of "faith," his larger corruptions of spirit which more than match the lies and deceptions Raffles happens to have known and threatens to reveal. A pompous banker who preaches Jesus Christ's message, then goes on to the next bit of cynical, financial double-dealing, Bulstrode may not be the first hypocrite in the history of the novel, but one might have thought him irresistible to George Eliot. She has never been really cruel to any of her characters, but she is a teacher and a moralist, and Bulstrode offers her the resort to a serviceable tradition of edifying satire.

Properly restrained, yet deftly used, such satire can be enormously suggestive. The world is full of show and pretense, and we crave their unmasking. Particularly helpful is the novelist who doesn't ruin the job with scorn; then we become uncomfortable because we feel somehow cheated. Insincerity and sanctimony are not as flagrant and extraordinary as some satirists make them out to be. Anyway, we fancy ourselves sophisticated, and we want a subtle if not gentle analysis; that way a lot more ground can be covered, many more connections made. After all, Bulstrode was not Middlemarch's only liar or crook dressed up in good clothes and married well and able to intimidate people not only financially but morally. Pharisees plagued Christ; and this side of heaven they persist everywhere--certainly in churches all over that bear His name. He was betrayed by His disciple; He is betrayed every day by those who call on others to believe in Him. It is an old story, and Middlemarch is no special place where a different twist to the story will be found. Or so it seems for a while, as Raffles wields his power and Bulstrode begins to crumble--though he fights back with every resource at his command.

Yet, gradually the author introduces a new element in her narrative. She reveals how skilled a story-teller she can be; as mentioned, the narrative quickens, and plenty of action takes place. But more than that happens. At a certain point we begin to lose Bulstrode as the object of scorn. We even begin to sympathize with him, however obvious his crimes. Indeed, as he plots and calculates, tries everything his mind, well versed in tricks and bluff, can come up with, we almost wish him success. Raffles is a no-good, and not in any way explored psychologically, so good-riddance to him is easy. But the way Bulstrode's mind is revealed to us contrasts with the level and range of analysis given every other character in the novel. The motives of others are brought to light in a leisurely fashion, and to a great extent, in order to build up a variety of individuals, each of them different in a number of respects. In the case of Bulstrode something else is done. His complexity of character, his anguish, his malevolence, all of it virtually explodes upon us, and before we know it we are strangely caught up--implicated is perhaps the word. The crucial turn in the narrative occurs in chapter 68:

> For Bulstrode shrunk from a direct lie with an intensity disproportionate to the number of his more direct misdeeds. But many of these misdeeds were like the subtle muscular movements which are not taken account of in the consciousness, though they bring about the end that we fix our mind on and desire. And it is only what we are vividly conscious of that we can vividly imagine to be seen by Omniscience.

We already know that Bulstrode is quite able to deceive people, yet the author now brings up this distinction of "a direct lie." Furthermore, words like "consciousness" and "conscious" appear. Even God becomes Omniscience. The question of awareness gets linked to that of "a direct lie" or "more indirect misdeeds." Bulstrode may not only fool others; it is quite possible that he himself does not know exactly what his intentions are, what he is aiming at, trying to accomplish. We know for sure that this man is no vague, wondering, self-deluded failure. Nor is he a mental case. He seems all too effective and directed in manner. More than others in Middlemarch he seems to have a clear idea of what he is after. Yet, of all things his mind's activity is called into question--almost as if he were alive today and some of our lawyers and psychiatrists, concerned about the issue of right-versus-wrong in the light of psychoanalytic determinism, were not quite sure how to regard the man. To some extent Raffles' behavior, steadily worse, makes us move closer to Bulstrode. Raffles is appeased, bought off, then reneges and makes new demands and threats. He also begins to deteriorate, break his part of the bargain, drink to excess, and talk the same way. And soon he is very sick, quite possibly on his death bed. It is natural for us to feel that Bulstrode may deserve our contempt, but not the injury an alcoholic confidence man and ne'er-do-well wants to impose.

While all that is going on in *our* minds, George Eliot is moving closer and closer toward Bulstrode's private mental life. His "nervous energy" under the strain is mentioned. There is a marvelous scene in which one kind of liar confronts another. Bulstrode mobilizes his "cold, resolute bearing" and Raffles, so full of swagger, so convinced he has the upper hand, melts. Bulstrode's servants imagine Raffles "a poor relation," rather a nice moment for Bulstrode, given what he is afraid of. And by this time we are enough with Bulstrode to settle for that as a proper punishment: let Raffles properly embarrass him. That way the banker will come off his high horse, and stop preaching all the time. He will have to attend his own before he finds fault with others.

But matters go from bad to worse. Raffles becomes more garrulous, hence dangerous. He also starts becoming a victim of his success. Ever greedy, he demands more from Bulstrode, then drinks away what he has secured. For "various motives" Bulstrode stiffens his defenses, squarely threatens to call Raffles bluff, but is generous with him, noticing the man's decline and perhaps hoping against hope for more of it. None of that is especially revealing to us, but it is rendered forcefully and tersely. Even when the author comes up with one of her especially pointed paragraphs of a single sentence, ("Who can know how much of his most inward life is made up of the thoughts he believes other men to have about him, until that fabric of opinion is threatened with ruin?") we are still relatively detached from Bulstrode. We have simply been reminded once again that no one's life is all that private; that a society like Middlemarch's works its way into everyone's mind and heart, exacts tributes, prompts attitudes and desires, generates assumptions, imposes restrictions or inhibitions, expects and to a degree obtains a form of allegiance, a code of behavior--all of it, as the rhetorical question indicates, the more influential because submerged in life's everyday flow of feeling and action, rather than noticed and considered.

Relentlessly the author pushes on, however. She goes from those "other men" to Bulstrode. She has this particular person examine himself, wonder why Raffles has come with his threats as well as when he will leave and stay away. "Divine glory" comes to mind: can God have his purposes, unapparent to man? Bulstrode the man of piety had always thought God's purposes could be ascertained--proven visible, even, by a show of religious devotion. Now a more inscrutable and devious God is conjured up by the desperate man. And in such desperation he becomes a deeper, more reflective man. Rather as Adam and Eve must once have, he wonders to himself what God does see: everything? only so much? Anyway, might an apparent disaster be but the advance sign of some good news? Might the Lord visit and chastise those he has singled out for eventual recognition of quite another kind? Is submission to a tormentor like Raffles in truth obedience to God? Or ought one be more self-protective, so that the good Lord sees quite clearly the justice of one's cause, and one's faith in oneself?

As Bulstrode asks himself such questions, directly or by implication, his mind moves back and forth from the things of this world to an almost Biblical resignation before the felt presence of an altogether different World. God's mysterious ways, and Satan's obsess him; and his mental activity does not disintegrate into psychopathology or into cowering religious ingratiation, a last-ditch effort to stave off disaster through Divine intervention. His ruminations and moments of confrontation, not long and not overly dramatic, are nevertheless worthy of St. Augustine's. A sinner, he is also a sincere believer--but also a thoroughly imperfect one. A moral hypocrite and a man capable of being mercilessly out for himself, he can be conscientious, open to new ideas, genuinely self-critical in his own stop-and-go journey toward repentence. He never loses his scheming, vastly materialistic side. He can pray hard and long, while all the time estimating what to do with his various properties. Yet his prayers, his desperate effort to meet with God and understand His purposes, are an unquestionable part of him, and significantly, are not subjected to the author's mockery. Even the obvious irony of his conflicting dispositions begins to wilt under the heat of his scrupulous self-examination before God: we become, with him, totally immersed in a supplicant's religious fervor, and begin to forget his other qualities. In his own way he asks why--not only why Raffles has appeared thus to curse and quite possibly destroy him, but why God tempts man with possibilities, moments of triumph, situations just ambiguous enough to allow the worst to be done in such a way that it seems not so bad, after all, and maybe even, all things considered, rather virtuous.

As Bulstrode struggles with himself, a number of such philosophical and theological issues became subtly absorbed into his moment of intense and prayerful introspection--a psychological "crisis" we would call it. He wonders how God can possibly permit him, a man of avowed faith, to be destroyed by an obvious heathen. He prays, whereas Raffles drinks and has nothing to do with any church. He prays with all his heart and soul, whereas others, his self-righteous creditors, who he fears will soon enough be gossiping about him, go to church on Sundays, but that is that. But if he can be quite self-righteous himself, he can also feel himself to be in the very midst of a riddle which none of us can ever resolve. "He knew that he ought to say, 'Thy will be done'; and he said it often." On the other hand, he hoped against hope that "the will of God might be the death of that hated man."

Raffles ultimately disintegrates and goes into what we would call "delirium tremens" (perhaps even "alcoholic encephalopathy"), and know how to treat, if not necessarily reverse. Doctors then knew less to do. Often the patient was helped into coma with more liquor; even substantial doses of opium were given. Bulstrode called in Dr. Lydgate and the latter, ahead of his time and well read in the latest medical advances, explains what ought to be done: no brandy or anything else, and extremely careful administration of opium. The author has prepared the way for one of the great self-confrontations in the history of the novel.

She is no Dostoevsky; she goes about developing her characters with more restraint, and they never will speak with the dramatic intensity the Karamazovs possess as they reflect upon just about everything that has to do with heaven and earth. But in her quiet way she enables Bulstrode to look at himself and judge himself with exceptional subtlety. More than that, as mentioned, the reader is drawn into this self-indictment to an astonishing degree. Before George Eliot is through with Bulstrode he has become nothing less than an only slightly exaggerated version of everyone else, Caleb Garth included. In so doing a scapegoat is denied us, and as well a romantic hero. What we are left with, of course, is Middlemarch, with its many different sorts of people, some better and some worse, but none without sins and very definite limitations as human beings, even as none are without impressive if not redeeming virtues. Interestingly enough, the one character in the novel who has none of the latter, the one character who lends himself to easy and unqualified categorization, is John Raffles. In a stroke the author through him distinguishes herself from other authors, and makes her point rather clear. This outsider is not part of Middlemarch's world, so his seeming lack of complexity, his outright evil, itself left unexplored, is not to be taken for granted. Rather, Raffles is outside not only the "provincial life" of Middlemarch, but the province of *Middlemarch*. He is an outsider such as Bulstrode or Dr. Lydgate or Ladislaw is not. They have come into the community and tried in their various ways to become known. The more of themselves they reveal, the more complicated they become, the less clear-cut their involvements with others turn out to be. The author takes the trouble to delve into them, and as she does, we feel ourselves going up and down, in this direction or that direction. Is Dr. Lydgate "strong" or "weak"? Does he suffer from some "fatal flaw," and if so, precisely what is its nature? Alternatively, is the well-intentioned doctor simply the victim (eventually, rather than at any particular moment) of a series of developments no one could have foreseen; a series not at all "determined" by anything in his "personality"? Ought we subscribe to the author's preface, and her conclusion as well, and see Dorothea hopelessly entangled in the structures and blind spots of a given time and place? Should we, on the other hand, give full vent to our occasional feeling that Dorothea needs a good shaking, or after our fashion, an extended "course" of psychotherapy--so that she stops thinking or saying or doing any number of things that only lead to trouble and her enfeeblement, for which we are then asked to grieve? In the case of Rosamond, are we to see her as a self-centered shallow, but thoroughly resourceful woman who has a certain kind of emotional make-up, which Dr. Lydgate, to his own sorrow, caught glimpses of rather late in the game, or is she one of many examples of what a materialistic social system does to those who are part of it?

V

Those kinds of questions, to the author's great credit, never really get an answer. We are left unsatisfied, floundering even, and at a loss to figure out the author's intentions. And maybe she herself had to struggle with a conflict or two--and had the sense not to try to resolve within herself as a writer some contradictions that must have presented themselves to her as she wrote. The novelist in her may well have tried to portray particular individuals, but there is that need in all of us I have mentioned earlier on--one which philosophers, theologians and moralists often show quite clearly: to tidy up life's hodgepodge, sort out the irritating jumble of ideas and passions and forces that go to make up a person's existence, so that we can make a judgment, not only in the Calvinist fashion, but out of a less ambitious, more humdrum desire simply to feel we have got our bearings.

It is all the more ironic, therefore, that as Bulstrode becomes distinctly and with justice known as a kind of imposter--he has falsified his past, pretended and dissembled even to his wife--he concurrently begins to win us over, not as admirers, but as fellow sufferers. The closer he looks at himself the closer the author asks us to look at him, get to know him from within and at some length, the harder it gets to square what we know he has done with what we know about his "nature"--as it is discovered by the man himself, in the midst of this terrible moment in his life. He has all along had a good marriage; his wife has been devoted to him, and he to her. But the depth of their feeling, the strength of the bond between them, was unknown to either until this event tested them separately and together. Might they have, anyway, realized what they meant to one another? Do we ever find out abstractly--that is, in "analysis," done alone or with another's help--how we feel, or do our feelings emerge only in consequence of events, which not only bring out what is dormant but generate new possibilities for feeling? Again, such questions are never even asked until something has *happened*, brought us up short, made us stop and wonder about "human nature": exactly how much real freedom do we ever have, given all that is around us and all that we have experienced?

To all those questions George Eliot has no "answers"; only the richly suggestive fabric of her novel for us to gaze at and, more often than not, feel in awe of, rather than be made the recipients of "solutions." Her much discussed "wisdom" is not abstract, but tied to the particulars of individuals to whom she has virtually given the breath of life, so strikingly *themselves* are they! She has compelled us to regard their moral ambiguities and complexities of character and temperament with increasing relaxation. They emerge out of the context of their lives, yet they never become mere symbols for that context. One moment they are distinct types, or themselves and no one else, a bit later on they blur into the nearest available crowd. So far as the world and what it offers is concerned, that so-called "environment" (or "society," or "culture," or "historical era") which impinges upon all of us, she has given us Middlemarch, as hard to fasten down as it is easy to locate in space and time. Middlemarch is "provincial" all right, but no more so than any community; in it are the refined and the coarse, the thoughtful and the narrow-minded, the sophisticated and the ignorant, the urbane and the countrified or rude, the mostly honorable and the--well, less than honorable. If there was in the nineteenth century any community of grown-up people which didn't possess such a mixture of people, such a mixture of those qualities and others in *each* of its members, then George Eliot was no doubt unaware of the place when she wrote *Middlemarch*.

As for us today, will the "counter-culture" or "transcendence" or a place "where the wasteland ends" permit us at last to glimpse a community George Eliot never really expected any of us to find--this side of Heaven at least? No doubt if she were alive today she would keep her customary reserve, and refuse us an absolutely certain reply. She has such a habit of turning coins over, moving from one chair to another, looking out of every window she can find. She has such a habit of arguing for, then against--even when the "against" is, in turn, directed at a "for" previously held by her. She has such a habit of turning round on us, taking away what she has seemingly given for keeps--only to come forth with yet another gift, and a valuable one at that. She won't let up with her paradoxes and ambiguities, her complexities and contradictions; most of all there are ironies, so elusive and yet firmly instructive, so hard to see coming, but in retrospect, inevitable or seemingly foreordained. At the very end, she lets us know what it is all about, and the "finale" is not so different from the "prelude":

> Every limit is a beginning as well as an ending. Who can quit young lives after being long in company with them, and not desire to know what befell them in their after-years? For the fragment of a life, however typical, is not the sample of an even web; promises may not be kept, and an ardent outset may be followed by declension; latent powers may find their long-waited opportunity; a past error may urge a grand retrieval.

It is not exactly a definitive statement, nor one congenial to an age like ours, when determinants are deemed so precious, when the slightest tinge of mystery is felt to represent a "problem" to be "solved" when any leeway we have, any openness to each day's flow of events and circumstances is seen as a phantom, a bit of pretense on the part of the deceived, a posture meant to buttress an illusion. *Middlemarch* gives us nothing authoritative or definitive. Indefiniteness of character becomes indefiniteness of wisdom. The word is "may," not "will." Those who have Dorothea's "soul hunger" may not be offended, but those who hunger to put the life of the mind squarely in its place may well cringe or walk away in search of more "relevant" approaches. As for a word like "maturity"--and *Middlemarch* is concerned with grown-up, serious, intelligent people--no novelist like George Eliot is going to bandy that one around, not in its present-day meaning. "Maturity" has become part of our preaching vocabulary; it is demanded of people and all too rigidly defined, rather than regarded as a many-splendored thing: present as a series of values even in those lacking a good deal of it, absent suddenly among those who have a right to take it for granted much of the time, but for all of us a state of being, a condition that has to do with age, the assumption of certain responsiblities, the experience of achievements or disappointment--and a coming closer to the end.

So, it is left for one more irony to vex us, and maybe give us the solace that "indefiniteness" (the haziness of George Eliot's "every limit") is meant to provide: a century that has hovered over children and talked itself hoarse about its young people doesn't quite know what to do with the longest stretch of life that follows those two "periods." Psychological reflection and analysis of various kinds meant to give us leverage on ourselves as the grownup human beings who do the reflecting, undertake the analysis, leave us unaccountably diminished: we are called, in our thirties or forties or fifties, mere after-thought to what has made us as we are. We are regarded as fixed once and for all by the past of childhood and its spill-over of sorts, youth. A quest by full-grown men and women perhaps deserves better of itself than such renunciation or potentially vindictive self-arraignment. We are destined to be more than pietistic alternatives like "mature" or "immature" allow. We are also destined to be more than lucky survivors or sad victims of an ever receding "infantile conflict" or "complex." We are destined to stumble into "indefiniteness," and not always to bad or good effect. If that is no completely pleasing design, it provides for possibilities and fortuitous moments as well as hazards and casualties. "Every limit is a beginning as well as an ending," that important passage in the "finale" of *Middlemarch* starts out saying. The ultimate limit, of course, is our last breath; and speaking of that, one is left to wonder whether George Eliot, evangelical Christian become tentatively optimistic rationalist and naturalist, would claim for that particular limit the same alternatives presented us by all the other limits we come across in the course of our lives.

CRITICAL RESPONSE TO
DANIEL DERONDA

THE STRONG SIDE OF
DANIEL DERONDA

The Spectator, 29 July 1876

R.H. HUTTON

. . .The most inadequate part of the book has been the part in which Mordecai has canvassed his politico-religious enterprise, and tried to demonstrate that the Jewish nation might still have a national work to do in the world in interpreting to the East the wisdom of the West, as modified by the higher conceptions of the Jewish faith. But the greatest fault of the book has been very close, at least, to its greatest secret of power,--a kind of power in which no previous book of George Eliot's has been nearly so rich as this. If the conception of Mordecai's religious and political mission has transgressed the bounds of what even George Eliot can accomplish in fiction, there is yet a religious element in the story far surpassing in power and in the skill with which it is developed, anything corresponding to it in any other of her books. We refer to the very great power with which the over-ruling influence of a spirit which moulds human wilfulness to its higher purposes is brought out, in the story both of Gwendolen and of Daniel Deronda and his ancestors, not only without any interference with the naturalness of the story, but even with very great advantage to the connection of its incidents and the unity of its effect. Indeed, whatever may be the faults of this last work of George Eliot's, we do not think that any of her books, not even *Adam Bede*, has been so powerfully constructed in point of plot. And it is precisely because the shadow of a higher conception has been thrown over the plot, because the various lives, and the various parts of lives in this book, have been conceived and determined in relation to the demands of a purpose which, so far from being defeated by the resistance of human wilfulness, finds in these caprices the opportunity of effecting something even larger and higher than, apart from that resistance, might have been possible, that we read the whole with so intense an interest, and find both a naturalness and grandeur in the threading-together of the successive generations and the individual lives brought before us, which very few stories of any author's have seemed to contain, and which certainly none of George Eliot's have ever before aimed at in any high degree.

There is in this tale more of moral presentiment, more of moral providence, and more of moral subordination to purposes higher and wider than that of any one generation's life, than in any previous story of this author's, and the effect certainly has been to weld the whole together, in a way that is very unusual with her brilliant but somewhat loosely-knitted sketches of character. Nothing can be finer, now we have seen the issue of Gwendolen's wicked self-will in the number just published, than the connection between her girlish dread of the supernatural--the horror with which the white dead face from which a figure is fleeing in horror in the old panel-picture, struck her--and the destiny which she works out for herself, by her selfish persistence in a course which she knew to be both opposed to all pure womanly instincts, and treacherous to one to whom she had pledged her faith. And perhaps the finest part of this fine picture is the careful, subtle moderation with which it is worked out. Gwendolen, after all, realises the fate of which she had had so dim and dreadful a presenti-ment, only in a very modified form. While, in one sense, she has been offending more and more consciously against her sense of right, it has been partly because the sense of right itself has been growing in her even faster perhaps than the evil will which has outraged it; so that when at last she finds herself fleeing from the silent accusation of a dead face, the accusation it brings against her is not so fearful as it might have been, and is more likely to bear fruit in humility and penitence than in mad horror of inexpiable remorse. Whatever we may think, too, of the character of Daniel Deronda,--and to us it remains at the end what it was from the beginning, far too much of an elaborate study and too little of a vivid picture,--no one can deny that the power of the personal influence which passes from his into Gwendolen's life is very finely portrayed, and that the mode in which his evident nobility of nature becomes to her, as it were, a sort of moral inspiration, and a living standard of inward obligation, is very finely conceived and executed. But after all, it is the working-out of the retribution which her sin brings upon her, and the growing hatred of the sin, even while the very life of it seems to be growing, too, in her, which is the finest thing in her story. Her interviews with Deronda, after she has faced the fulfilment of her dread, her terror lest he should think her guilt too deep to be expiated, and his fear lest, in trying to give her nature the support it needed, he should be accepting for himself a burden greater than he could support, are all painted in a mood higher than even with this author we were prepared for. And it is curious to notice that, in this last and finest part of her tale, the vein of cynical, and sometimes almost flippant observation, in which she had so often indulged before, almost wholly disappears. She rises to the dignity of tragedy when she passes into the tragic scenes.

And to our minds, the conception of Deronda's mother, of her hatred of her lot as a Jewess, of her inability to resist the iron will of her father, and yet her determination somehow to escape its galling and oppressive yoke; of her apparent conquest over destiny, her career as a great singer, her desire for bringing up her son without the taint of the Jew upon him, and the collapse of her whole resolve as age and disease come on, beneath the inward spell exerted over her conscience by her dead father's imperious fidelity to duty, is still more finely painted. You see the physique of the great singer and actress in all she says and does. You see that she is what she calls herself, an unloving woman, to whom high dogmatic conscientiousness seems a gadfly which pursues us in our madness, rather than one of the noblest of human attributes; and yet you see, too, that she recognises, the nobility of the ideas which dominated her father's life, and that she acquiesces (though unwillingly) in the duty of giving them a chance with her son. And the author's evident intention to hint that Deronda, instead of losing by his mother's faithfulness to her father's will, had gained greatly by it in capacity to become precisely what that father had fondly hoped him to be, a new leader for his people, a leader with wider conceptions of what lay outside his race's nature and deeper conceptions of what lay inside it, is a nobler indication of her faith in a power which consciously overrules human errors for its own higher purposes, than any we can recall in any of her other works.

If we may judge by the story of *Daniel Deronda*, George Eliot has real faith in a power which anticipates the end from the beginning, and moulds our nature so as to fit it for a life above nature,--a faith which is the condition not merely of finding any true significance in art, but of seeing any perennial interest in the vicissitudes of history and that 'web of human things' which make up human life. What has been mostly wanting in George Eliot's books is this faith in the larger purpose which moulds men into something higher than anything into which they could mould themselves. And now that it is powerfully presented in one of her stories, though a story in which some of the elements of her genius are less visible than before, it certainly lends to her writing a force and a unity and a grandeur of effect which make up for many faults of execution, and even for occasional evidences of that weariness, which, more than anything in a great writer's works, excites the solicitude and the regret of the reader.

THE SATURDAY REVIEW

16 September 1876

UNSIGNED REVIEW

. . .Of course in the design of *Daniel Deronda* we are reminded of the part played by Fedalma in the *Spanish Gypsy*. Fidelity to race stands with this author as the first of duties and of virtues, nor does it seem material what the character of the race is. Fedalma feels her gipsy blood, as soon as she is made aware of her origin, to be as strong and imperious a chain as his Jewish descent is with Deronda. In each, race, as linking past and future together, is the idea of an earthly perpetuity. In obedience to this sentiment, the one throws over faith and lover and takes ship with her people; the other, except that he is lucky in a Mirah, follows the same course, throws over every previous association, and takes ship to the vague East.

It is not often that the poet or novelist sets himself to draw a perfect man. The effort is commendable, for it is mostly its own reward. . . .Deronda is so far successful as a portrait that we believe no other writer of our day, inspired by the same intention, could have imparted the degree of amiability, life, and reality which our author has infused into her ideal. It has evidently been a labour of love to apply her special talents to the embodiment of cherished ideas in an external form; to dramatize them, as it were, and make them speak for themselves, through the person and action of her hero; and no one is more successful in helping her readers to realize, not through elaborate and ineffective description, but by conveying an image through its effect on others. Deronda does nothing, but he has a curious influence. Thus "there was a calm intensity of life and richness of tint in Deronda's face, that on a sudden gaze from his was rather startling, and often made him seem to have spoken; so that servants and officials asked him automatically, 'What did you say, sir?' when he had been quite silent." And, again, his eyes "had a peculiarity which has often drawn men into trouble; they were of a dark but mild intensity, which seemed to express a special interest in every one on whom he fixed them, and might easily help to bring on him those claims which ardently sympathetic people are often creating in the minds of those who need help." And the qualities of his mind are indicated with the same characteristic art. We are left to assume his intellectual elevation, but his moral nature is the thing to be described, as inevitably resulting in a certain view of life. His youth suffers under the pain and social disadvantage of not knowing his birth, "such as easily turns a self-centred unloving nature into an Ishmaelite. But in the rarer sort the inexorable sorrow takes the form of fellowship, and makes the imagination tender," "raising a strong array of reasons why he should shrink from getting into that routine of the world which makes men apologize for its wrong doings." Persons attracted him in proportion to the possibility of his defending them. He had to resist an inclination to withdraw coldly from the fortunate. "What I have been most trying to do," he says, "for fifteen years is to have some understanding of those who differ from myself." His imagination had so wrought itself to the habit of seeing things as they probably appeared to others, that a strong partisanship, unless it were against an immediate oppression, had become an insincerity to him." Hence there was, as his mind ripened, a tolerance towards error. Few men were able to keep "themselves clearer of vices than he; yet he hated vices mildly, being used to think of them less in the abstract than as a part of mixed human natures, having an individual history which it was the bent of his mind to trace with understanding and pity." In all these things Deronda acknowledges no teacher. No state of mind can be described more incompatible with strong dogmatic convictions.

But what is wanting in himself Deronda yet seems to supply to others. The author invests him with many spiritual functions, not scrupling to add certain adjuncts impressive to the imagination, as where it is noted, in Gwendolen's confession in the library, that a joint fragrance of Russian leather and burning wood gave the idea of incense, "of a chapel in which censers have been swinging." Not only is he Gwendolen's preacher, confessor, and director, but he is her conscience, and in this capacity she calls his eye dreadful. There are occasions even when he arrives at an elevation higher than this; when he suggests the idea of a Providence, when he is a Being with a capital B, and is foretold by his grandfather as Deliverer with a capital D, and finally he represents to Mordecai, whose inward need of a prolonged self had been dwelt on, something beyond even this. The dying Jew commits his soul into his charge. "Where thou goest, Daniel, I shall go. Is it not begun? Have I not breathed my soul into you? We shall live together." It is not easy to reconcile these qualities, functions, or attributes--whatever we may call them--with the costume of the day, whether evening full dress, which he sets off so well, or that morning drab suit which sets off him. The task which the author has set herself to accomplish in these volumes is to bring together past and present; to modify, by certain explanatory analogies, ancient beliefs into modern doubt, and in her own case to show how the keenest insight into the world's doings may work side by side with a vein of speculation far removed and alien from ordinary sympathies.

ELIOT TO MME. EUGENE BODICHON

The George Eliot Letters, 1978

2 OCTOBER 1876

. . .I have had some very interesting letters both from Jews and from Christians about *Deronda*. Part of the scene at the club is translated into Hebrew in a German-Jewish newspaper. On the other hand a Christian (highly accomplished) thanks me for embodying the principles by which Christ wrought and will conquer. This is better than the laudation of readers who cut the book into scraps and talk of nothing in it but Gwendolen. I meant everything in the book to be related to everything else there. . . .

ELIOT TO HARRIET BEECHER STOWE

The George Eliot Letters, 1978

29 OCTOBER 1876

. . .As to the Jewish element in *Deronda*, I expected from first to last in writing it, that it would create much stronger resistance and even repulsion than it has actually met with. But precisely because I felt that the usual attitude of Christians towards Jews is--I hardly know whether to say more impious or more stupid when viewed in the light of their professed principles, I therefore felt urged to treat Jews with such sympathy and understanding as my nature and knowledge could attain to. Moreover, not only towards the Jews, but towards all oriental peoples with whom we English come into contact, a spirit of arrogance and contemptuous dictatorialness is observable which has become a national disgrace to us. There is nothing I should care more to do, if it were possible, than to rouse the imagination of men and women to a vision of human claims in those races of their fellow-men who must differ from them in customs and beliefs. But towards the Hebrews we western people who have been reared in Christianity, have a peculiar debt and, whether we acknowledge it or not, a peculiar thoroughness of fellowship in religious and moral sentiment. Can anything be more disgusting than to hear people called "educated" making small jokes about eating ham, and showing themselves empty of any real knowledge as to the relation of their own social and religious life to the history of the people they think themselves witty in insulting? They hardly know that Christ was a Jew. And I find men educated at Rugby supposing that Christ spoke Greek. To my feeling, this deadness to the history which has prepared half our world for us, this inability to find interest in any form of life that is not clad in the same coat-tails and flounces as our own lies very close to the worst kind of irreligion. The best that can be said of it is, that it is a sign of the intellectual narrowness--in plain English, the stupidity, which is still the average mark of our culture.

Yes, I expected more aversion than I have found. But I was happily independent in material things and felt no temptation to accomodate my writing to any standard except that of trying to do my best in what seemed to me most needful to be done, and I sum up with the writer of the Book of Maccabees--'if I have done well, and as befits the subject, it is what I desired, but if I have done ill, it is what I could attain unto'. . .

INTERNATIONAL REVIEW

January 1877

R.R. BOWKER

. . .Considering then that a novel with a purpose and with a personality may still be recognized as a novel and as a work of art, we may take as a chief element of George Eliot's greatness that her books are so persistently occupied with the greatest of problems--the problem, old as humanity, that must forever be set before each man as his question of life or death. As unreligious in the personality of her novels as Shakespeare the dramatist, George Eliot is always dealing with the most profound of practical religious questions. That truceless conflict which the Persians deified into alternating gods of Light and of Darkness; which Protestantism has philosophized into the problem of free-will *vs.* predestination; which is presented in history by the sustaining faith of the Jew on the one hand and the disintegrating fatalism of the Turk on the other; which in the experience of the individual is figured by the immortal parable of St. Anthony's strugglings between the spirit and the flesh--this clashing of the universe, one through its many phases, fought out now with the world for its battle-field, but oftenest in the inmost recesses of the human heart, presents itself to the rationalistic mind of George Eliot as the conflict between character and circumstance. Through all the full harmony of her writings is heard this theme.

Daniel Deronda not only treats of this question; it is built upon it. The novel has two centres, Gwendolen and Mordecai, between whose circles the author's hero is the connecting link. The evident difference of opinion between the author and her readers, as to which is the leading person of the story, grows out of this pervasive problem. She concentrates her attention upon Deronda because he represents character, force--originative in its relations to Gwendolen, transmissive in its relations with Mordecai. The reader looks upon him more as a force than as a person. On the other hand, the reader's attention is concentrated upon Gwendolen, this throbbing, bleeding heart, torn by the thwarting circumstance we all know to our pain, herself the product of circumstance and the battle-field of opposing character--because this is human and near to us. On either hand are the angel and the demon--not above, shadowy in the clouds, but called Deronda and Grandcourt. The one is indeed the messenger of life, the quickener; the other, the mocking spirit of negation which Goethe pictures as truly devil. Both of these men are evidently intended to represent 'character' in Emerson's sense. 'This is that which we call Character,' says this seer, 'a reserved force which acts directly by presence and without means.'[1] Tito Melema, the antipodes of Deronda, we know through his deeds, but neither Deronda nor Grandcourt *do* any thing. George Eliot has thus set to herself the most difficult task before creative art. There is more in these men than can be told of them, even in real life, and in endeavoring to give to the reader her own impression of Deronda she has returned again and again to the picture, only to find that, with all her pains, the reader must take something for granted. The reader who will take nothing for granted--in the heavens or under them, who, in a word, has no sense of spiritual force--finds Deronda a nonentity and Grandcourt an impossibility. Gwendolen knew, and we knew, that this is not true; these men are those who are able to successfully oppose circumstance, and get the better of events. Perhaps if George Eliot had been content just to give us her word for Deronda, to elaborate him less, she would have accomplished more. We might then have seen him through the eyes of Gwendolen.

There are other readers who pronounce Grandcourt a living realization, but Deronda an unreal and objectionable prig. But Deronda is neither unreal nor a prig. There may be some to whom George Eliot has not made him evident, partly because literary art fails her to paint the real being she knows; partly because they could not, by their nature, know this real being in actual life. We can not make a photograph of a sunbeam, because it is the sunbeam which makes the photograph; we can not make any photograph evident to the blind. But some of us have known these Messianic men--we speak reverently--of whom Deronda is a type: strong with man's strength, tender with the tenderness of woman, touching no life that they did not lighten and inspire. Yet what could we tell of them that should make our friends know them as we know them? It is

Deronda's literary misfortune that he is placed in conditions which in many minds attribute to him effeminacy: it doesn't look very manly to treat a woman as if she were in love with you. It is provoking also to poor humanity to gaze long upon too near an approach to unstained goodness, nor do men take kindly to that unpartisan catholicity which, seeing good on both sides as well as ill on both, seems to each party a defender of the other. Thus Deronda arouses manifold prejudices, but they are prejudices and not judgments. His character is justified as the book reaches its real climax and conclusion in that touching sentence of Gwendolen, the noblest testimony a noble soul can have: 'It is better--it shall be better with me--because I have known you.'

To most readers it goes without saying that this problem of character and circumstance is the mainspring of the Gwendolen side of Daniel Deronda's double history; it will be seen also that what is commonly known as 'the Jewish business' no less grows out of it, while even in a side personage like Klesmer we are shown the triumph of character over social circumstance. The history of the Jews appealed powerfully to the imagination of George Eliot, because it presented at once the most remarkable proof of the abidingness of character, in its broader relations, and the most striking illustration of that contact of ideal character and every-day circumstance which, as in the frequent suggestion that Deronda has a modern tailor, she is so fond of pointing out. The Jewish is so far the one race in history that can lay claim to immortality--because the earlier Ezras founded its national life upon a Rock. It was these Prophets of Judea, strong in faith, and defying circumstance, who, with that fire of soul that blazed into the most splendid and fervent oratory the world has known, gave to their petty state that principle of life which could never be quenched by the whole power of the magnificent empires that one after another fell to pieces around it. And it is this people, the chosen of God, who time and time again have turned aside, betrayed by the lusts of the flesh, into the entanglement of circumstance--who, to-day, leave the ancient and splendid ritual of their synagogues, to cheat Jehovah and the Gentiles on the street. 'Seest thou,' says Mordecai, in one of the great passages of the book, 'our lot is the lot of Israel. The grief and the glory are mingled as the smoke and the flame.' The very name of Mordecai and his contrasting fellow-Cohens itself tells the story. Associated in our minds with a common order of people, Cohen is the Hebrew word for priest. Always, as in *The Spanish Gypsy*, emphasizing the idea of race, the thought of Judaism came also personally home to George Eliot, not so much in the influence of her husband, as has been suggested, as in that of her friend Emanuel Deutsch,[2] whose *Literary Remains* have shown to the world one whose kindling enthusiasm, thwarted aspirations, and gentle, pathetic life bring to mind both Deronda and Mordecai. For the latter, the direct suggestion came of course from that Cohen who was the leader of the philosophical club described in Lewes's *Fortnightly* article on 'Spinoza,'[3] but it is doubtless the life of Deutsch that has given life to Mordecai. In his influence upon George Eliot, as in that of

Mordecai upon Deronda, is seen that transmissive inspiration and 'apostolic succession' of character that is a chief factor and proof of greatness. It is perhaps his enthusiasm for the East, also, that unfortunately started off Deronda upon a mission, of the geographical reunion of the Jews, which, in the light of modern relations, seems useless and absurd, as well as chimerical, and runs counter not least to the usual philosophy of George Eliot herself. . . .

NOTES

1. In his essay 'Character' (1844).
2. Emanuel Deutsch (1829-73), Jewish orientalist and friend of George Eliot.
3. *Fortnightly Review* (1 April 1866), iv, 395-406.

DANIEL DERONDA AND THE VICTORIAN SEARCH FOR IDENTITY

Studies in the Humanities, October 1972

ARLENE M. JACKSON

In the Victorian world conveyed through the provincial setting of *Middlemarch* (1871-72), George Eliot stressed the lack of a "coherent social order or faith" and lamented the passing of a world which had supported man in his search for an epic, or heroic, identity. An even greater incoherence exists in the later, London world of *Daniel Deronda* (1876), and that world denies not only epic identity but identity itself. Through Daniel--a prototype of the kind of man that Thomas Hardy would later describe as suffering from "the ache of modernism"--George Eliot wished to present her concept of the New Man, product of an age of increasing disorder. Daniel's particular response to modernism is a weakness or vacillation of will, and it is precisely this deficiency, its causes and possible consequences, that George Eliot understood as a most serious danger to the Victorian man. Daniel Deronda is a Victorian in search of a literal, familial identity, but this search also has psychological and social dimensions and is closely related to George Eliot's theory of "separateness with communication."

Like Dorothea Brooke of *Middlemarch*, Daniel Deronda desires to perform some great good, to find some duty which would give meaning to his life, but cannot define what that duty should be. As a male, urban aristocrat who has reached his majority, the possibilities for a commitment to society would seem to be immense. Daniel Deronda, however, must solve problems which are much more serious than Dorothea's had been. Raised by Sir Hugo Mallinger, Daniel suspects he is the illegitimate son of Sir Hugo, and whether his suspicions are true or false, ignorance of his lineage becomes a very prominent obstacle to knowledge of social duty. Burdened by the thought that he is different from his peers because he has no knowledge of his lineage, Daniel feels he has been grafted onto London society because of Sir Hugo's efforts. Daniel thus senses the artificiality of his life. With no class traditions to uphold, no class dignity to fight for, no family lineage to give him pride in the knowledge of who and what he is, Daniel believes that he is set apart from the rest of society, and this estrangement and artificiality cause him many hours of painful introspection.

What Daniel does not know is that his Jewish identity has been deliberately withheld because society has decreed that it is shameful to be a Jew. Daniel's mother, Alcharisi, had given her infant son to Sir Hugo in an effort to erase the stigma of Jewishness from her son's life. Through Daniel's suffering, however, George Eliot shows her belief that the attempt to erase this identity does not strengthen man's union with society, but actually increases his loneliness. Young Deronda yearns to become "an organic part of social life, instead of roaming in it like a yearning disembodied spirit. . .without fixed local habitation to render fellowship real" (I,547).[1]

Daniel Deronda has a premonition that knowledge of his origin will bring pain, but he is willing to undergo such pain if the knowledge will put an end to his uncertainty and estrangement, "if it helped him to make his life a sequence which would take the form of duty--if it saved him from having to make an arbitrary selection where he felt no preponderance of desire" (II,104). Daniel longs to become involved with mankind, but until he knows who he is, in terms of familial, class, and national origin, he does not know what his future should be.

The disappearance of the literal identity is only one level of meaning here. In a larger sense, Sir Hugo and Alcharisi are conspirators who represent the forces of the modern world which attempt to deface any kind of identity. The familial rootlessness of Daniel Deronda is a manifestation of the aimlessness, bewilderment, and estrangement which result when traditional values are no longer viewed as sacrosanct, no longer seen as relevant to nineteenth-century life. George Eliot believed that traditional social, intellectual, and religious patterns of thought had provided men with the framework for an ordered life. The destruction of these patterns, just as surely as ignorance of his particular lineage, causes Daniel's loneliness and confusion, qualities of the New Man who is the product of an age of increasing fragmentation. Although George Eliot does not wish for a reincarnation of the past world with all its faults and errors, *Daniel Deronda* reveals her lament that the Victorian world does not give man the psychological and social identity provided by the ordered world of the past.

George Eliot criticizes her disordered, fragmented world, but she also finds serious defects in the Victorian man himself. At the same time that Daniel suffers and even fears loneliness, he also fears commitment and union with humanity. Something within him causes Daniel to shrink from commitment-- some fear, perhaps, that he will be less than perfect. The first sight of Mirah, with her appearance of "helpless sorrow," blends with what seemed to Daniel "the strong array of reasons why he should shrink from getting into that routine of the world which makes men apologize for all its wrong-doing, and take opinions as mere professional equipment--why he should not draw strongly at any thread in the hopelessly-entangled scheme of things" (I,281). For Daniel, commitment means that he must be prepared to accept sorrow and failure, must take a chance at being affected by an expedient world; and he is not prepared to face this hazard. Fear at risking the integrity of the self impedes Daniel from actively engaging in the business of the world, and if man is unwilling to expose himself to something less than perfect, if he fears that he will be liable to error or to the "common run of things," then he has no confidence in his own strength to withstand the pressures of his world. Enthusiasm, that moral energy which marks the Victorian man's plunge into the business of the world, depends on the consciousness of personal strength. Daniel Deronda's fear of commitment is due, in part, to the disorder of his world, but it is also caused by the New Man's lack of belief in himself.

This fear of commitment is demonstrated when Sir Hugo offers to help Daniel enter politics; Daniel's only answer is silence. Since George Eliot tells us in another context that Daniel questioned whether it were "worth while to take part in the battle of the world," his silence says much. His habit of looking for the poetry and romance in everyday things of life, furthermore, may be associated with his desire for some great good to which he can dedicate himself, but it is more likely to be a form of escapism in his unwillingness to commit himself to the reality of positive action.

Another form of escapism is what D.R. Carroll calls the "disease of sympathy."[2] Daniel is paralyzed by a particular attitude toward life, for he could always see two sides of a problem or question, see the disadvantages and advantages of so many things that he finds it difficult to take sides. The result of this "disease" is that his "plenteous, flexible sympathy had ended by falling into one current with that reflective analysis which tends to neutralize sympathy" (I,545). And when Daniel projects himself into objects which surround him, when he thinks "how far it might be possible habitually to shift his centre till his own personality would be no less outside him than the landscape" (I,282), sympathetic identification has taken place to such an extent that Daniel has destroyed his own ability to act. Daniel Deronda thus exhibits a peculiar form of self-consciousness which has the intent and result of effacing individual identity;[3] and he takes refuge in self-consciousness because he fears to commit himself to the tangled web of life.

There is, of course, a strong relationship here between the forces of society and the reaction of the self, for George Eliot shows through this novel that the Victorian man is hindered from seeing and acting because a disordered world has blurred, even withheld, his literal as well as social and psychological identity. But though the forces of the world may stifle the Victorian into passivity, there is never the feeling in *Daniel Deronda* that man is not responsible for his particular plight. Even though the general situation of the world is a cause of frustration, George Eliot reveals through Daniel's plight that the greater burden of responsibility rests on the Victorian man because he has the potential which would enable him to cope with the pressures of life. The existence of this potential, and thus a clarification of Daniel's own responsibility for his refuge in self-consciousness, is first evident in his relationship with Mirah and Gwendolen. In aiding these two women, Daniel begins to commit himself to the unpleasant, problem-filled world outside the self.

With this commitment, Daniel Deronda achieves one level of the "separateness with communication" theory that is George Eliot's answer to the plight of the Victorian man. She is to develop this theory more extensively and on different levels in the final stages of her novel, but on this first plane, she demonstrates that feeling has a twofold relation with "doing." Feeling, or "sympathetic identification," can move man to act, as well as cause paralysis of the will, and the particular effect feeling will have depends on the deliberate choice of the Victorian man: feeling paralyzes the will only when man allows it to do so.

Sympathy ceases to be an illness and can result in positive action, however, when man consciously wills an I-Thou relationship based on an awareness of the needs of suffering humanity. The distaste of the "I" for the suffering, for the "tangled scheme of things," is the basis of the Victorian man's fear of commitment. George Eliot believed that this fear could be overcome when and if man recognizes that the needs of humanity are more important than his own distaste or fear of involvement. Feeling can negate action, however, when man shrinks from an I-Thou relationship, uses feeling in its diseased form of sympathetic identification as a shield to fend off a chaotic, unpleasant world, and finds that, while he has protected himself, he has also isolated himself. The direction of sympathy into its proper channel of human fellowship is the first kind of "communication" that George Eliot believes is necessary to the Victorian man if he is to emerge from his refuge and his fear. Through "communication," through recognizing the needs of Mirah and Gwendolen and overcoming his distaste at becoming involved in the confusion of their lives, Daniel Deronda discovers one part of both his psychological and social identity; and though this one level of discovery does not solve all his fears, though it has certain restrictions, it brings Daniel a happiness he had never before experienced.

While Daniel has overcome one part of his fear of commitment, that victory does not extend beyond the boundaries of his immediate life. Like Dorothea Brooke, Daniel Deronda yearns for a greater involvement with the world; unlike Dorothea's task of learning to accept restriction, Daniel's lot involves learning to commit himself to *potential*, to the uncertainty of an heroic action, once it is offered through the hands of Mordecai. "Visions are the creators and feeders of the world" (II,147), explains Mordecai, but Daniel cannot commit himself to Mordecai's mission because he fears the personal cost of that larger, heroic commitment. The vision of this holy man may be based, not on logic, but on emotion, Daniel realizes. If men accept missions to serve humanity, he continues to ask, and those missions are not based on logic, how can truth be served? After much paralyzing introspection, Daniel arrives at the only conclusion he sees is possible: action based on logic may lead men into error because logical action may proceed from a false premise; action based on emotion, conversely, may lead men to truth because such action may proceed from sincere desire to improve the lot of mankind.

With this realization, George Eliot shows us how much Daniel Deronda has come to terms with a highly significant hazard: because man is human and therefore fallible, because action may lead man either to truth or falsehood,

George Eliot tells through Daniel that "we must be patient with the inevitable makeshift of our human thinking, whether in its sum total or in the separate minds that have made the sum" (II,171). With this acceptance of failure and error as possible parts of the tangled scheme of life, Daniel also sees the possibility of truth and success. More important than either, however, is his realization of individual responsibility: change is related to the will and actions of man as he chooses to hasten or retard change, and on individual man rests the responsibility of the wisdom to know and the strength to resist the false in life. At this point, Daniel ceases to shrink from meaningful involvement with the larger issues of life and accepts the hazards that come with committing himself to positive action--and only at this point in Daniel's growth is he worthy to learn the full nature of Mordecai's vision. Yet Daniel cannot help thinking that the painful questioning he has gone through would not have happened in some other day and age; the spiritual mission of Mordecai, he reminds himself, would have seemed quite believable, even natural, in a past era. George Eliot implies through Daniel's reference to the past, furthermore, that pre-modern man would have committed himself to the spiritual mission without the hesitation of modern man.

When Daniel has accepted uncertainty and individual responsibility, he has achieved full psychological "separateness"; now he must discover the full "communication" that will fulfill his yearning for his true identity. That Daniel has not yet seen his relationship with the world at large, that he interprets action, wisdom, and strength only as they apply to individual man, is evident when we compare his thoughts with those of Mordecai, for the latter speaks of a "new unfolding of life" which is checked when "the soul of a people, whereby they know themselves to be one, may seem to be dying for want of common action" (II,190). While Daniel speaks of *himself*, Mordecai speaks of a *people*, and the largeness of Mordecai's vision is due to the fact that he sees man imbedded in a social context. The consciousness of this larger identity is "as a seed of fire that may enkindle the souls of multitudes, and make a new pathway for events" (II,190). The man who knows his identity must strive to bring that knowledge to other men, George Eliot reminds us, for human progress has its roots in a sense of cultural tradition.

As Mordecai interprets the problems and needs of the modern world, the most immediate step in preserving tradition is to bring to life an "organic centre" for the Jew: "Let the unity of Israel which has made the growth and form of its religion be an outward reality" (II,199). If this organic center is made into geographic reality, the Jewish people will then share in the dignity of having a "national life which has a voice among the peoples of the East and the West-- which will plant the wisdom and skill of our race so that it may be, as of old, a medium of transmission and understanding" (II,200). This restoration of the Jewish nation thus becomes another stage, both literal and symbolic as Daniel's individual search for his familial identity had been, in George Eliot's theory of "separateness with communication."

On the cultural level, George Eliot conveys her belief in the need for union and diversity in the modern world: the Jew as well as the Gentile must keep his heritage intact, for the world is culturally richer if the Jew remains Jew, Gentile remains Gentile. Mordecai's vision embraces not only the errant Jew and the guidance and stability--derivatives of cultural identification--that a national center will provide for him, but includes also the contribution a Jewish homeland will make to a more extensive unity. From the separateness of distinct cultural traditions comes an enriched and strengthened civilization.

Because the Jewish homeland would contain within it the diversity of national origin as well as the cultural similarity of the Jewish people, the East will have a community which would unite the "culture and the sympathies of every great nation in its bosom" (II,207). And because of this diversity within union, a Jewish homeland would be to the East as Belgium is to the West: a place where enmity is halted. A New Judea would, in fact, be "poised between East and West" and would therefore serve as a force of reconciliation for a fragmented world (II,207). George Eliot thus sees Judea as a symbol of the moral order that can be carved out of chaos. Transcending its more immediate interpretation as Jewish unity, Judea has for its most extensive meaning the union of the human race, and this union, as well as the literal restoration of the Jewish nation, is the idealistic vision that Mordecai bequeaths to Daniel Deronda.

As George Eliot presents this vision, however, she also adds a warning: just as the "separateness" of national origins within the Jewish nation will strengthen the unity of Palestine, just as the "separateness" of a Jewish homeland will strengthen world unity, so too must there be diversity of thought in any society which aspires to the New Order where the quality of life is enriched and where men are no longer fearful, confused, or debilitated. From the "separateness" of individual thought within any nation comes strength, for diversity provides not only a richness of thought but a safeguard for truth and a means of discerning falsehood. George Eliot sees great dangers in chaos, but she also sees danger in a unity which does not allow diversity of thought: in this kind of restrictive unity, there is the danger of falsehood reigning unchallenged.

This necessity of the "separateness" of thought within a society which seeks and values union answers the question Daniel poses to the members of "The Philosophers" debating club. Disturbed by the implications of the evolutionary process, Daniel wonders how man can define or know truth. How can man distinguish, for example, between an inevitable change and a change which only *seems* to be inevitable? While Daniel has already answered this question on one level by realizing that he, as individual man, must make decisions and bear responsibility for finding truth, George Eliot offers another answer through her concept of separate identity within a culture, diversity within the union of nations, and the diversity of thought--differing social relations, economic approaches, philosophic concepts--within a society which commonly accepts as its uniting bond the belief in the free will and dignity and, therefore, the *humanity* of man. "Separateness with communication," distinction within union on several levels of life, is a safeguard for truth, and is George Eliot's proposal for the restoration of a coherent social order and faith in the modern world.

This "separateness with communication," when applied to individual men, has a more immediate result: Daniel Deronda's understanding of his personal identity gives him the courage to face the hazards of the world, and his realization of his social identity--his discovery of his Jewishness as well as his bond with all men, everywhere--enables him to find Duty. In more specific terms, Daniel joyfully perceives: "I hold that my first duty is to my own people, and if there is anything to be done towards restoring or perfecting their common life, I shall make that my vocation" (II,493).

Daniel also seeks to have all men know their identities. When he discovers he is a Jew, something he has suspected ever since meeting Mordecai, he speaks out against the attempts of his mother and Sir Hugo to hide this identity from him. It is man's right to know his heritage, he believes, since knowledge of cultural and familial heritage--man's union made manifest in the social context--enables man to know his duty in life. Daniel's mother, Alcharisi, has spent a lifetime trying to erase the Jewess in herself, and although she is unsuccessful in this attempt, she surely has succeeded in destroying her capacity for love and sympathy. Through her failure to erase her particular bonds with humanity and through Daniel's gradual recognition of that heritage and bond, it is apparent that George Eliot believes this cultural consciousness and basic union between men can never be completely destroyed, that it is stronger than the will of men, stronger than the pressures of a disordered world, and will eventually emerge once more. What this Victorian does see as a present reality, however, is the chaos and dehumanization which result when man seeks to destroy his social identity or has this identity, these marks of his distinction within as well as union with humanity, withheld from him by forces of his world which operate through the will of men.

Daniel Deronda's new knowledge of his personal and social identity enables him to realize it is his duty to travel to the East to become more familiar with his cultural heritage before he can seek to establish a geographical home for the Jew. And while this last goal in his immediate plans gives rise to the charge of excessive optimism, no such charge can really be aimed at George Eliot. She presents Daniel as clearly aware of the restrictions of his world: the animosity toward the Jew, and particularly the Jew with Zionist ambitions, the fear of the idealist, and the dislike of any man who would dare to upset the *status quo* of the world. The geographical establishment of a Jewish nation is only a vague possibility, he realizes. If he cannot establish this, however, he will do what he can to create what he sees as more important: the awakening of a "movement in other minds, such as has been awakened in my own" (II,616). That Daniel's hopes are tempered by realism is again evident in his remark that he will seek to establish "faithful tradition where we can attain it" (II,535). Although he realizes this quest will be most difficult and that failure may result, he now understands the real failure would be not to undertake the quest. And it is fit that this man who has conquered his own fear of failure, this man who has discovered his own personal strength and social bonds, who no longer fears to commit himself to the "tangled scheme" of life, devotes his life to helping other men find out who and what they are.

As George Eliot guides Daniel Deronda from rootlessness and uncertainty to the "separateness with communication" of a personal and social identity, she is critical of a world which helps to create these New Men, and she is critical yet sympathetic toward those men who withdraw into self-consciousness and passivity because they fear involvement at the same time as they long for it. The theory of "separateness with communication" is George Eliot's proposal for the psychological and social salvation of those men who painfully perceive they live in a chaotic world, who fear loneliness and confusion, but who find commitment difficult because they fear terror and entanglement. In her understanding of the difficulties of living in a Victorian world, in her analysis of Daniel Deronda's psychological states, and in the various dimensions of her theory of "separateness with communication," George Eliot demonstrates a depth of thought she had not reached in any of her previous novels.

NOTES

1. *George Eliot's Works*, Warwick edition, 12 vols. (New York, 1901-03). *Daniel Deronda* volume and page references will accompany the quoted passage.

2. D.R. Carroll, "The Unity of *Daniel Deronda*," *Essays in Criticism*, 9 (1959), 378-379. Carroll explains how experimental empathy turns into the disease of sympathy.

3. Maurice Beebe, in "Visions are Creators': The Unity of *Daniel Deronda*," *BUSE*, 1 (1955), 173, relates Daniel's abhorrence of a career as a concert singer to this negation of individuality. Daniel rejects this career "apparently because he fears to assert further the individuality which he finds already too conspicuous."

THE RHETORIC OF MAGIC IN
DANIEL DERONDA

Studies in the Novel, Spring 1983

JAMES CARON

An overview of criticism of George Eliot's *Daniel Deronda* since its publication reveals two schools of thought. One holds that there are actually two stories contained in the novel, one about Gwendolen Harleth, the other about Daniel Deronda, and that the former is far superior to the latter. This position implies that the book contains no unifying design. The other critical view is that the novel is far more organically constructed. This essay attempts to demonstrate the organic view by delineating a pattern of diction, imagery, and dramatic scenes I call the rhetoric of magic. By this I mean a conscious effort on Eliot's part to assimilate concepts which are associated with romance, legend, and folk tales--witches, sorcerers, divination, potions, curses, auguries, demons--to the purposes of the novel's narration and themes. Eliot uses this techinque to describe the psychology of interpersonal relationships as well as attitudes toward shaping individual destiny and the destiny of humanity. The technique not only provides evidence for the notion that *Daniel Deronda* was conceived as a totality, but, by revealing the extent to which elements of romance are mixed with the realistic conventions of Eliot's style, it also suggests why the novel has been judged an overall failure.

Among the themes of *Daniel Deronda* one is particularly relevant to the rhetoric of magic. The core of the theme is the notion of world-community. Specifically, it is an ideal of brotherhood and ecumenical history which seeks to minimize political and religious boundaries so that people might apprehend the truth of one fact--humanity's essential unity.

The embodiment of such a large conception is Deronda, and it is mainly the weight of this ideal that flattens his presentation toward ideality. Conceiving Deronda in this way depends upon a realization of what lies at the center of his personality: "a habit of thinking himself imaginatively into the experience of others."[1] This "many-sided sympathy," with its echoes of Shelley's idea of the imagination's moral dimension, is meant to be the ground of plausibility for Deronda's acceptance of Mordecai, which is also intimately bound up with his love of ecumenical history--his "fibre of historic sympathy." Characteristic of Deronda's mental life, this ecumenism is employed in his internal debate as to the meaning of Mordecai.

In Deronda's physical demeanor this imaginative sympathy is manifested by his "calmly penetrative eyes," a phrase that points to the essence of this all-important feature: the inability to discern relations where none are thought to exist--to penetrate to the center of people and events. In the rhetoric of magic this is divination.

If one judges the first chapter as representative, the rhetoric of magic, with its hints of evil and sorcery, is clearly not a mere arbitrary schema, but a basic mode of presentation Eliot will use to further her thematic concerns. The ambiance of the gambling resort in the opening scene takes its tone from this rhetoric: for example, the casino's "well-brewed" atmosphere and spellbound players ("as if they had all eaten of some root that for the time compelled the brains of each to the same narrow monotony of action" [p.37]). In addition, there is a kind of sorcery to the act of gambling itself, the stakes magically swept away or doubled according to the unseen power, Luck. Gwendolen feels this sorcery when she imagines herself "as a goddess of luck and. . .her play as a directing augury" (p.39). Gwendolen also clothes Deronda's imaginative sympathy with the rhetoric of magic when she feels his gaze "to have acted as an evil eye," disrupting her luck.

The rhetoric of magic marks Deronda, with his historic and imaginative sympathy, as a benevolent sorcerer figure, a person who uses his power of divination only to aid and to understand those whom he sees into. His opposite is, of course, Henleigh Grandcourt, whose divining power is propelled not by warm sympathy, but rather by a coldblooded, reptilian desire for mastery. The scope of his power stands in stark contrast to Deronda's wide horizons: "[Grandcourt] had no imagination of anything in her but what affected the gratification of his own will; but on this point he had the sensibility which seems like divination" (p.616).

The goal of Grandcourt's power is to control those into whom he sees and to subdue them to his will. Gwendolen is his chief victim, and his effect upon her is mesmeric. The prominent horse imagery of the story conveys the idea of mastery, of course, but the idea of divination, when linked with Grandcourt, exposes the violent underside of this control by suggesting the mental powers of an evil sorcerer. Grandcourt's limited but powerful insight is like a mental stranglehold, paralyzing Gwendolen and robbing her of her will to act. Thus, when she senses the violence of Grandcourt's mastery, the feeling is often presented, appropriately enough, through a motif of strangulation.

This strangulation of will is evident even in Gwendolen's first conversation with Grandcourt at the archery contest, where he makes her feel "less mistress of herself than usual" (p.148), revealing words as a prime source of his mesmeric power. Another example of evil-word magic is the proposal scene, where his speech again acts like an opiate, subtly drugging Gwendolen's will. "As the words penetrated her, they had the effect of a draught of wine. . . Yet when Grandcourt had ceased to speak, there was an instant in which she was conscious of being at the turning of the ways" (p.347). At one point in this scene they exchange glances. In doing so, Grandcourt's eyes mysteriously arrest Gwendolen's, echoing her initial exchange with Deronda in the casino where her eyes are also "arrested." In both cases a mental probing is suggested, but with Grandcourt its aim is to immobilize. Once they are married, his divining power soon resembles, as the reptile imagery associated with him indicates, the effect of a snake upon a rabbit--a stasis of terror. The essence of Grandcourt's mesmeric divination, then, is his ability to circumscribe the will of another within his own narrow orbit--to transfix his victim with a word or a glance, like a hypnotist.

If the rhetoric of magic is useful in schematizing the natures of Grandcourt and Deronda into types of the evil and benevolent sorcerers, then it is less straightforward in regard to Gwendolen in the role of sorceress. In relation to the two men, the rhetoric of magic is something akin to a suit of clothes, something external that is most useful in describing their characteristic mode of behavior. With Gwendolen this rhetoric is internal as well as external; it is her characteristic mode of perceiving and thinking as well as a mode of description by others.

The internal or perceptual half is apparent throughout the book: Gwendolen's initial encounter with Deronda; her description of and reaction to Grandcourt; her perceptions of Lydia Glasher as a sorceress, the Grandcourt family diamonds as a curse, and horses and gambling as potions against ennui. Gwendolen also perceives herself in terms of such rhetoric. For example, she thinks of herself as "witching the world with her grace on horseback" (p.68). Though she sees herself in such terms, she does not actually possess the power of divination, either mesmeric or sympathetic. In her adolescent self-confidence Gwendolen believes she is possessed of such power, yet her marriage to Grandcourt is based upon a fundamental misperception: she mistakes his manners for malleability. Indeed, it is part of Gwendolen's immaturity that she lacks a true perception of the world. Instead of her possessing knowledge of a penetrative kind, of seeing *through* to the center of people and events as do Deronda and even Grandcourt in his limited way, her knowledge is of a reflected kind. Her self-knowledge is simply self-image: the image she sees in a mirror, or the illusion of a role which the mirror of others (e.g., her family) gives her. For most of the story she does not look into herself, but is contented with her imagined effect upon others. "She meant to do what was pleasant to herself in a striking manner; or rather, whatever she could do so as to strike others with admiration and get *in that reflected way* a more ardent sense of living" (p.69, my emphasis). Her knowledge of the world is also derivative, gathered from the literature which she implicitly believes to be a mirror of reality. "[A]nd what remained of all things knowable, she was conscious of being sufficiently acquainted with through novels, plays, and poems" (p.70).

All of this points to a theme of George Eliot's which dominates *Middlemarch*: the ego that romanticizes and inflates itself. Yet the rhetoric of magic through which this theme is developed in *Daniel Deronda* adds a new tone, one which suggests both the demonic side of people and the mystery of events as they impinge upon the narrow, ego-constructed view of the world. Part of Gwendolen's moral education consists of being divined by various people and becoming mature through these experiences. Thus, Deronda's gaze alerts her to a "region outside and above her" (p.38) while Grandcourt's gaze forces her to see the folly of imagining herself as the driver in the marriage chariot. Gwendolen's fanciful idea of herself as an actress or stage singer is similarly swept away by Klesmer, who, with his "magic spectacles," lucidly analyzes her potential for such careers. The effect of these successive divinations upon the enclosed world of the immature ego can be seen by comparing the imagery which expresses Gwendolen's fear of wide open spaces with her subsequent sense of the larger world.

Gwendolen's role as a witch, then, is highly complex in its irony. Though her mind dresses events and people, including herself, with a clothing of magic, this does not indicate a power of insight, nor even a truly poetic imagination that transforms what it sees, for these are active interpretations of the world. The rhetoric of magic with which Gwendolen describes self and world is mere reaction; it is essentially superstitious (that is, a belief in the power of outside forces, not an inner power). When she extends this rhetoric to herself, Gwendolen ironically reveals her basic immaturity since she mistakes this habit of superstitious description for an active power of will. For the reader, the irony deepens as others see Gwendolen in the sorceress role. The references to her as Lamia or a snake, as a witch, as a devil, or as possessing a divinatory power are all to be seen as ironic contrasts to those characters who do possess the traits associated with these epithets. The most pointed irony is Vandernoodt's mention of the Medea legend in connection with Lydia Glasher. Gwendolen is cast not in the Medea-sorceress role, but in the Creusa role, the victim of the sorceress's "poisoning skill" (p.616). These references are integral with Gwendolen's immature idea of her own powers.

Mordecai is the apex of the sorcerer figures, for his power of divination is that of the prophet; whereas Deronda possesses imaginative sympathy for the present (the people he meets) and for the past (his sense of universal history), Mordecai has a finely tuned vision of the future. In effect, his imaginative will has the power to shape future events. "[T]here are persons whose. . .conceptions. . .continually take the form of images which have a foreshadowing power; the deed they would do starts up before them in complete shape, making a coercive type" (p.527). This statement clearly refers to Mordecai since the rest of the chapter has two purposes: to impress upon the reader the quality of Mordecai's imagination, and to state explicitly what his "foreshadowing" conception is.

The first goal is accomplished by dramatic as well as expository means. Mordecai is not only referred to as a Djinn, a poet, and a prophet, but in the scene with little Jacob Cohen he overtly assumes the role of prophet: the man who is touched by a transcendent, burning vision and is carried out of himself. "[I]t was as if the patient, indulgent companion had turned into something unknown and terrific" (p.535). Mordecai's foreshadowing conception is the notion of spiritually prolonging himself by transmitting his vision to an ideal heir.

Mordecai's power to divine the future is demonstrated in Chapter 40, where this conception of an ideal heir is fulfilled in its exact terms; Deronda fits the description of the heir to the letter, even though at this point in the story the question of parentage remains unanswered. The entire scene at Blackfriars Bridge is fraught with mystical significance. The bridge itself (from which Mordecai sees Deronda--"the face of his visions") is a "meeting place for the spiritual messengers" and the habitual place for Mordecai's meditations. The time is sunset, symbolic of Mordecai's physical decline, yet also a sign of a spiritual beginning, for sunset is the commencement of the Jewish Sabbath. Thus, it symbolizes the spiritual transmission that will take place between the two men.

The mystery and magic of unexpectedly seeing Mordecai on the bridge are not lost upon Deronda. Though he believes Mordecai's statement of having waited on the bridge for him for five years to be a fabrication, a moment later Deronda senses the power of the visionary. "[T]his claim brought with it a sense of solemnity which seemed a radiation from Mordecai. . .as if he had been that preternatural guide seen in the universal legend, who suddenly drops his mean disguise and stands for a manifest Power" (p.551).

In effect, Mordecai now holds Deronda spellbound and will-less much as Grandcourt affects Gwendolen, though with vastly different purpose. "[H]e foresaw that the course of the conversation would be determined by Mordecai, not by himself: he was no longer confident what questions he would be able to ask" (p.552). Deronda has become passive, in a state of "complete superstition," as if awaiting the pronouncement of his destiny. Indeed, this pronouncement has already been provided by Mordecai, his faith in Deronda as his heir being tantamount to the revelation of Deronda's heritage; the transmission has already begun.

In a sense we are to see Mordecai as a manipulator of events through intense imaginative will. This notion of him as an example of the ultimate power of divination leads to a consideration of the relationship between event and the individual's will, to a consideration of how history takes shape and what conscious role humanity has in that shape. This in turn brings up a philosophical question which was very important to George Eliot: the question of a person's ability to act in a deterministic universe.

Within the rhetoric of magic framework, this question resolves itself into two positions, one essentially passive, the other active: first, a superstitious dread in which events seem to occur outside one's ken and therefore have a threatening kind of magic about them; second, the sorcery of the conscious, imaginative will in which events are seen as a dialectic of planning and circumstance, and the sense of magic comes from circumstances conforming to the plan.

Gwendolen is the type for the passive attitude. Despite her feelings of mastery early in the book, superstition rules her consciousness; events and even personal motives seem to be outside her. "Why she should suddenly determine not to part with the necklace was not much clearer to her than why she should sometimes have been frightened to find herself in the fields alone. . ." (p.321).

When she is married to Grandcourt, this "streak of superstition" nearly stifles her existence. Grandcourt completes Gwendolen's passivity through a total abrogation of her will. She becomes a beautiful statue, afraid to move because of her "almost superstitious [feelings] about his power of suspicious divination. . ." (p.670). Moreover, Gwendolen senses that outside influences have compelled her into marriage, that the combination of circumstances called Fate made the choice for her and held her spellbound to it. The proposal would be an excellent example of this: Gwendolen enters intending to reject Grandcourt and emerges having accepted him. Though Gwendolen may feel spellbound as she wonders what happened to plans of gaiety, freedom, and mastery within marriage, Eliot will allow no such denial of responsibility. "She seemed to herself to be, after all, only drifted towards the tremendous decision:--but drifting depends on something besides currents, when the sails have been set beforehand" (p.348). Surely, this is no necessitarian world where human choice is futile. Eliot accomplishes two things with the idea of superstition: she portrays that kind of magic called Destiny, which seems to have been preordained as a person looks back at the chain of events that has brought him or her to the present; she also implies the role of the human will in shaping events.

Chronic passivity is also common with Deronda. His essential characteristic, sympathetic imagination, gives him the ability to help Gwendolen (among others) as well as to divine Mordecai, yet its negative side creates a problem Deronda himself recognizes: a propensity for carrying his habit of introspection into a "meditative numbness" (p.414) that precludes a practical, energetic life. Though Mordecai's power as the ultimate kind of diviner--the prophet--is beyond realistic bounds, the ideal his sorcery represents serves an important function in the story: it moves Deronda out of this realm of "reflective hesitation" and into a course of action.

The rhetoric employed to move Deronda can best be summed up with a portion of Mordecai's impassioned speech at the workingman's symposium in Chapter 42. "The divine principle of our race is action. . . .Let us contradict the blasphemy, and help *to will our own better future and the better future of the world.* . . .The vision is there; it will be fulfilled" (p.598, my emphasis). This can also be seen as an implicit condemnation of Grandcourt, of whom Gwendolen thinks that "it was perhaps not possible for a breathing man wide awake to look less animated" (p.145). Grandcourt's ideal--yachting--with "its dreamy do-nothing absolutism, unmolested by social demands," completes the censure (p.732).

Deronda, however, had already exhibited a desire for action before he met Mordecai; he only needs to find the proper channel for the impulse (e.g., his preference as a boy for Washington and Pericles--men of action--over Porson and Leibnitz--men of thought). Mordecai's vision will provide the desired channel, yet we continue to see an inclination for action originating solely from Deronda even as late in the story as Grandcourt's death. Deronda's advice to Gwendolen about her role in the drowning demonstrates his association of morality with action: "no evil dooms us hopelessly except the evil we love, and desire to continue in, and make no effort to escape from" (p.765). The need to act, to seize one's destiny, is the core of Mordecai's vision as well as the lesson that Gwendolen must learn and enact. Nevertheless, as the repeated stress on vision clearly insists, merely blind action is unacceptable; this is as bad as "reflective hesitation." Mordecai represents the ideal type since his most profound action-- his spiritual transmission into Deronda--is itself wrought by an intense imaginative vision. An "emotional intellect" stands as the ideal, a person in whom a "wise estimate of consequences is fused in the fires of *that passionate belief which determines* the consequences it believes in" (p.572, my emphasis). Deronda, with a "keenly perceptive emotiveness which ran along with his speculative tendency" (p.553), is actually already balanced to that ideal. Mordecai's rhetoric and the discovery of Deronda's heritage are only catalysts which activate an already formed personality: the reader is not allowed to see any real growth of Deronda's character toward the ideal balance of passionate action tempered with careful planning. Furthermore, since Deronda is virtually that which Mordecai's influence is supposed to make him, the plot device of spiritual transmission is weak: it is stunted and sketchy--dramatically deficient.

As an ideal, however, this fusion of thought and action is the impulse behind the novel's master-theme: universal history and brotherhood of humanity, or, to borrow Brian Swann's felicitous phrase, the "march to the millenium in psychic and social terms."[2] The strong coloring of idealization in the so-called Jewish half of the book comes from Eliot not only trying to embody this large idea in fictional terms, but also trying to point out the need for vision and ideals in the practical realm of social and political change. The insistence upon vision and practicality is summed up neatly by Herr Klesmer, who, in an echo of Shelley's "Poets are the unacknowledged legislators of the world," unites poetics and politics in his comments to Mr. Bult on artists. "We help to rule the nations and make the age as much as any other public men. We count ourselves on level benches with legislators" (p.284).

The breadth of the ideal of universal history, to be accomplished by ideal men of impassioned intellect, obviates, to some degree at least, the epithet Jewish that has been applied to the non-Gwendolen part of the novel. Most of Mordecai's thoughts are not so much those of a patriotic Jew with a nationalist's feeling, as those of a visionary who sees Judaic tradition as a symbolic nucleus for a future world community: "[T]his [confession of divine Unity] made our religion the fundamental religion for the whole world; for the divine Unity embraced as its consequence the ultimate unity of mankind" (p.802). This de-emphasis in ethnicity is symbolized by the status of Deronda as both Christian and Jew. The transmission of Mordecai's ideals to him suggests their universal aspects will come even more into the foreground. Allowing her ideas to weaken characterization may be bad art, but it nevertheless indicates Eliot's larger intentions.

These larger intentions remind us George Eliot was not simply an artist who wrote fine novels; she was also a thinker who possessed a subtle mind. In one role she is committed to the conventions of realistic fiction; in the other she is a visionary concerned with promoting the value of visions. From the biographer's point of view, *Daniel Deronda* may be seen as an exercise to fuse these two roles. On a formal level, however, the tension of the exercise becomes apparent. The denseness of empirical particulars that is the very weave of realistic fiction clashes with the nonperceptual dimension of the thematic pattern --ideals of universal brotherhood, ecumenical history, and men of impassioned intellect. At the universal level, the rhetoric of magic suggests two truths--the mystery of human destiny and the need for vision--which stretch to the utmost the realistic fibers that embody them; at the individual level, theme and technique work much better. When employed for psychological portraiture--as analogues for states of mind--the fanciful and demonic elements of the rhetoric of magic are believable; when employed for a representation of the idea of vision's power, the rhetoric of magic's romance and ideality fail the test of probability. It is here that the seam of *Daniel Deronda* shows, not so much along the Gwendolen/Jewish division. Perhaps that seam is inevitable, given the natures of quotidian detail and transcendent vision. But the failure is also one of characterization and plot, for Deronda is essentially static (a violation of Eliot's own idea of novelistic character portrayal), and this weakness in turn undermines the plot device of spiritual transmission.

Daniel Deronda is an artistic gamble, one intended to expand horizons, unlike the gambling metaphor in the story. It represents a vigorous, though imperfect event; itself the kind of vision Eliot hoped would discover the future ways of humanity. "[E]vents are as a glass where-through our eyes see some of the pathways" (p.818).

NOTES

1. George Eliot, *Daniel Deronda*, ed. Barbara Hardy (Harmondsworth: Penguin Books, 1967), p.570. All parenthetical references are to this edition.

2. Brian Swann, "George Eliot's Ecumenical Jew, or, the Novel as Outdoor Temple," *Novel*, 8, (Fall 1974), 38-54.

SELECTED ADDITIONAL READINGS

Adam, Ian. "Character and Destiny in George Eliot's Fiction." *Nineteenth-Century Fiction*, 20 (1965), 127-143.

apRoberts, Ruth. "*Middlemarch* and the New Humanity." *George Eliot: A Centenary Tribute*. Ed. Gordon S. Haight and Rosemary T. VanArsdel. Totowa: Barnes & Noble, 1982. Pp.38-46.

Auster, Henry. "George Eliot and the Modern Temper." *The Worlds of Victorian Fiction*. Ed. Jerome H. Buckley. Cambridge: Harvard University Press, 1975. Pp.75-101.

____. *Local Habitations: Regionalism in the Early Novels of George Eliot*. Cambridge: Harvard University Press, 1970.

Bamber, Linda. "Self-Defeating Politics in George Eliot's *Felix Holt*." *Victorian Studies*, 18 (1975), 419-435.

Bedient, Calvin. "The Fate of the Self: Self and Society in the Novels of George Eliot, D.H. Lawrence, and E.M. Forster." DA, 25:1187. (University of Washington).

____. "The Social Self." *Architects of the Self: George Eliot, D.H. Lawrence, and E.M. Forster*. Berkeley: University of California Press, 1972. Pp.33-69.

Beer, Gillian. "Myth and the Single Consciousness: *Middlemarch* and *The Lifted Veil*." *This Particular Web: Essays on Middlemarch*. Ed. Ian Adam. Toronto: University of Toronto Press, 1975. Pp.91-115.

Bellows, John A. "Religious Tendencies of George Eliot." *Unitarian Review*, 16 (1881), 125-134, 216-229.

Bennett, Joan. "Vision and Design." *George Eliot: Her Mind and Her Art*. Cambridge: Cambridge University Press, 1948. Pp.77-101.

Bodenheimer, Rosemarie. "Mary Ann Evans's Holy War." *Nineteenth Century Literature*, 44 (December 1989), 335-363.

Bolstad, R. Montelle. "The Myth of Sensibility in George Eliot."*Recovering Literature*, 1 (Fall 1972), 26-39.

____. "The Passionate Self in George Eliot's *Adam Bede, The Mill on the Floss*, and *Daniel Deronda*." DA, 37:980A. (University of Washington).

Bonaparte, Felicia. *Will and Destiny: Morality and Tragedy in George Eliot's Novels*. New York: New York University Press, 1975.

Bourl'honne, Paul. *Essai de Biographie Intellectuelle et Morale, 1819-1854*. Paris: Librarie Ancienne Honore Champion, 1933; repr. New York: AMS Press, 1973.

Bradley, Anthony Gerard. "Family as Pastoral: The Garths in *Middlemarch*." *Ariel,* 6 (October 1975), 41-51.

_____. "Pastoral in the Novels of George Eliot." DA, 33:4334A. (State University of New York at Buffalo).

Brody, Selma B. "Physics in *Middlemarch*: Gas Molecules and Ethereal Atoms." *Modern Philology*, 85 (August 1987), 42-53.

Brown, John Crombie. *The Ethics of George Eliot's Works*. Philadelphia: George H. Buchanan, 1885.

Bullen, J.B. "George Eliot's *Romola* as a Positivist Allegory." *Review of English Studies*, 26 (November 1975), 425-435.

Burns, John Sandidge. "The Wider Life: A Study of the Writings of George Eliot." DA, 25:1903-04. (Rice University).

Butwin, Joseph. "The Pacification of the Crowd: From 'Janet's Repentence' to *Felix Holt*." *Nineteenth-Century Fiction*, 35 (December 1980), 349-371.

Campbell, Thomas J. "From Country to Town: The Growth of Abstract Consciousness in *The Mill on the Floss*." *Research Studies of Washington State University*, 49 (June 1981), 107-115.

Carpenter, Mary Wilson. "The Apocalypse of the Old Testament: *Daniel Deronda* and the Interpretation of Interpretation." *PMLA*, 99 (January 1984), 56-71.

Carroll, David R. "*Felix Holt*: Society as Protagonist." *Nineteenth-Century Fiction*, 17 (1962), 237-252.

_____. "An Image of Disenchantment in the Novels of George Eliot." *Review of English Studies*, 11 (1960), 29-41.

_____. "The Unity of *Daniel Deronda*." *Essays in Criticism*, 9 (1959), 369-380.

Carter, Duncan Albert. "The Drama of Self: Role-Playing in the Novels of George Eliot." DA, 35:4420A. (University of Illinois at Urbana-Champaign).

Carter, Margaret Larrabee. "George Eliot's Early Fiction: The Movement from Alienation to Integration." DA, 45:188A. (University of Illinois at Urbana-Champaign).

Chase, Karen. "The Modern Family and the Ancient Image in *Romola*." *Dicken Studies Annual: Essays on Victorian Fiction*, vol. 14. Ed. Michael Timko, Fred Kaplan, and Edward Guiliano. New York: AMS Press, 1985. Pp.303-326.

Collins, K.K. "G.H. Lewes Revised: George Eliot and the Moral Sense." *Victorian Studies*, 21 (1978), 463-492.

Cottom, Daniel. "The Romance of George Eliot's Realism." *Genre*, 15, no.4, (Winter 1982), 357-377.

____. *Social Figures: George Eliot, Social History and Literary Representation.* Vol. 44. Theory and History of Literature. Ed. Wlad Godzich and Jochen Schulte-Sasse. Minneapolis: University of Minnesota Press, 1987.

Costabile, Rita Mary. "Moral Authority: George Eliot's Politics." DA, 46:2298A. (Columbia University).

Cox, C.B. "George Eliot: The Conservative-Reformer." *The Free Spirit: A Study of Liberal Humanism in the Novels of George Eliot, Henry James, E.M. Forster, Virginia Woolf, Angus Wilson.* London: Oxford University Press, 1963. Pp.13-37.

Craib, Ian. "*Criticism and Ideology*: Theory and Experience." *Contemporary Literature*, 22 (Fall 1981), 489-509.

Craig, David M. "Fiction and the 'Rising Industrial Classes.'" *The Real Foundations: Literature and Social Change.* New York: Oxford University Press, 1974. Pp.132-142.

Dale, Peter. "Symbolic Representation and the Means of Revolution in *Daniel Deronda*." *Victorian Newsletter*, 59 (Spring 1981), 25-30.

Dentith, Simon. *George Eliot.* Atlantic Highlands, New Jersey: Humanities Press, 1986.

Di Pasquale, Pasquale, Jr. "The Imagery and Structure of *Middlemarch*." *English Studies*, 52 (1971), 425-435.

Doyle, Mary Ellen. *The Sympathetic Response: George Eliot's Fictional Rhetoric.* East Brunswick, New Jersey and London: Associated University Presses, 1981.

Eagleton, Mary and Pierce, David. "Aspects of Class in George Eliot's Fiction." *Attitudes to Class in the English Novel: From Walter Scott to David Storey.* London: Thames & Hudson, 1979. Pp.53-68.

Ermarth, Elizabeth Deeds. *George Eliot.* Ed. Herbert Sussman. Boston: Twayne, 1985.

____. "George Eliot's Conception of Sympathy." *Nineteenth-Century Fiction*, 40, no.1, (June 1985), 23-42.

____. "George Eliot's Invisible Community." *Realism and Consensus in the English Novel.* Princeton: Princeton University Press, 1983. Pp.222-256.

____. "Incarnations: George Eliot's Conception of 'Undeviating Law.'" *Nineteenth-Century Fiction*, 29 (December 1974), 273-286.

Fairey, Wendy Westbrook. "The Relationship of Heroine, Confessor and Community in the Novels of George Eliot." DA, 36:1523A. (Columbia University).

Fairlay, E. "The Art of George Eliot in *Silas Marner*." *English Journal*, 2 (1913), 221-230.

Faulkner, Peter. "George Eliot, George Meredith and Samuel Butler." *Humanism in the English Novel.* New York: Barnes & Noble, 1976. Pp.42-70.

Feltes, N.N. "Community and the Limits of Liability in Two Mid-Victorian Novels." *Victorian Studies*, 17 (June 1974), 355-369.

_____. "George Eliot's 'Pier-Glass': The Development of a Metaphor." *Modern Philology*, 67 (1969), 69-71.

Fisher, Philip. *Making Up Society: The Novels of George Eliot*. Pittsburgh: University of Pittsburgh Press, 1981.

Fitzpatrick, Terence Daniel. "Alienation and Mediation in the Novels of George Eliot." DA, 40:266A. (Rutgers University).

Fuchs, Eva. "The Pattern's All Missed: Separation/Individuation in *The Mill on the Floss*." *Studies in the Novel*, 19 (Winter 1987), 422-434.

Goldberg, S.L. "Morality and Literature; with Some Reflections on *Daniel Deronda*." *Critical Review*, 22 (1980), 3-20.

Gordon, Jan B. "Affiliation as (Dis)semination: Gossip and Family in George Eliot's European Novel." *Journal of European Studies*, 15 (September 1985), 155-189.

Gould, Carol S. "Plato, George Eliot and Moral Narcissism." *Philosophy and Literature*, 14 (April 1990), 24-39.

Graver, Suzanne. *George Eliot and Community: A Study in Social Theory and Fictional Form*. Berkeley: University of California Press, 1984.

Halperin, John. "George Eliot." *Egoism and Self-Discovery in the Victorian Novel: Studies in the Ordeal of Knowledge in the Nineteenth Century*. New York: Franklin, 1974. Pp.125-192.

Hanlon, Bettina Louise. "Supporting Characters and Rural Communities in the Novels of George Eliot and Thomas Hardy." DA, 44:2772A. (Ohio State University).

Hardy, Barbara. "*Middlemarch*: Public and Private Worlds." *English* 25 (Spring 1976), 5-26.

_____. "Objects and Environments." *Particularities: Readings in George Eliot*. London: Owen, 1982. Pp.147-173.

Henry, Maria Louise. "The Morality of Thackeray and George Eliot." *Atlantic Monthly*, 51 (February 1883), 243.

Herrick, Jim. "John Stuart Mill and George Eliot: A Religion of Humanity." *Against the Faith: Essays on Deists, Skeptics, and Atheists*. Buffalo, New York: Prometheus, 1985. Pp.170-181.

Holloway, John. "*Silas Marner* and the System of Nature." *George Eliot*. Ed. Harold Bloom. Modern Critical Views. New York: Chelsea House, 1986. Pp. 37-44. Reprinted from *The Victorian Sage: Studies in Argument*. New York: Macmillan, 1953.

Hornback, Bert G. "The Organization of *Middlemarch*." *Papers on Language and Literature*, 2 (1966), 169-175.

Horowitz, Lenore Wisney. "Present, Past, and Future: The Vision of Society in George Eliot's Novels." DA, 32:4567A. (Cornell University).

Huzzard, John A. "The Treatment of Florence and Florentine Characters in George Eliot's *Romola*." *Italica*, 34 (1957), 158-165.

John, Joseph. "Pan-Humanism in the Novels of George Eliot." DA, 36:316A. (Marquette University).

Johnstone, Peggy Ruth Fitzhugh. "Narcissistic Rage in *The Mill on the Floss*." *Literature and Psychology*, 36, no.1/2, (1990), 90-109.

____. "Self-Disorder and Aggression in *Adam Bede*." *Mosaic*, 22 (Fall 1989), 59-70.

Klieneberger, H.R. "George Eliot and Gottfried Keller." *The Novel in England and Germany*. London: Wolff, 1981. Pp.87-107.

Knoepflmacher, U.C. "*Middlemarch*: An Avuncular View." *Nineteenth-Century Fiction*, 30, no.1, (June 1975), 53-81.

____. *Religious Humanism and the Victorian Novel: George Eliot, Walter Pater, and Samuel Butler*. Princeton: Princeton University Press, 1965.

Kovalevskaia, Sophia V. "A Memoir of George Eliot." Trans. Miriam Haskell Berlin. *Yale Review*, 73 (Summer 1984), 533-550.

Kucich, John. "George Eliot." *Repression in Victorian Fiction: Charlotte Brontë, George Eliot, and Charles Dickens*. Berkeley: University of California Press, 1987. Pp. 114-200.

Langland, Elizabeth. "Society and Self in George Eliot, Hardy, and Lawrence." *Society in the Novel*. Chapel Hill: University of North Carolina Press, 1984. Pp.80-123.

Lerner, Laurence. "The Education of Gwendolen Harleth." *Critical Quarterly*, 7 (1965), 355-364.

____. *The Truthtellers: Jane Austen, George Eliot, D.H. Lawrence*. London: Chatto; New York: Schocken, 1967.

Levine, George. "Determinism and Responsibility in the Works of George Eliot." *PMLA*, 77 (1962), 268-279.

____. "Intelligence as Deception: *The Mill on the Floss*." *PMLA*, 80 (1965), 402-409.

Liebman, Sheldon. "The Counterpoint of Characters in George Eliot's Early Novels." *Revue des Langues Vivantes* (Bruxelles), 34 (1968), 9-23.

Lyons, Richard S. "The Method of *Middlemarch*." *Nineteenth-Century Fiction*, 21 (1966), 35-48.

Mann, Karen B. "Self, Shell, and World: George Eliot's Language of Space." *Genre*, 15, no.4, (Winter 1982), 447-475.

Marcus, Steven. "Literature and Social Theory: Starting in With George Eliot." *Representations: Essays on Literature and Society*. New York: Random House, 1975. Pp.183-213.

Mason, Michael Y. "*Middlemarch* and Science: Problems of Life and Mind." *Review of English Studies*, 22 (1971), 151-169.

McCobb, E.A. "*Daniel Deronda* as Will and Representation: George Eliot and Schopenhauer." *Modern Language Review*, 80 (July 1985), 533-549.

McCullough, Bruce. "The Psychological Novel: George Eliot's *Middlemarch*." *Representative English Novelists: Defoe to Conrad*. New York: Harper, 1946. Pp.197-214.

McLaverty, James. "Comtean Fetishism in *Silas Marner*." *Nineteenth-Century Fiction*, 36 (December 1982), 318-336.

Miller, J. Hillis. "Optic and Semiotic in *Middlemarch*." *The Worlds of Victorian Fiction*. Ed. Jerome H. Buckléy. Cambridge: Harvard University Press, 1975. Pp.125-145.

Milner, Ian. "The Quest for Community in *The Mill on the Floss*." *Prague Studies in English*, 12 (1976), 77-92.

Molstad, David. "*The Mill on the Floss* and *Antigone*." *PMLA*, 85 (1970), 527-531.

Myers, W.F.T. "Politics and Personality in *Felix Holt*." *Renaissance and Modern Studies* (University of Nottingham), 10 (1966), 5-33.

Nadel, Ira Bruce. "The Alternate Vision: Renunciation in the Novels of George Eliot and Thomas Hardy." DA, 31:2929A. (Cornell University).

Nawalanic, Lillian Antoinette. "George Eliot's Ecological Consciousness in *Middlemarch*." DA, 40:4057A. (University of Houston).

Newton, K.M. *George Eliot, Romantic Humanist: A Study of the Philosophical Structure of Her Novels*. Totowa, New Jersey: Barnes and Noble, 1981.

Nicholes, Joseph. "Vertical Context in *Middlemarch*: George Eliot's Civil War of the Soul." *Nineteenth-Century Literature*, 45 (September 1990), 144-175.

Pangallo, Karen. *George Eliot: A Reference Guide, 1972-1987*. Boston: G.K. Hall, 1990.

Paris, Bernard J. *Experiments in Life: George Eliot's Quest for Values*. Detroit: Wayne State University Press, 1965.

____. "George Eliot's Religion of Humanity." *English Literary History*, 29 (1962), 418-443.

Parrinder, Patrick. "The Look of Sympathy: Communication and Moral Purpose in the Realistic Novel." *Novel*, 5, no.2, (Winter 1972), 135-147.

Postlethwaite, Diana. "'The Many in the One, the One in the Many': George Eliot's *Middlemarch (1871-1872)* as Victorian Cosmology." *Making It Whole: A Victorian Circle and the Shape of Their World*. Columbus: Ohio State University Press, 1984. Pp.232-266.

Poston, Lawrence, III. "Setting and Theme in *Romola*." *Nineteenth-Century Fiction*, 20 (1966), 355-366.

Preston, John. "The Community of the Novel: *Silas Marner*." *Comparative Criticism: A Yearbook*. Vol. 2. Ed. Elinor Shaffer. Cambridge: Cambridge University Press, 1980. Pp.109-130.

Preyer, Robert. "Beyond the Liberal Imagination: Vision and Unreality in *Daniel Deronda*." *Victorian Studies*, 4 (1960), 33-54.

Putzell-Korab, Sara M. *The Evolving Consciousness: An Hegelian Reading of the Novels of George Eliot*. Ed. Dr. James Hogg. Salzburg: Institut fur Anglistik und Amerikanistik, Universitat Salzburg, 1982.

____. "Role of the Prophet: The Rationality of *Daniel Deronda*'s Idealist Mission." *Nineteenth-Century Fiction*, 37, no.2, (September 1982), 170-187.

____. "The Search for a Higher Rule: Spiritual Progress in the Novels of George Eliot." *Journal of the American Academy of Religion*, 47 (September 1979), 389-407.

Redinger, Ruby V. *George Eliot: The Emergent Self*. New York: Knopf, 1975.

Reisen, Diana Mary Cohart. "Pilgrims of Morality: The Quest for Identity in the Novels of George Eliot." DA, 35:6730A. (Columbia University).

Robbins, Larry M. "Mill and *Middlemarch*: The Progress of Public Opinion." *Victorian Newsletter*, 31 (Spring 1967), 37-39.

Roberts, Neil. *George Eliot: Her Beliefs and Her Art*. Pittsburgh: University of Pittsburgh Press; London: Elek, 1975.

Robinson, Carole L. "The Idealogy of Sympathy: A Study of George Eliot's Later Phase." DA, 27:1383A. (Brandeis University).

____. "The Severe Angel: A Study of *Daniel Deronda*." *English Literary History*, 31 (1964), 278-300.

Sabiston, Elizabeth Jean. "Dorothea Brooke: The Reluctant Aesthete." *The Prison of Womanhood: Four Provincial Heroines in Nineteenth-Century Fiction*. New York: St. Martin's, 1987. Pp.81-113.

Sambrook, A.J. "The Natural Historian of Our Social Classes." *English*, 14 (1963), 130-134.

Scott, James E. "George Eliot, Positivism, and the Social Vision of *Middlemarch*." *Victorian Studies*, 16 (September 1972), 59-76.

Shuttleworth, Sally. "Fairy Tale or Science? Physiological Psychology in *Silas Marner*." *Languages of Nature: Critical Essays on Science and Literature*. Ed. L.J. Jordanova. New Brunswick: Rutgers University Press, 1986. Pp. 244-288.

Simpson, Peter. "Crisis and Recovery: Wordsworth, George Eliot, and *Silas Marner*." *University of Toronto Quarterly*, 48 (Winter 1978), 95-114.

Spivey, Ted R. "George Eliot: Victorian Romantic and Modern Realist." *Studies in the Literary Imagination*, 1 (1968), 5-21.

Steele, Karen Beth. "Social Change in George Eliot's Fiction." DA, 35:7329A. (Brown University).

Stoneman, Patsy. "George Eliot: *Middlemarch* (1871-1872)." *The Monster in the Mirror: Studies in Nineteenth-Century Realism*. Ed. D.A. Williams. Oxford: Oxford University Press, 1978. Pp.102-130.

Sudrann, Jean. "*Daniel Deronda* and the Landscape of Exile." *English Literary History*, 37 (1970), 433-455.

Svaglic, Martin J. "Religion in the Novels of George Eliot." *Journal of English and Germanic Philology*, 53 (1954), 145-159.

Tesler, Rita Weinberg. "George Eliot and the Inner-Self." DA, 36:2229A. (New York University).

Thompson, Andrew. "George Eliot, Dante, and Moral Choice in *Felix Holt, the Radical*." *Modern Language Review*, 86 (July 1991), 553-566.

Thompson, David Owen. "Fiction and the Forms of Community: Strauss, Feuerbach, and George Eliot." DA, 40:5881A. (Yale University).

Thomson, Fred C. "Politics and Society in *Felix Holt*." *The Classic British Novel*. Ed. Howard M. Harper and Charles Edge. Athens: University of Georgia Press, 1972. Pp.103-120.

_____. "The Theme of Alienation in *Silas Marner*." *Nineteenth-Century Fiction*, 20 (1965), 69-84.

Tomlinson, Thomas Brian. "*Middlemarch* and Modern Society." *The English Middle-Class Novel*. London: Macmillan; New York: Barnes & Noble, 1976. Pp.102-113.

Vance, Norman. "Law, Religion and the Unity of *Felix Holt*." *George Eliot: Centenary Essays and an Unpublished Fragment*. Ed. Anne Smith. Totowa: Barnes & Noble, 1980. Pp.103-123.

Vogeler, Martha S. "George Eliot and the Positivists." *Nineteenth-Century Fiction*, 35 (December 1980), 406-431.

Wedgwood, J. "The Moral Influence of George Eliot." *Contemporary Review*, 39 (February 1881), 173-185.

Williams, Raymond. "Knowable Communities." *The Country and the City*. Oxford and New York: Oxford University Press, 1973. Pp. 165-181. Reprinted in *George Eliot*. Ed. Harold Bloom. New York: Chelsea House, 1986. Pp.81-97.

_____. "The Knowable Community in George Eliot's Novels." *Novel*, 2 (1969), 255-268. Reprinted in *Towards a Poetics of Fiction*. Ed. Mark Spilka. Bloomington: Indiana University Press, 1977. Pp.225-238.

Wright, T.R. "George Eliot and Positivism: A Reassessment." *Modern Language Review*, 76 (Spring 1981), 257-272.

Yeazell, Ruth Bernard. "Why Political Novels Have Heroines." *Novel*, 18 (Winter 1985), 126-144.

INDEX

About the Editor

KAREN L. PANGALLO is a reference librarian at the Lynn Campus Library of North Shore Community College in Massachusetts.

ISBN 0-313-28773-2

90000>

EAN

9 780313 287732

HARDCOVER BAR CODE